Yesterday, Today, and Tomorrow

School Desegregation and Resegregation in Charlotte

Roslyn Arlin Mickelson
Stephen Samuel Smith
Amy Hawn Nelson

Editors

HARVARD EDUCATION PRESS
CAMBRIDGE, MASSACHUSETTS

Library of Congress Control Number 2014949034

Paperback ISBN 978-1-61250-756-9
Library Edition 978-1-61250-757-6

Published by Harvard Education Press,
an imprint of the Harvard Education Publishing Group

Harvard Education Press
8 Story Street
Cambridge, MA 02138

Cover Design: Saizon Design
Cover Photo: © 145/John Cardasis/Ocean/Corbis
The typefaces used in this book are Bembo and Lucida Sans.

For Julius LeVonne Chambers
and the many who struggled alongside him
for racial and social justice

Contents

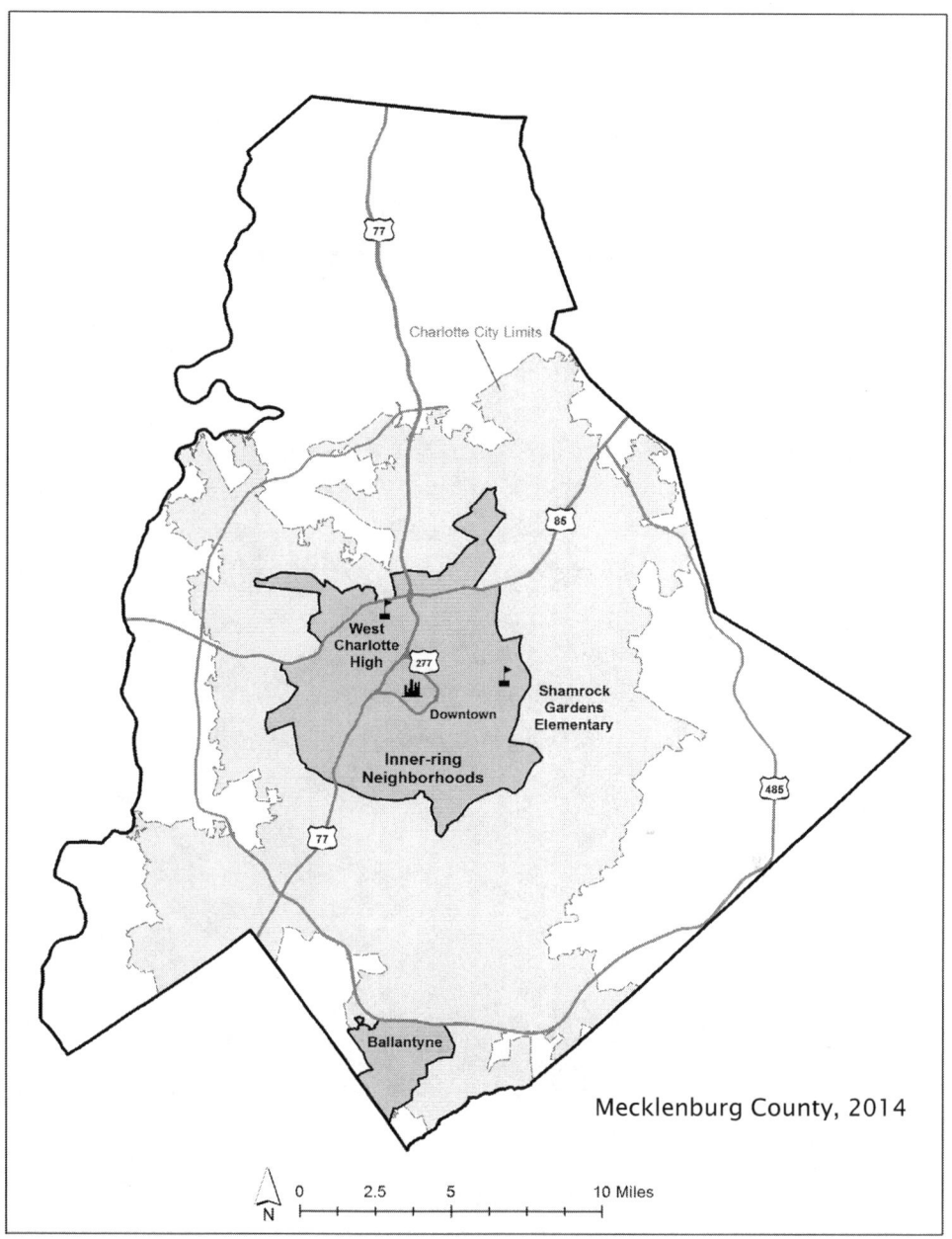

Charlotte City Limits

West
Charlotte
High

77

85

277

Downtown

Shamrock
Gardens
Elementary

Inner-ring
Neighborhoods

77

485

Ballantyne

Mecklenburg County, 2014

0   2.5   5   10 Miles

N

Source: Laura Simmons and Jacob Schmidt, UNC Charlotte Urban Institute.

Preface

Our professional and personal lives are intertwined with Charlotte-Mecklenburg Schools (CMS) and each other. In many ways this book is a natural vehicle to tell the CMS desegregation and resegregation story and for us to wrestle with the significance of that story for our own lives. Our personal histories embody the experiences and struggles over desegregation in Charlotte that many families have faced during the past four decades.

Amy Hawn Nelson was born in Charlotte and participated in the CMS mandatory desegregation plan as a K–12 CMS student. After graduating from South Mecklenburg High School in 1997, she attended North Carolina State University. She became a CMS teacher and school leader after working for Teach For America in Baltimore, Maryland. When Hawn Nelson entered the University of North Carolina at Charlotte's Urban Education PhD program she met Roslyn Arlin Mickelson, who went on to chair Hawn Nelson's PhD dissertation about 1997 CMS graduates' lived experiences with desegregation. Several years after completing her doctorate in urban education, Hawn Nelson assumed the directorship of UNC Charlotte's Institute for Social Capital (ISC), a unit of the UNC Charlotte Urban Institute. One mission of the ISC is to connect CMS data with the community that it serves. In many ways, this book does just that. Hawn Nelson was promoted to the position of Director of Research for the UNC Charlotte Urban Institute in 2014, and she continues to serve as the director of ISC.

In 1985 Roslyn Arlin Mickelson and Stephen Samuel Smith left Ann Arbor, Michigan, and arrived in Charlotte with their two children, who were enrolled in CMS as a fourth grader and a first grader. From that time until they graduated from high school, both children attended schools involved in CMS's desegregation plan. Mickelson and Smith's daughter went on to graduate from UNC Chapel Hill, and their son graduated from UNC Charlotte.

Mickelson, a professor of sociology and public policy at UNC Charlotte, and Smith, a professor of political science at Winthrop University, began to examine desegregation in Charlotte as part of their scholarly inquiries into the social context of schooling and urban politics, respectively. They both served as expert witnesses in the 1999 reopening of the *Swann v. Charlotte-Mecklenburg Board of Education* litigation that resulted in the vacating of the original *Swann* orders and the declaration that CMS was unitary (i.e., that CMS had eliminated as much of the *dual* system—state-mandated segregation—as was feasible).[1] Mickelson was one of CMS's expert witnesses, while Smith served as an expert witness for the NAACP's Legal Defense and Educational Fund, which had intervened in the case on behalf of the new black plaintiffs.

This volume is the natural outgrowth of our personal and professional interests and connections. We share a critical appreciation for CMS's herculean accomplishments since 1971 and a growing concern about CMS's future. We are also devoted to policy and scholarship that foster wider understanding of the tension between education's role in both alleviating existing inequalities and reproducing them for individuals and in the larger society. The history of desegregation and resegregation in CMS reflects such reproduction *and* social transformation.

CMS did many things right while it operated under *Swann*; the district also did a number of things very poorly. Learning from these successes and failures and telling the story of the district's journey through desegregation to resegregation is important, especially in a manner that emphasizes, as this book does, how yesterday's agency—both what was done right and what was done poorly—became structures that constrain our choices today and tomorrow. We hope the lessons learned from this case study inform and challenge the Charlotte-Mecklenburg community, the state of North Carolina, and perhaps the nation.

Finally, we want to bring readers' attention to the book's Web site, yesterday todaytomorrowcms.com, where we have placed supplemental materials for many of the chapters. The Web site offers detailed tables, figures, and technical appendixes about the chapters' research designs and statistical analyses. When such material is relevant to a passage in the text, an endnote directs readers to the Web site. The Web site also includes an edited transcript of an interview with Julius LeVonne Chambers conducted by Roslyn Arlin Mickelson several months before his death in 2013. We offer these supplements for two reasons. First, because we conceived this book for a wide audience, we do not want more technical discussions of research design, sampling, analytic approaches, and statistical models to detract from readers' appreciation of the chapters' arguments. At the same time, as social scientists, we wanted these technical materials to be available to readers who are interested in them. Second, the Web site offers us the option of providing documentation, figures, tables, and other supplemental materials that would otherwise be unavailable given Harvard Education Press's understandable constraints on the number of pages in this book.

Roslyn Arlin Mickelson
Stephen Samuel Smith
Amy Hawn Nelson

CHAPTER 1

Yesterday, Today, and Tomorrow

Structure and Agency in the Resegregation of the
Charlotte-Mecklenburg Schools

Roslyn Arlin Mickelson
Stephen Samuel Smith
Amy Hawn Nelson

FEW SCHOOL REFORMS have been as fully implemented and successful as
the Charlotte-Mecklenburg Schools' (CMS) desegregation plan. Yet forty years
after the plan was first implemented, the school system has largely resegregated
by race and class. CMS's resegregation notwithstanding, three decades of desegregation accomplished several goals. CMS achieved high levels of racial balance, and desegregation benefited both black and white students academically,
but especially blacks. The city and nation moved incrementally closer to racial
and educational justice. Moreover, there was widespread pride in Charlotte in
CMS's school desegregation accomplishments, and Charlotte gained a national
reputation as a progressive New South city that had a favorable business climate
and was a good place to work and raise a family. *Yesterday, Today, and Tomorrow:
School Desegregation and Resegregation in Charlotte* is about these many aspects of
the Charlotte school desegregation experience and, looking forward, what this
experience suggests for school reform, public policy, and desegregated education's relationship to racial and social justice in Charlotte and the nation.

Accounts of Charlotte's desegregation experience frequently call attention
to a 1984 campaign stop in Charlotte by President Ronald Reagan during
which he denounced busing for desegregation as a failed "social experiment

that nobody wants." Reagan's otherwise enthusiastic audience responded with a silence that "was uncomfortable, embarrassed, almost stony."[1] Shortly thereafter, the *Charlotte Observer* ran an editorial headlined "You Were Wrong, Mr. President," saying that "Charlotte-Mecklenburg's proudest achievement of the past 20 years is not the city's impressive new skyline or its strong, growing economy. Its proudest achievement is its fully integrated school system . . . [that] has blossomed into one of the nation's finest, recognized through the United States for quality, innovation, and, most of all, for overcoming the most difficult challenge American public education has ever faced."[2]

Now, three decades later, there's a quaintness to that editorial that is as noteworthy as the stoniness that greeted Reagan's denunciation of busing. The downtown skyline features many more impressive buildings, which were amply displayed to the worldwide audience that tuned in to watch the 2012 Democratic National Convention. The convention and subsequent appointment of Charlotte Mayor Anthony Foxx as Secretary of Transportation exemplify the city's growing prominence in national affairs. But while Charlotte's skyline and economy may have soared, its school desegregation accomplishments have plummeted. Within a year or two of Reagan's visit, Charlotte-Mecklenburg Schools began a slow drift toward resegregation that continued until the end of the last century and rapidly accelerated in the first decade of the twenty-first century. In 2014 Charlotte's schools are certainly not as segregated as they were in the era of Jim Crow education, but they are a long way from what they were when the *Observer* was touting them as being "fully integrated."

Charlotte is not the only city whose schools have experienced considerable resegregation since the 1980s. Resegregation has increased nationally.[3] But Charlotte's resegregation deserves special attention because of the city's historic prominence in the country's school desegregation efforts. It is the city that gave rise to the *Swann v. Charlotte-Mecklenburg Board of Education* litigation, a case in which the Supreme Court unanimously—and in an opinion written by Chief Justice Warren Burger, a Nixon appointee—affirmed the decision of Federal District Court Judge James McMillan. Although CMS had made limited progress in desegregating its schools, McMillan drew on a 1968 Supreme Court decision to say that CMS had a constitutional obligation to eliminate all racially identifiable schools.[4] Noting how governmental action had facilitated residential segregation and the building of schools in residentially segregated neighborhoods, McMillan said that the "neighborhood school concept never *prevented* statutory racial segregation; it may not now be validly used to *perpetu-*

ate segregation."[5] McMillan was wise enough not to order CMS to pursue any particular strategy or method of eliminating racially identifiable schools. But given the extent of residential segregation, such strategies and methods would inevitably involve significant amounts of busing, and the *Swann* litigation is often called "the school busing case."

In the aftermath of the *Swann* decision, CMS desegregated. The district adopted a desegregation plan that relied heavily on a system of paired elementary schools, with the K–3 schools located in predominantly white neighborhoods (to which black children were bused) and the grades 4–6 schools located in black neighborhoods (to which white children were bused).[6] The attendance zones of junior and senior highs could be sufficiently large that pairing was neither necessary nor feasible at the secondary school level. Rather, a secondary school's attendance zone was typically an area contiguous to the school, supplemented, if necessary, by one or more satellite (i.e., noncontiguous) areas. Most of the high schools that remained open were in white neighborhoods, and most of the satellites were in black neighborhoods.[7]

Of the many school districts whose desegregation was triggered by the Supreme Court's decision in *Swann*, CMS's experience was often viewed as among the most successful because of both the high levels of racial balance that were achieved in the 1970s and early 1980s, and according to the best available information, improved educational outcomes.[8] In the early 1990s CMS again attracted attention from education policy makers around the county when, under the leadership of a nationally prominent superintendent, John Murphy, the district voluntarily dismantled much of the mandatory busing plan in favor of a system of magnet schools ostensibly aimed at maintaining the desegregated school system. Under the magnet plan, most schools still met CMS's desegregation guidelines even though racial imbalance continued to drift upward in the 1990s.

Although the magnets were designed to preserve CMS's commitment to desegregation, the use of racial guidelines in magnet school assignments prompted a lawsuit seeking to end CMS's desegregation efforts. A white parent, William Capacchione, later joined by six other white families, challenged the use of race in pupil assignment, claiming these guidelines were unconstitutional. Julius Chambers's law firm, (which had represented Darius and Vera Swann in the original lawsuit against CMS), along with the NAACP, intervened to protect the original *Swann* orders. The lawsuit resulted in the reopening of the *Swann* case and an examination of the constitutionality of CMS's continuing to consider race in pupil assignment. In the original *Swann* litigation CMS had vigorously opposed efforts to increase desegregation. But in the 1999 trial, CMS—by a 6–3 vote of the school board—took a very different position; that is, it argued in court that it should be allowed to continue to consider race in pupil assignment because it had not yet fully complied with the original *Swann* order. Few, if any, school boards have ever fought to remain under desegregation orders as vigorously as CMS did in the 1999 trial.

The case was heard by a Reagan appointee, Judge Robert Potter, as McMillan had died in 1995. As a private citizen, Potter had been active in the antibusing movement of the 1960s, having drafted a petition to the school board on the movement's behalf and publicly spoken against it.[9] Given that background, it is perhaps not surprising that Potter found CMS *unitary*—that is, CMS had eliminated as much of the *dual* system (state-mandated segregation) as was feasible—and ordered the district to cease using race in pupil assignment.[10] Although some aspects of Potter's decision were overturned on appeal, the most important parts—that CMS was unitary and had to stop considering race in pupil assignment—were not. In the aftermath of Potter's ruling, in 2002 CMS implemented a race-neutral pupil assignment plan that was heavily based on neighborhood schools. In the wake of that decision, black/white segregation jumped to a level approaching what it had been prior to the Supreme Court's 1971 *Swann* decision, as figure 1.1 illustrates by depicting changes in the dissimilarity index, a widely used measure of desegregation.[11]

FIGURE 1.1   Black/white dissimilarity index: CMS elementary schools

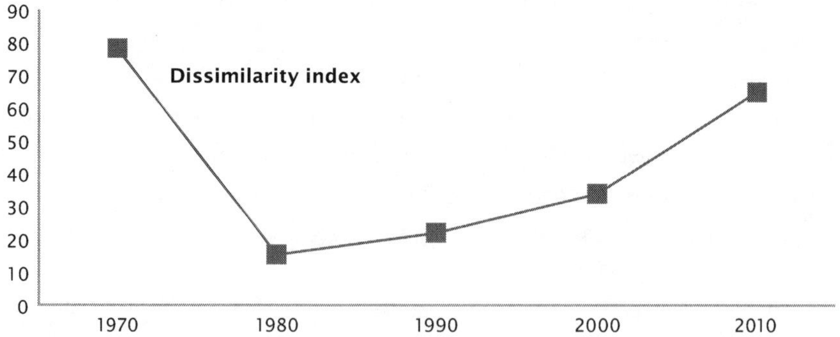

Source: American Communities Project and Charlotte-Mecklenburg Schools

THE IMPORTANCE OF THE CMS STORY

The fact that CMS looms so large in the nation's school desegregation history is in and of itself sufficient to justify a book about the desegregation and resegregation of its schools, especially because, as noted earlier, CMS is hardly the only school district to experience considerable resegregation. A more compelling reason, however, is what can be learned from how a district, previously noted for its desegregation accomplishments, attempts to boost educational achievement in its resegregated schools. Such knowledge may very well be relevant for other districts' similar efforts and for larger issues of educational reform, public policy, and racial justice.

For example, CMS received the 2011 Broad Prize for Urban Education and was lauded by Secretary of Education Arne Duncan as "a model for innovation in urban education."[12] Two years later a 2013 study of National Assessment of Educational Progress (NAEP) scores indicated that CMS outperformed the other twenty urban districts in the study.[13] Taken in conjunction, the comparison of NAEP scores and the Broad Prize would seem to indicate that CMS is doing a lot of good things from which other urban districts could learn. But a more relevant lesson may come from putting such accolades and accomplishments in perspective. CMS's poverty rate was the lowest among the school districts in this study of NAEP scores, which raises the strong possibility that it played a key—perhaps decisive—role in explaining why the district's scores were the highest.[14]

As for the Broad Prize, test scores dropped sharply, as CMS candidly admitted, in the academic year immediately following those upon which the Prize was based.[15] The academic year in which the Prize was awarded saw the district rocked by a brutal controversy over school closings that bitterly divided the community and required poor children of color to bear the brunt of such closings.[16] Moreover, Peter Gorman, CMS's superintendent at the time, was a 2004 graduate of the Broad Academy for Superintendents, and the year the prize was awarded he was a member of the Broad Center's board of directors.[17] These considerations accord with the critique that the Broad Prize is less a recognition of programs and policies that contribute to genuine and longstanding educational progress, and more a reflection of rewards bestowed among members of a professional network with a shared perspective on urban education reform that the Broad Foundation has carefully cultivated.[18]

Although lower profile than Broad Prizes and NAEP studies, another aspect of resegregated CMS's experience may hold many lessons. This aspect is a partnership between CMS and Project LIFT, which a lengthy *Education Week* article calls "unique" and, as the article's headline indicates, "blurs the line between public [and] private."[19] An acronym for Project Leadership & Investment For Transformation, Project LIFT is conceived roughly along the lines of the Harlem Children's Zone (HCZ), but unlike HCZ, does not utilize any charter schools. Instead, Project LIFT involves local foundations raising and spending $55 million over a five-year period to improve educational outcomes in CMS's lowest performing high school and its feeder schools, all of which are hypersegregated racially and socioeconomically.

Implemented in the 2012–2013 school year, Project LIFT includes educational programs and support for teachers, social and dental services for students, efforts to boost parent and community involvement, a plan for robust evaluation, and a governance structure in which some Project LIFT personnel, including its director, report to CMS but are paid with Project LIFT funds and whose performance must satisfy Project LIFT's board of directors as well. How Project LIFT fares and the extent to which it succeeds in improving educational outcomes for students in a hypersegregated, low performing set of schools will likely affect CMS education policy, one way or the other, for years to come and could easily influence the likelihood of such partnerships continuing in CMS and developing elsewhere in the nation.

In addition to these primarily educational reasons for studying CMS, demographic and economic developments make the district worthy of attention. Charlotte is a rapidly growing New South city that plays an increasingly important role in national economic and political affairs. The area's sweeping demographic shifts, captured by its label as a Hispanic hypergrowth center, are emblematic of the future challenges of many urban districts. CMS is currently the seventeenth largest public school system in the country, and the ways in which its demographic shifts influence the contours of schools, neighborhoods, and curricular and programmatic diversity in CMS and the larger community have implications for many other large urban districts.

STRUCTURE AND AGENCY

Telling the CMS story requires a multidisciplinary approach because the district's experiences with desegregation and resegregation have political, educational, legal, economic, demographic, and normative dimensions that have unfolded over four decades. Thus, this book features chapters by historians; sociologists; political scientists; social geographers; economists; public policy, legal, and education scholars; and practicing attorneys and educators. Yet, despite this range of disciplinary perspectives, the book's chapters are linked by a common theme that illustrates the interplay of what social scientists often call *agency* and *structure*. *Agency* typically refers to "individual or group abilities (intentional or otherwise) to affect their environment."[20] *Structure* typically refers to the conditions that "define the range of actions available to actors."[21] Three aspects of this interplay between structure and agency are of interest to us. First, and most generally, to what extent does yesterday's agency become the structure that influences today's agency? Second, what is the nature of that influence (i.e., to what extent does structure tend to constrain or expand various actors' agency)? Third, and especially related to the focus of this book, to what extent has the iterative relationship between structure and agency across four decades affected the history of desegregation and resegregation in CMS?

Federalism, Structure, and Agency

The interplay between structure and agency is especially complicated in the case of school desegregation because pupil assignment decisions are generally made by local school boards whose agency is affected by a series of nested structures. Many of these structures are a consequence of the federal nature of the U.S. political system, which results in developments at the national and state level establishing many of the parameters within which local boards must work. Especially evident at the national level is the role of court decisions such as those in *Brown v. Board of Education* and *Swann*. These decisions facilitated desegregation in the civil rights era, and more recently—as in the case of Judge Potter's 1999 decision in the reopened *Swann* litigation—have made it much more difficult for local boards to pursue desegregation even when so inclined.[22] But also important at the federal level are acts of Congress. The 1964 Civil Rights Act and the 1965 Elementary and Secondary Education Act facilitated desegregation. The latter gave the federal government the carrot of increased aid to local districts, while the former gave it the stick of withholding such aid to segregated districts. But more recent national legislation has largely cut the other way. Neither of the two most recent federal education initiatives—the No Child Left Behind Act of 2001 (NCLB) and Race to the Top—places any emphasis on diversity, much less desegregation.[23] Moreover, Race to the Top's emphasis on charter schools generally militates against desegregation because charter schools tend to be more segregated than traditional public schools, and the growth of charters affects the demographic mix in all public schools, charters and noncharters, and contributes to the segregation by race and socio-economic status in both.[24] NCLB's requirement that test scores be disaggregated by student subgroup has had the crucial benefit of making class, race, linguistic, and ability disparities in test scores crystal clear. However, since NCLB was implemented all state standardized tests have become high stakes. While not all the costs are readily visible or equally shared, all children, educators, and schools suffer.[25] To illustrate, if the Obama administration had not issued NCLB waivers to states beginning in 2011, it is likely that every school in America would have failed to meet NCLB goals in 2014.[26] Well-publicized ostensible failures of public education fuel the middle class flight from traditional public schools into charters and private schools, exacerbating race and class segregation.

The growing federal role in education notwithstanding, local school districts are creations of state governments and thus their local boards are empowered and constrained by state constitutions, and actions of state courts, legislatures, and governors. Approximately 60 percent of CMS's operating budget comes from the state, and the extent to which the state is appropriately funding CMS and many North Carolina school districts has been the subject of the long-running educational adequacy litigation *Leandro v. State of North Carolina*.[27] State legislation also governs the operation and existence of charter schools, and North Carolina's 2011 decision to eliminate the cap on charter schools has encouraged their proliferation. If the past is prologue, the expansion of charters will further segregate CMS students by race and socioeconomic status.

Important as is the role of structures rooted in federal and state decisions, this book is primarily about the history of CMS itself. Local history, too, bespeaks the interplay between structure and agency, and the dynamics of this interplay over time. A straightforward illustration of how agency at one point in time created structures that at subsequent points in time affected other actors' perceived range of options includes choices about "brick-and-mortar structures" (e.g., the location of roads, schools, and residential development). In particular, the decisions in the 1970s and 1980s about the location of an interstate highway on Mecklenburg's periphery (the I-485 Outerbelt) affected residential development, families' choices of where to live, and CMS's decisions about where to build schools, all of which created facts on the ground (i.e., physical as well as social structures) that have greatly affected CMS pupil assignment decisions, making it harder to pursue desegregation in the 1980s and 1990.

A more complex but equally telling example involves how various actors' agency has been affected by the relationship between CMS's political structure and *Swann*. As indicated by its name, CMS is a consolidated district encompassing all 524 square miles of Mecklenburg County, the principal city of which is Charlotte. Consolidation resulted from a 1959 referendum, the main push for which came from the advocacy (i.e., agency) of civic leaders concerned about improving rural schools and increasing administrative and fiscal efficiency. In 1959, some Charlotteans might have realized the implications that consolidation could have for desegregation given the Supreme Court's decision in *Brown* five years earlier. But such implications received little public discussion, perhaps because southern resistance to *Brown* seemed so effective.

Given the legal conditions created by the Supreme Court's *Swann* decision, the political structure created by consolidation had the largely unforeseen consequence of facilitating desegregation. The district's large size deprived whites seeking to avoid desegregation easy access to the close-in, primarily white suburbs that have characterized many other urban areas with smaller, more balkanized, and more racially homogenous school districts. By constraining (though certainly not eliminating its possibility, because moving out of Mecklenburg County was still possible) the agency of such whites, consolidation and the Supreme Court's decision markedly expanded the opportunities for civil rights advocates to pursue their goal of ending segregation in CMS; that is, consolidation and *Swann* enhanced the latter's capacity to act.

However, four decades later, because of the changed legal conditions resulting from Judge Potter's 1999 order, the consolidated nature of CMS is now more likely to cut both ways when it comes to education policy and desegregation. The district's large size and consolidated nature continue to allow CMS to avoid some of the political, fiscal, and social problems that are intensified, if not created, by the fragmented character of many contemporary metropolitan areas.[28] In other words, because it is consolidated, CMS has access to more resources—a wealthier tax base and more middle-class white families—than do many urban districts. But the same middle-class white families who help boost CMS's fiscal resources are also claimants upon CMS funds and other policy outputs. At present, the political structure created by consolidation is less determinative of education policy than it was during the *Swann* era. When a structure is less determinative at any particular time, there's more opportunity for the agency of various actors to influence the development of future structures, as the chapters in this book will explain.

The Economy, Demography, Normative Climate, and Role of Foundations

In addition to being affected by the structures resulting from federal, state, and local decisions, CMS's decisions are also enmeshed in conditions created by the economy, the district's changing demography, the normative climate, and the role of foundations, both local and national. Most obvious is the role of the economy, especially the ongoing high childhood poverty rate and growing economic inequality.[29] As is well known, children from impoverished backgrounds often face educational challenges, and a large concentration of poor children in a particular school poses marked challenges for educators. Moreover, as economic inequality increases, the "haves" gain additional resources to pursue educational options other than traditional public schools and, perhaps additional motivation for doing so given the high concentration of "have-nots" in many CMS schools.[30]

Moreover, CMS's decision makers must currently make decisions under much more complex racial/ethnic conditions than in the past. As opposed to the *Swann* era, students of color now constitute a majority of the district's enrollment, and many are English language learners. Thus, CMS must consider desegregation and diversity from a multiracial, multiethnic perspective at the same time that it considers how much its decisions should propitiate the middle-class white families whose economic resources, social networks, cultural capital, and political clout it generally prizes.

The normative environment in which CMS educational decision makers craft and implement school policy has changed over the forty years since *Swann* was first implemented. The local culture that embraced desegregation and politely ignored President Reagan has changed, in part because of the influx of newcomers to the area who do not share in the community's history and in part because of larger national trends. Since the 1980s, the normative climate for public policy has been evolving from equity-based to market-based approaches and this is especially apparent in education, as evidenced by the growth of reforms that embrace choice, privatization, standards, and accountability.[31] The market-based approach to educational reform drives local policies including CMS's post-unitary pupil assignment plans, state-level reforms including Common Core State Standards and the embrace of charters, and national reforms including NCLB and the Race to the Top initiative.[32]

Last but not least is the role of think tanks and foundations, both of which are playing an increasingly prominent role in shaping the national dialogue over education and the direction of education policy itself.[33] Local foundations such as the Foundation for the Carolinas and the C. D. Spangler Foundation have a prominent role in setting some of the parameters within which CMS makes decisions. Large national philanthropic organizations including the Gates, Walton, and Broad Foundations affect the environment in which school systems make decisions by offering grants with significant financial incentives to districts whose goals and policies accord with the foundations' priorities. For financially pressed school districts, grants are especially appealing, and grant applicants are generally aware of a particular philanthropy's philosophical bent and theory of change. It is common for successful applicants to act in tune with that bent and theory of change.[34] For example, many CMS board members and senior administrators have attended Broad Foundation trainings, and the district received the Broad Prize in 2011, as noted earlier. It is probably not surprising that CMS's current theory of action, managed performance empowerment, is consistent with the Broad Foundation's approach to school reform.[35] School board member Reverend Thomas Tate explained why foundations influence the direction of reform in CMS: "I'll just say it: the money is what drives it."[36] Given the scant attention that local and national foundations pay to desegregation and diversity, it is perhaps understandable that such issues have dropped so low on CMS's list of priorities even though the district's vision statement once proclaimed the aspiration to be the "premier integrated urban school system in the nation."

DO DESEGREGATION AND RESEGREGATION MATTER? WHAT SOCIAL SCIENCE TELLS US

As compelling as Charlotte's experience is, the reader may be asking, *Why study school desegregation now?* Or, more specifically, setting aside issues of racial justice and the broader merits of societal and educational diversity—to the extent these issues can be put aside—does desegregation improve educational outcomes? After all, many people agree with President Reagan that busing was a failed social experiment. More recently, Supreme Court Justice Clarence Thomas said as part of a lengthy and presumably informed opinion in an important school desegregation case that the social science evidence on the question of educational effects of diverse schooling is inconclusive and, thus, there is no empirical foundation to argue that integrated schools are a compelling state interest.[37]

Justice Thomas is wrong.[38] To be sure, as he notes, there are studies questioning the relationship between the racial/ethnic composition of schools and classrooms and students' academic achievement. But the preponderance of scholarly studies, especially those that are recent and methodologically sound, offers consistent findings that irrespective of their ethnicity, race, or social class, students are more likely to make academic gains in mathematics, reading, and often in science by attending diverse schools and learning in diverse classrooms rather than in segregated ones. Students who attend diverse K–12 schools are more likely to attend and graduate from college. The most disadvantaged youth receive the greatest academic benefits from diverse schooling. At the same time, there is overwhelmingly consistent evidence that youth from all racial, ethnic, and socioeconomic backgrounds benefit socially from attending diverse schools and none suffer from it. Students who attend desegregated schools exhibit greater levels of intergroup friendships, demonstrate lower levels of racial fears and stereotypes, and experience less intergenerational perpetuation of racism and stereotypes across multiple institutional settings.[39]

In addition to the benefits of desegregation and harms of segregation in the studies summarized in the preceding paragraph, there is also compelling evidence for the benefits of desegregation and harms of segregation in CMS itself, as chapters 3, 4, 8, and 9 of this book indicate. Equally striking are results from additional studies that exploited the natural experiment presented by Charlotte's operating as a unitary system beginning in 2002, which permitted researchers to isolate the effects of resegregation by examining student outcomes before and after the lifting of *Swann*. Research from post–unitary CMS specifically about elementary school, middle school, high school achievement, and the freshman GPA of the CMS graduating class of 2004, is consistent with the previously summarized research showing a negative relationship between segregation and achievement.[40]

These additional studies showing the negative effects of resegregation on CMS students' academic outcomes are not surprising. Along with rigorous curricula, components such as academically oriented peers, access to Advanced Placement courses, and highly qualified and experienced teachers are essential for academic achievement and college preparation. Yet the likelihood of access to these opportunities to learn varies with a school's racial and socioeconomic profile. A study of teacher quality in post–*Swann* CMS, which also exploited the natural experiment presented by the end of desegregation, reinforces our understanding of this dynamic. The study found that as the student populations in CMS schools became more black, the most highly qualified teachers transferred out, leaving the resegregated schools with less qualified teachers.[41]

The broad corpus of social science research we summarized earlier indicates nonacademic outcomes of schooling also are affected by school and classroom socioeconomic and racial composition. They show that the importance of cross-racial friendships and the reduction of racial fears and stereotypes extends beyond the school campus into neighborhoods, the marketplace, and civil society. Attending diverse schools has a positive effect on adults' understanding of race in their lives, the lives of others, and in the larger society. Multicultural navigation skills learned in diverse schools are essential for employment in an increasingly globalized economy where clients, customers, and coworkers are from diverse backgrounds.[42] Not surprisingly, a multimethod study of 1997 CMS graduates found positive intergroup relations were particularly evident among graduates of the most racially diverse high schools.[43]

Given the disproportionate numbers of blacks, Latinos, and the poor who are both victims of crimes and incarcerated for committing them, there are sound reasons to investigate whether there is a relationship between the racial and socioeconomic composition of their schools and involvement with the criminal justice system. Research clearly indicates desegregation is associated with lower probability of involvement with the criminal justice system.[44] Indeed, the *PICS* (Parents Involved in Community Schools) amicus brief filed by U.S. police chiefs in support of voluntary desegregation in the 2007 Seattle and Louisville cases argued that integration reduces truancy and dropout rates, both of which are linked to crime.[45] One author of this brief was Charlotte's then Chief of Police, Darrel Stephens. In fact, the natural experiment provided by the end of desegregation in CMS confirmed the argument advanced in the police chiefs' amicus brief. In Charlotte, black males' likelihood of involvement with the criminal justice system increased with the resegregation of their high schools.[46]

The decreased involvement with the criminal justice system, higher graduation rates, greater employability, and higher earnings that result from desegregation all point to another of its very important benefits: it is cost effective. Outcomes such as higher earnings increase tax revenues, and outcomes such as decreased incarceration rates lower government expenditures. These fiscal benefits to the public are significantly greater than whatever additional start-up and operational costs a desegregation plan might entail.[47]

PLAN OF BOOK

The first few chapters of this book address crucial aspects of Charlotte's desegregation experience prior to the implementation of the race-neutral pupil assignment plan in 2002. Chapter 2's analysis of the political economy of desegregation, development, and school reform in Charlotte, authored by political scientist Stephen Samuel Smith, chronicles the political economy of CMS's recent history. Smith shows how the district's desegregation and resegregation were not due to a series of uncontrollable forces like the weather; rather, they were the result of the choices of actors operating in a complicated environment that shaped, and often limited, the possibilities to develop diverse schools once development and demography triggered political, logistical, and normative challenges in Mecklenburg County.

During the heyday of the busing plan, West Charlotte High School epitomized the district's success. In chapter 3, historian Pamela Grundy offers a narrative of iconic West Charlotte High School's journey from a segregated to desegregated school. West Charlotte became a place where blacks and whites learned how to work and live together, excelling in academics, sports, and the arts.

Chapter 3's case study of West Charlotte High School's successes during desegregation sets the stage for chapter 4's case study of the same high school when, after unitary status, it became hypersegregated and performance plummeted. In this chapter, Roslyn Arlin Mickelson and Stephen Samuel Smith are joined by education policy scholars Stephanie Southworth and S. Lorén Trull in showing how the end of *Swann* in 2002 ushered in two related phenomena in CMS's most challenged schools: a striking drop in performance, and programmatic and policy responses that largely ignored the intensifying socioeconomic and racial segregation. Emblematic of this response is Project LIFT, the five-year, $55 million intervention loosely based upon the Harlem Children's Zone that makes no effort to address the extreme racial and socioeconomic isolation of West Charlotte.

The book continues with chapter 5's assessement of levels of between-school and within-school segregation in CMS during the post-unitary period. Economists Charles Clotfelter, Helen Ladd, and Jacob Vigdor describe and analyze contemporary CMS's school- and classroom-level segregation in terms of both the white/nonwhite imbalance and free-lunch/non-free-lunch imbalance in CMS. They also compare CMS levels with those in Wake County, the state's largest district, and the state of North Carolina overall.

Wake and Mecklenburg are North Carolina's largest countywide school systems. The counties have many things in common, including rapid population growth, striking demographic change, and histories of successful desegregation plans. But they differ in one very stark way: CMS has resegregated and its board has no program in place to create diverse schools, while Wake continues to have desegregated schools and its citizens support their board's struggles to maintain diversity. In chapter 6, sociologists Toby Parcel and Joshua Hendrix join political scientist Andrew Taylor to compare and contrast the interplay of the political, legal, and demographic conditions that shaped the perceived policy options and school assignment choices made in Wake and Mecklenburg Counties during the past forty years.

School policy influences housing patterns; housing patterns shape school diversity; school composition influences residential choices—and the cycle continues. In chapter 7, educator and scholar David Liebowitz and economist Lindsay Page make use of the natural policy experiment, the judicial decision to end CMS's court-ordered desegregation, to examine these dynamics in Mecklenburg County. Their chapter illustrates how the school assignment choices of policy makers triggered an increase in residential segregation in post-unitary CMS.

The last four chapters of the book look to policy and practice options for CMS as the district wrestles with the demographic, curricular, legal, policy, and normative challenges it faces in the immediate and distant future. CMS was essentially a black and white school system at the time of the 1971 *Swann* decision. No longer: in 2014, Mecklenburg County is a colorful mixture of ethnic, linguistic, and racial diversity. For example, the Charlotte area is the nation's fourth largest center of Latino hypergrowth. In chapter 8, urban educator Michelle Plaisance and social geographers Elizabeth Morrell and Paul McDaniel describe and analyze Mecklenburg County's spatial demographic shifts during the forty years since the Court's decision in 1971 and these shifts' striking implications for CMS, especially its policies for English language learners.

Despite its many problems, the resegregated CMS can claim some important successes, including the transformation of Shamrock Gardens Elementary School from one of the lowest performing schools in the state to a model "turnaround school" even though it remains a high poverty, racially isolated school. In chapter 9, urban educator and scholar Amy Hawn Nelson chronicles the school's ten-year journey to sustained improvements. The chapter problematizes test-score snapshot assessments of reform success, suggests instead that a longitudinal and multifaceted success trajectory be used, and explores the likelihood for implementing Shamrock's model across CMS and urban schools nationally.

For decades, civil rights and educational equity advocates have relied on the federal courts as allies in their struggle. As attorneys Mark Dorosin and Luke

Largess argue in chapter 10, the federal judiciary has largely retreated from this historic role. But the North Carolina constitution and the state courts' interpretation of their role may yet offer remedies to school socioeconomic and racial segregation and their sequelae. Drawing upon North Carolina court decisions in the state's educational adequacy cases *Leandro v. State of North Carolina* (*Leandro I*; 1997) and *Hoke County Board of Education v. State of North Carolina* (*Leandro II*; 2004), and the 2007 U.S. Supreme Court decision in *Parents Involved in Community Schools v. Seattle School District No. 1* (2007), the authors examine the legal parameters and options for achieving an integrated, sound, basic education for every child in North Carolina.

In the book's concluding chapter, we draw upon the earlier chapters to discuss the prospects for integrated, equitable, high-quality education in CMS. We reflect upon how CMS's experiences inform the book's larger theoretical argument about the relationship of structure and agency for social action and public policy, and we consider how implications of CMS's experiences during the past four decades might inform the prospects for, and obstacles to, creating genuinely integrated education in this increasingly multiethnic democratic society. We pay particular attention to the opportunities and barriers to educational reform presented by the complexities of the nested structures in which decision makers set policies and attempt to implement them. Finally, we analyze the lessons CMS holds for other large urban school systems, for twenty-first-century public education nationwide, and more generally, for race-neutral approaches to public policy.

As the chapters in this volume demonstrate, the policy of mandatory desegregation had striking effects on a host of outcomes for the students, parents, businesses, and community in Charlotte and Mecklenburg County. And as the chapters also indicate, the return to racially and socioeconomically isolated schools has also had marked effects on the people, the neighborhoods, and the larger community. Yesterday, CMS was the nation's desegregation bellwether. Today, it is struggling, with varying degrees of success and failure, to avoid becoming a separate and unequal school district like Atlanta, Chicago, Detroit, or Newark. To what extent will tomorrow's CMS be the bellwether for education policy, school reform, and desegregation or resegregation? This book provides a basis for exploring that question.

CHAPTER 2

The Price of Success

The Political Economy of Education, Desegregation, and Development In Charlotte

Stephen Samuel Smith

*The success of Charlotte, N.C. and Mecklenburg County, all this economic success
. . . has been based on what I would call racial harmony . . . Had we taken a different
course in 1972 (when schools were desegregated), then we would not be enjoying the
prosperity that we now have.*[1]

> —Statement prior to the 1999 reopening of the *Swann* litigation by C. D.
> Spangler Jr., business executive, member of Charlotte's school board in the
> 1970s, one of North Carolina's wealthiest individuals, president of the Uni-
> versity of North Carolina, and president of Harvard's board of overseers

*Almost immediately after we integrated our schools, the southern economy took off like a
wildfire in the wind. I believe integration made the difference. Integration—and the diversity it began to nourish—became a source of economic, cultural, and community strength.*[2]

> —Statement in 2000 by Hugh L. McColl Jr., at the time CEO and chair-
> man of Charlotte-based Bank of America and the person widely credited
> for spearheading the bank's emergence as a global financial powerhouse

THESE STATEMENTS BY TWO of Charlotte's most preeminent business
executives have been widely echoed by numerous other civic leaders as well
as by virtually every journalist and scholar (including me) who has written
about the Charlotte-Mecklenburg Schools (CMS). CMS gave rise to the *Swann*
decision of 1971 in which the Supreme Court upheld the constitutionality of
mandatory busing for school desegregation in a unanimous decision whose

opinion was authored by Chief Justice Warren Burger, a Nixon appointee. That landmark decision facilitated desegregation nationwide, and CMS developed one of the nation's most successful mandatory busing plans.

Given that contemporary Charlotte is much more of a global city than it was in the 1970s and 1980s—the heyday of the mandatory busing plan—and that desegregation is usually touted as preparing students to deal with the increasingly diverse workplaces and societies resulting from globalization, one might assume that school desegregation would be even more necessary for Charlotte's development at the start of the twenty-first century than it was a generation ago. But that assumption is contradicted by Charlotte's recent history, which has been characterized not by increasing racial and socioeconomic desegregation, but *re*segregation.

This chapter's goal is to discuss how the contrasting trends in desegregation and development—the former decreasing, the latter increasing—have been affected by the interplay of structure and agency. Especially important structural influences include the aftermath of court decisions and the consequences of the construction and location of highways, schools, and so forth—what chapter 1 called "brick-and-mortar structures." Discussion of the agency aspect of the interplay will focus on the choices and actions of Charlotte's corporate class, the single most influential social formation in the city. Also considered will be the agency of CMS board members and administrators, civil rights advocates, and the many people who moved to Charlotte because of its flourishing economy.

The chapter's discussion of the interplay between structure and agency in Charlotte's desegregation saga can be usefully prefaced by being put in broad historical perspective. In the post–World War II era, the South's economic development, the political stability of the region, and Cold War competition with the Soviet Union required transformation of many aspects of southern race relations, especially because of the determination with which blacks were challenging these relations. This transformation's national aspects included landmark court decisions and legislation such as *Brown v. Board of Education* and the 1964 Civil Rights Act. But the particular route this transformation took in any given locality was heavily affected by the specifics of the local situation. In Charlotte, these specifics involved school desegregation. However, once the transformation of race relations together with Charlotte's political and economic development had crossed certain thresholds, the city's future development no longer hinged as heavily, if at all, on school desegregation. Thus, although CMS's desegregation accomplishments once facilitated development, public schools in Charlotte increasingly resemble the systems in the many other U.S. cities whose successful participation in the global economy is scarcely affected by their public education systems' de facto segregation.

THE ADOPTION OF CHARLOTTE'S DESEGREGATION PLAN

The Supreme Court's *Swann* decision was an affirmation of the April 1969 decision by Federal District Court Judge James McMillan. CMS appealed McMillan's decision, triggering legal battles as well as upheavals that included fighting at newly desegregated schools, frequent bomb threats at these schools, and the nighttime torching of the offices of Julius Chambers, the black attorney who represented the *Swann* plaintiffs. Antibusing sentiment also manifested itself in a wide spectrum of legal activities that included demonstrations, petitions signed by thousands of parents, and the formation of an antibusing organization, the Concerned Parents Association (CPA), which fielded three candidates for the three seats at stake in the 1970 school board election. All three of the CPA's candidates won.[3]

The virulence of the opposition to McMillan's desegregation order and the racism often accompanying this opposition helped unite the black community in support of school desegregation, and between the early 1970s and mid-1980s there were not any significant challenges from within Charlotte's black community to desegregation's hegemonic position. To be sure, the inequities of the busing plan (discussed shortly) occasioned opposition from many blacks, but that opposition was aimed at making the busing plan work more fairly, not ending it.

Although the almost exclusively white antidesegregation fervor triggered by McMillan's 1969 decision helped unify the black community in support of school desegregation, the same cannot be said of Charlotte's corporate class. While the corporate class had quickly come together to desegregate public accommodations in the early 1960s, on school desegregation it remained on the sidelines and divided until the Supreme Court's decision. "It was," as one business leader remarked, referring to Charlotte's historically black university, "one thing to go to lunch with a Johnson C. Smith professor; it was quite another to send one's child to school in a black neighborhood." But the Supreme Court's decision convinced the corporate class that court-ordered busing was virtually inevitable, and that only the effective implementation of a desegregation plan could restore stability to CMS and tranquility to the community. As the struggle to put CMS on a new course unfolded from 1972 to 1976, the corporate class became deeply involved in the process. The Chamber of Commerce, in the words of the school board chair, William Poe, "played sort of a partnership with local government."[4] The Chamber funded surveys and provided assistance to a citizens committee trying to devise a busing plan, and its chair, Cliff Cameron, lobbied fellow business leaders.

An especially powerful illustration of the corporate class's change in perspective is provided by the 1972 school board election. This was the first to take place after the Supreme Court's decision and followed the 1970 election in which opponents of busing had won all three seats that were at stake. The corporate class had made no coherent attempt to influence the 1970 school board election, but the 1972 election proved very different. A *Charlotte Observer* article, headlined "Slate-Makers Tap Candidates for Funds," described how a "lower-level executive of a large Charlotte-based bank . . . wrote a $500 check to the 'Committee for Better Government,'" a group that consisted largely of influential businessmen and had existed for twelve years. However, in a "departure from tradition," the group, for the first time, provided support to candidates for the school board, deciding that it was their "responsibility as community leaders to endorse persons who will join the bitterly divided board's present majority bloc, which is willing to live with court-ordered busing." All three of the candidates supported by the Committee for Better Government were elected, and it was this newly constituted board that took the decisive steps in developing Charlotte's busing plan, the specifics of which are discussed in chapter 1. Although one of the three members of the victorious 1970 CPA slate would be reelected in 1976, no candidate with an explicitly antibusing platform would again secure election to the school board until 1988.[5]

SCHOOL DESEGREGATION, LOCAL POLITICS, AND ECONOMIC DEVELOPMENT

Although it was only after the Supreme Court's decision that Charlotte's corporate class threw its support behind CMS's desegregation efforts, corporate executives and their spokespeople would soon milk the school system's desegregation accomplishments for all they were worth in the national competition among localities to attract investment capital. The success of the busing plan allowed civic boosters to publicize Charlotte as a progressive southern city with tranquil and enlightened race relations, and these boosters got a lot more mileage from touting Charlotte as the "City That Made It (school desegregation) Work" than they could have gotten from calling Charlotte just another city, like Atlanta, that was "too busy to hate."

Corporate executives' support for the busing plan was part of a broader political alliance between these executives and the political leadership of the black community. This alliance was a defining characteristic of Charlotte's urban regime through the 1970s and most of the 1980s, and it played a frequently decisive role in the election of pro-growth local officials and the successful passage of bond referenda for roads, sewers, and other infrastructure necessary for Charlotte's growth. The political clout of the alliance of the corporate class and black political leadership was exemplified by the mayoral elections of 1983 and 1985, in which Harvey Gantt became the first black to be elected mayor of a large, predominantly white southern city.

Development Undermines Desegregation

Although school desegregation facilitated development, when there was a conflict between the two, development typically trumped desegregation, as illustrated by the population growth that occurred in the south of the county. As early as the 1979–1980 school year an *Observer* columnist noted, "If some of the city's explosive suburban growth could be shifted around to the north and west, it would be much easier to deal with school [racial] imbalances."[6] Based on recognition that the high-growth areas in south Mecklenburg were distant from neighborhoods with large numbers of blacks, the columnist's point was an obvious one. Its prescience is illustrated by the history of McAlpine Elementary School, built in the mid-1980s. Located in predominantly white southeast Charlotte, McAlpine was planned as a response to growth, but it also fueled development. "When that site was selected," a developer testified in the reopened *Swann* litigation, "almost overnight there were major subdivisions that came on line. Land values certainly started increasing."[7] The CMS administration did have reservations about the site, but felt that the judicious drawing of attendance boundaries and the pairing of McAlpine with other schools would allow it to be racially balanced. This hope was realized, sometimes barely, until the 1990s when, as will be discussed shortly, most of the mandatory busing plan was scrapped. CMS stopped pairing elementary schools and McAlpine's black population plummeted to 4 percent in 1995–1996, an academic year in which blacks constituted 41 percent of CMS's enrollment.

A year after McAlpine opened, CMS made a similar decision with equally dire consequences for desegregation. It purchased another parcel of land—this one even farther south than McAlpine. The site's considerable distance from any sizeable concentration of black neighborhoods notwithstanding, CMS planners claimed that an appropriate black/white ratio could be obtained by busing black students from an inner-city neighborhood. That claim provoked considerable skepticism, and the board's two black members and one white member voted against acquiring the site. Their skepticism proved justified. Although the school, McKee Road, was racially balanced during its first year of operation (the 1989–1990 school year), it became racially imbalanced the next year and remained so. With the completion of the depairing of elementary schools in 1996–1997, McKee's black enrollment plummeted to 1 percent, making it CMS's most racially imbalanced school at the time of the trial in the reactivated *Swann* case.[8]

In addition to illustrating the difficulty of desegregating a school built in such an outlying region of the county, the McKee Road story calls attention, as did that of McAlpine, to the self-fulfilling character of school siting decisions; they can both contribute to development as well as respond to it. In the case of McKee Road, much of the development near the site may have been planned prior to the school board's decision to acquire it. But as with McAlpine, another portion of the major development in the area followed CMS's decision to acquire the land for McKee. In particular, the preliminary plans for the 141-residential-unit Providence Arbours Development, located one-half mile from the school, were not filed until five months after CMS decided to acquire the land.

An event of much broader consequences than the acquisition of land for the McAlpine and McKee Road elementary schools involves the debate over the location in southern Mecklenburg County of the Outerbelt (an interstate highway), which also provides an especially graphic illustration of the corporate class typically choosing development over desegregation. Beginning in the mid-1970s and not fully resolved for a decade, the debate saw the Chamber of Commerce and most of Charlotte's major developers and builders push for the more southern of the two proposed routes, despite the fact that this route would greatly lengthen the bus rides necessary for desegregation between white outlying neighborhoods and closer-in black neighborhoods. The debate over the Outerbelt's construction was finally resolved with the help of Johnny Harris, an influential developer who wanted to develop his vast landholdings in southern Mecklenburg into the two-thousand-acre residential, commercial, and recreational development called Ballantyne. Harris took advantage of his fund-raising activities in the 1984 gubernatorial campaign to secure appointment to the state's board of transportation. Once on the board, the *Observer* reported, Harris "pushed for completing the southern leg of the Outerbelt . . . It will border Ballantyne, increasing the land's value. Harris donated 110 acres in Ballantyne for the Outerbelt, U.S. 521, and other roads. In return, the state will relocate and widen U.S. 521 through Ballantyne. That is how the system works . . . Harris's advantage over most developers is the family land."[9] The eventual opening of the southern leg of the Outerbelt in the 1990s helped suck development from mid-ring neighborhoods and contributed to widespread demographic changes in these neighborhoods' schools.[10]

Attempts at Residential Desegregation

The unfortunate (for *school* desegregation) consequences of development in outlying, predominantly white neighborhoods might have been ameliorated had public policy aimed at increasing *residential* desegregation been more successful. In this respect, Charlotte had a promising start. In 1973, Julius Chambers filed suit in federal court charging the Charlotte Housing Authority with furthering residential discrimination by concentrating public housing in predominantly black neighborhoods. Despite initial resistance to the suit by many local officials, a settlement was reached several years later. Charlotte's initial scattered-site public housing project opened in 1978, making it one of the first localities in the country to coordinate its school desegregation and public housing efforts. Nine hundred units were eventually built in about twenty projects, but a combination of local and national developments brought the scattered-site program to an end about a decade later.

Subsequent efforts were even less successful, the most notable occurring in 1993–1994 as the busing plan was being phased out in favor of the increased use of magnets. At the request of school board member Arthur Griffin, the staff of the planning commission prepared a report, *Housing Strategies to Racially Integrate Schools.* Some of the proposed measures, such as monitoring and enforcing fair housing laws, were unexceptional and provoked little controversy. However, other strategies were both more ambitious and controversial, with the suggested exploration of "the use of regulatory techniques and incentive programs such as inclusionary zoning, linkage ordinances, density bonuses, and low interest loans" provoking a storm of criticism. The school board supported the report and passed a resolution calling for the creation of an Affordable Housing Policy Task Force that would include members of the school board, city council, county commission, and representatives of the real estate, banking, and housing industries. But other elected officials were less favorably inclined.

In a lengthy memo, Charlotte Republican Mayor Richard Vinroot wrote that while many of the goals were appealing, the overall tone and approach smacked of "social engineering." Rather than create a special committee, he successfully urged that the matter be left in the hands of the planning commission. The *Observer* endorsed that proposal as a way to nurture the city and "get past the hot rhetoric." But leaving matters in the hands of the planning commission—which was much more responsive than its staff to developers' concerns—effectively killed any attempt to implement the report's more ambitious strategies. It is thus hardly surprising that a year later the *Observer* could report: "There has been talk of building affordable housing throughout the county as a way to naturally desegregate the schools, but there are no formal plans."[11] More recent efforts to disperse affordable housing throughout the county have sometimes succeeded but more frequently have not.[12]

Newcomers Change Things

The ongoing housing issues and the importance of the Outerbelt's opening in the 1990s notwithstanding, both the busing plan and the alliance between the corporate class and black political leaders were already facing significant challenges by the late 1980s. In the 1987 mayoral election, Gantt, a Democrat, was upset by Republican Sue Myrick. Gantt's defeat had many reasons, the most relevant here being the changes in Charlotte's electorate and political geography wrought by the development that attracted newcomers from the North and Midwest. The white Republicans among the newcomers were more likely than others to settle in outlying areas of the county whose incorporation into the city of Charlotte was facilitated by North Carolina's liberal annexation laws. Education politics were also significantly affected by the white newcomers. Moving to Charlotte from outside the South, many were accustomed to predominantly white, suburban school districts; and, not having lived through CMS's desegregation battles, they lacked the pride of more established Charlotteans in the busing plan. Local unhappiness with busing resonated with the national dissatisfaction with public education that had been triggered by the 1983 publication of *A Nation at Risk*. Dissatisfaction with CMS was especially manifest in the 1988 school board election, which saw the defeat of three incumbents who were strong supporters of busing. Among their replacements was the first candidate in more than a decade to get elected on a platform calling for an end to busing for desegregation.[13] Turnover on the board increased in the 1990 election, and this dramatically different (from what it had been prior to 1988) board brought further changes to CMS with the hiring in 1991 of a new superintendent, John Murphy, who had a national reputation for being a "change agent."

Murphy lived up to that reputation in Charlotte, instituting a high-stakes accountability program and dismantling much of the mandatory busing plan in favor of a system of magnet schools, which was an effort to have the cake and eat it too; that is, to maintain desegregation but placate those, especially whites, opposed to mandatory busing. The plan also sought to hitch CMS's wagon to the rising star of school choice and thus help increase public confidence in the district. Although Murphy touted the magnet program as a way to maintain desegregation, the drift toward resegregation continued during his administration, in part because the magnets were creaming resources from other schools. Murphy began his tenure with strong support from the corporate class and many other sections of the community. But his frequent flirtations with superintendent jobs in other districts, abrasive management style, and preoccupation with his financial compensation eroded much of this support, and he resigned his position in December 1995. Moreover, as noted in chapter 1, the use of racial guidelines in magnet school pupil assignment decisions triggered a lawsuit by a white parent, William Capacchione, reflecting, as had the 1988 school board election, the special challenge to CMS desegregation policy posed by newly arrived whites. Capacchione had recently moved to Charlotte, as had five of the six other whites who joined him as plaintiffs in the 1999 trial that stemmed from his lawsuit.[14] At that two-month trial, CMS—as a result of a 6–3 vote by a sharply divided school board—vigorously defended its desegregation goals and fought to continue them. Presiding at the trial was Federal District Court Judge Robert Potter, who, as a private citizen, had been active in Charlotte's 1960s antibusing movement. Three months after the trial ended, Potter issued his ruling declaring CMS unitary and ordering it to stop using race in pupil assignment.

INITIAL AFTERMATH OF THE 1999 TRIAL

Potter's ruling ushered in several years of turmoil as CMS struggled with the ruling's aftermath. Key aspects of this turmoil were prefigured by a rally in downtown Charlotte featuring many political and business leaders that took place shortly between the trial's conclusion and Potter's announcement of his ruling. Resulting from fears that the trial had exacerbated doubts about the quality of education and the stability of pupil assignment, the self-proclaimed

Unity Rally was billed as an event that would unite Charlotteans whatever the outcome of the court case. Indicative of the corporate class's diminishing interest in pushing for desegregation was a statement by Allen Tate, a leading local realtor, chair of the Charlotte Chamber, and one of the main organizers of the rally: "The business community is anxious to get on with this business of education . . . We know we've got to move on."[15]

However, efforts "to move on" were stymied by other dynamics, many of which were illustrated by another rally several months later that packed one of Charlotte's largest black churches. Initiated by black religious, civic, and political leaders, this rally reflected alarm at the widespread resegregation portended by Potter's ruling. With a spirit reminiscent of the civil rights era, the prevailing sentiment of the rally was exemplified by remarks of one of its organizers: "We will not go back to a segregated system. There is a storm in Charlotte, and there can be no peace without justice."[16]

All four black members of CMS's school board attended this rally, as did one of its white members. Constituting a (bare) majority of CMS's nine-member board, these five people fought—during the subsequent exhaustive courtroom appeals of Potter's ruling and intense local controversy about a new pupil assignment plan—to preserve as much of CMS's historic commitment to desegregation as the changed legal environment would allow. The board majority's ability to wage this fight, indeed the continued existence of the majority, was made possible by the November 1999 election. Occurring a month after the school board voted to appeal Potter's ruling, the election was one in which the board's three at-large seats were at stake.[17] The board's two black at-large members, Arthur Griffin and Wilhelmenia Rembert, retained their seats despite their strong advocacy of this appeal and the high-profile campaigns of two challengers who opposed the appeal.

Initially, the board majority's efforts to preserve as much desegregation as was legally possible were accompanied by significant supportive grassroots mobilization, but this mobilization progressively diminished. With the legal appeals largely failing; CMS Superintendent Eric Smith, the corporate class, and most city and county elected officials pushing to "move on"; and increasing numbers of citizens dismayed by the ongoing uncertainty over pupil assignment, the school board adopted a new assignment plan in July 2001.

The Family Choice Plan, as it was called, can conveniently be summarized as a race-neutral choice plan that employed a complex system of magnet schools and geographically determined attendance areas. These areas gave every student a "home school," one near his or her residence, at which attendance was guaranteed. Students who did not wish to attend their home school could apply to other schools. But if a school lacked capacity to accommodate all applicants, preference went to those for whom it was the home school. Admittance to magnet schools was determined by a lottery, but in keeping with Potter's ruling, neither the lottery nor any other aspect of the pupil assignment plan took race into account.

The board's decision to adopt the plan lowered some of the stakes for the six district seats that were on the ballot in the November 2001 election. But important issues remained. The pivotal contest involved a challenge to Louise Woods, the white member of the five-person board majority that had sought to alleviate the district's pending resegregation. With considerable support from the corporate class, Woods's challenger raised more than three times the campaign funds that she did. But strong neighborhood organization and the advantages of incumbency helped her stave off the challenge by a 58–42 percent margin. The board's five-person majority thus remained intact.[18]

The results of the 2001 election illustrate an important point: despite claims about desegregation's unpopularity in Charlotte and elsewhere, the two school board elections (1995 and 1997) immediately prior to Potter's decision and the two school board elections immediately after it (1999 and 2001) resulted in CMS school boards whose majorities were committed to pursuing desegregation. This is not to say that these elections were referenda on desegregation; a lot of other considerations affected their outcome. But it is to emphasize that in Charlotte the workings of democratic local electoral politics resulted in school boards that advocated desegregation. In this respect, the situation at the end of the twentieth century was diametrically opposed to what it had been in the civil rights era, when desegregation proponents sought redress in the federal courts because local political venues were so hostile to civil rights.[19]

In Charlotte at the end of the twentieth century, it was the federal judiciary that was hostile to school desegregation and the local political venue that was supportive of it. Of course, there was considerable local opposition to CMS's desegregation efforts from 1995 to 2001. But despite this opposition, it was not until the 2003 school board election—by which time the Supreme Court had issued its final ruling in the reopened *Swann* case and Charlotte's black community experienced considerable demobilization over educational issues—that the school board's pro-desegregation majority was dismantled, resulting in the board's political perspective and racial composition changing dramatically.

The 2001 election provided a portent of this change. Although the board's pro-desegregation majority remained intact, this election also saw Larry Gauvreau—the most outspoken of the victorious white plaintiffs in the re-opened *Swann* litigation—win a seat on the board from the district in northern Mecklenburg. Gauvreau's opposition to CMS's desegregation policies was ac-companied by the combative scorn exemplified by his pre-election statement in the *Observer* denouncing the "diversity hucksters roaming the hallways of American education, business, and government."[20] His election augured the ongoing turmoil and greater political changes that would soon affect CMS.

THE EARLY YEARS OF THE POST-*SWANN* ERA

A discussion of these years best begins with an examination of resegregation followed by a historical narrative of this period's key events.

Resegregation

As figure 2.1 indicates, black/white segregation drifted upward through the 1990s, jumped sharply in 2002–2003, and has increased since then.[21] Similarly, white/nonwhite and white/Hispanic levels of segregation are also high.[22] Fig-ure 2.2 indicates that socioeconomic resegregation—as measured by the free or reduced lunch (FRL)/non-FRL dissimilarity index—has also increased, with the single sharpest jump occurring upon implementation in 2002–2003 of the new pupil assignment plan.

FIGURE 2.1   Elementary school black/white resegregation, 1997–2013

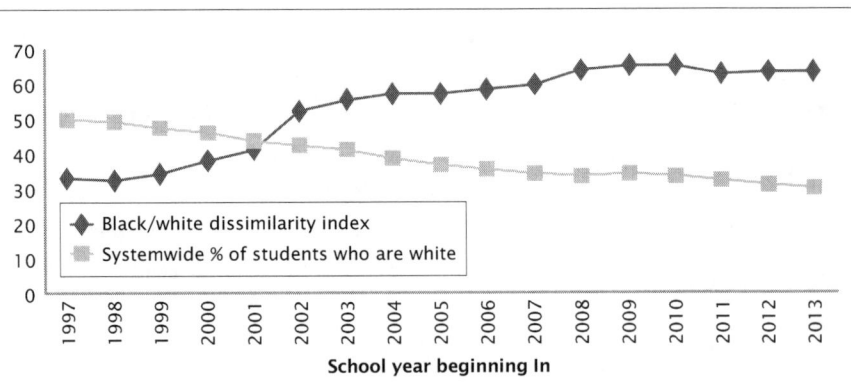

Source: Charlotte-Mecklenburg Schools

The increase in resegregation was paralleled by a change in CMS's self-definition. In 2006, the district revised its vision statement in a way that codified and inscribed on the district's self-definition the changes in pupil assignment that were taking place. For at least fifteen years, the statement had included the lofty aspiration of being "the premier, urban integrated school system in the nation in which all students acquire the knowledge, skills, and values" necessary to live full, enlightened, and productive lives. But the revised statement made no reference to integration or even implied the commitment to diversity and racial justice that was inherent in the inclusion of *integrated* in the abandoned statement. Rather, the revised statement rested content with saying that the district "provides all students the best education available anywhere, preparing every child to lead a rich and productive life."[23]

The abandonment of that lofty goal resembled another change that also recognized how CMS's reality now differed from its previously more grandiose aspirations. Whereas the post-*Swann* pupil assignment plan was initially called the Family Choice Plan, in 2004 it became simply the Student Assignment Plan. The change reflected the fact that, as an assistant superintendent commented in 2005, the plan's initial name erroneously conveyed the impression that families had more choice than they actually had.[24] The paucity of meaningful choices resulted from so many families choosing to exercise their guarantee of attendance at their home school. Thus, other than attending an underenrolled high-poverty school, there were very few choices available to students who did not want to attend their home school.

FIGURE 2.2   Elementary school socioeconomic resegregation, 1997–2013

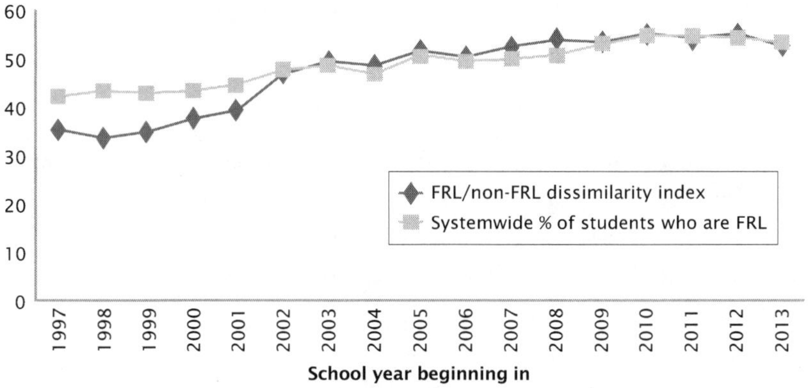

Source: Charlotte-Mecklenburg Schools

Academic Genocide, Overcrowding, and Attempts at Secession

The increased resegregation provided black members of the school board and their supporters, both black and white, with additional motivation to seek more instructional resources, more effective teachers, smaller class sizes, and better physical facilities at the increased numbers of schools with high concentrations of children of color from economically disadvantaged families. Thus, over the past fifteen years CMS has instituted a variety of programs to allocate these compensatory resources, such as providing high-poverty schools with additional funding. The longstanding concerns about academic achievement at CMS's high-poverty schools received dramatic judicial acknowledgment in 2005 when the judge in the long-running *Leandro I* educational adequacy case charged CMS with committing "academic genocide" on at-risk students in many of the district's high schools (see chapter 10 for a discussion of this case).[25]

The increased resegregation also fueled discontent in many outlying, predominantly white areas, but for different reasons. With large numbers of families in these areas opting for their home school, overcrowding increased in many schools in these outlying areas. Discontent gave rise in south Mecklenburg to Parents for Education in Charlotte-Mecklenburg Schools, and in the north to Families United for North Mecklenburg Education, whose acronym, FUME, bespoke these families' sentiments. Contributing to anger about the overcrowding was the claim by Gauvreau and other conservative activists that this overcrowding arose largely because CMS was spending too much money on renovating and building schools in neighborhoods of color in order to pursue desegregation and/or to please these neighborhoods' representatives.[26] Angry as members of these two groups were, most of their emphasis was on fixing CMS through school board elections, serving on task forces, and mobilizing parents to speak at school boards.

However, by early 2005, north Mecklenburg gave rise to an additional movement that was not so much concerned with fixing CMS as it was with dumping it—the group's website was titled dumpcms.com—by breaking it up into smaller districts. Fueling this movement were the severe overcrowding and complaints about discipline, safety, and the district's large size, many of the latter coming from newcomers to Charlotte who were accustomed to the smaller districts in other parts of the country. This group's initial meeting drew more than four hundred people. Larry Gauvreau supported deconsolidation, as did other conservative political officials including the county commissioner who represented northern Mecklenburg and the mayor of Matthews, a town in southern Mecklenburg County.[27] However, deconsolidation required the approval of the state legislature, which had generally promoted consolidation between a county district and any city district(s) located within the county. Thus, the state House's education committee killed the proposal with a near unanimous vote that was accompanied by statements from some members that deconsolidation would further segregate the district.

The 2003 School Board Election

Although efforts to secede from CMS failed, those to change the school board in the 2003 elections did not. With two longtime incumbents, including Arthur Griffin, deciding not to seek re-election in 2003, that election would of necessity bring two new faces to the at-large seats. However, it brought three new faces because of the defeat of Wilhelmenia Rembert, who was board chair. Rembert's loss stemmed from a variety of factors, probably the most important of which were indicated by her post-election analysis: "I believe there was a lot more anger in the suburbs and not the same sense of urgency in the black community."[28] Indeed, black mobilization in support of her campaign—as was the case with many other aspects of education politics—was weaker in 2003 than it had been in 1999. Part of the reason was a generically lower black turnout. However, there was also a more specific demobilization with regard to school board elections as measured by the fall-off in voting between contests at the top of the ballot (i.e., mayor and city council) and those further down the ballot (i.e., school board).[29]

Equally important as Rembert's defeat was the victory of Kaye McGarry, a white first-time candidate, who led the field with a stunning 18 percent more votes than the second-place finisher. She did especially well in Mecklenburg's outlying heavily white precincts, but in the heavily black precincts her vote total was less than 3 percent of Rembert's. Although voicing support for equity of resources in all schools, McGarry also claimed, "We do not have a funding problem; we have a spending problem. We do not need to be a transportation system; we need to be an education system."[30] Such claims, as well as her emphasis on preserving the home school guarantee, secured endorsements from prominent local conservatives, the Republican Party, and Parents for Education in Charlotte-Mecklenburg Schools and FUME. McGarry was also supported in a letter to the *Observer* and a thousand-dollar campaign contribution from Hugh McColl Jr., generally viewed as Charlotte's single most influential business executive of the past thirty years.[31] As noted by one of this chapter's epigraphs, McColl touted the effects of school desegregation in the 1970s and 1980s and its effect on economic development. Moreover, absent a scheduling conflict in the 1999 trial, McColl would have testified, at CMS's request, about the importance of diversity.[32] But given the outcome of the trial, he was unwilling to try to prevent the resegregation facing CMS since there was scant political or economic incentive to make that effort. Neither were other members of the corporate class, as indicated by the views of Kit Cramer, an executive of the Charlotte Chamber of Commerce, whose perspective typically reflects that of the corporate class. Recruited to run for school board by her boss, Cramer, too, was elected in 2003.[33] Several months into her term—by which time the resegregative consequences of the new pupil assignment plan were evident—the *Charlotte Business Journal* took note of this resegregation, indicated that the newly elected school board had shown "limited desire" to deal with the issue, and quoted Cramer, "'The last thing I'd like to see is us going into another pupil reassignment brouhaha,' she says. 'That instability is what drove a lot of people out of the system.'"[34]

CMS's Administration and the Corporate Class Try to Cope

Leading CMS during these tumultuous battles over resource allocation, claims of academic genocide, overcrowding, and secession was Superintendent James Pughsley. Previously CMS's deputy superintendent, he was appointed superintendent in May 2002 after Eric Smith announced his resignation. Superintendent since 1997, Eric Smith possessed formidable political skills, and successfully drew upon them in the battle to secure a majority of board members' support for the new pupil assignment plan. But with the plan not scheduled for implementation until the start of the 2002–2003 school year, Smith unceremoniously left the district before it took effect and any of its consequences could be assessed.

Smith's political skills allowed him to flourish in the goldfish bowl that came with being CMS's superintendent. Possessing a different kind of personality, his successor James Pughsley preferred, in his own words "to fly below the radar."[35] That preference, critics charged—some with great fury—helped explain why CMS, under his leadership, was not adequately addressing the many challenges it faced.[36] Many of these challenges stemmed from the political changes exemplified by the 2003 election, and Pughsley did not like these changes. Although a year remained on his contract, he announced his retirement in April 2005, calling attention to how "'the climate has shifted' away from commitment to equal education for all children."[37] That shift, he explained, was illustrated by recent decisions of the school board to change the guidelines for pupil assignment in a way that further strengthened the home school guarantee and that made it more difficult to address the dilemma of severe overcrowding at some schools and the concentrated poverty at others.

CMS's difficulty in dealing with the political turmoil rocking it, especially in outlying, predominantly white areas, triggered efforts by the city's political leaders and corporate class to quiet things down with the formation in March 2005 of a high-profile task force. However, unlike similar groups in CMS's history, this one was neither publicly chosen nor funded. Instead, local corporations contributed $500,000 to support the group's work. Co-chaired by one of Charlotte's most prominent black political figures, former mayor Harvey Gantt, and Cathy Bessant, a white, high-ranking Bank of America executive, the leadership of the task force embodied the alliance between the corporate class and Charlotte's black political leadership that had dominated local politics during the peak of the busing plan and prior to Harvey Gantt's upset in the 1987 mayor's race. But the task force's main concerns only minimally reflected the concerns that had given rise to the busing plan. Rather, its focus was on the governance issues that were especially dear to those seeking to dump CMS. While rejecting deconsolidation, the report's first four recommendations, calling for the sweeping decentralization of CMS, testified to the influence of the Dump CMS movement, as did the recommendation calling for CMS "to modify its K–8 student assignment plan toward a fixed assignment based on residence."[38]

Additional evidence of the differences between the local political and educational landscapes of the 1980s and the first decade of the twenty-first century came in the 2007 school board election, in which no people of color were on the ballot even though students of color composed a higher percentage of CMS's enrollment than ever before. Insofar as Hispanics, Asians, and Native Americans had rarely, if ever, sought election to the board, their absence on the 2007 ballot was perhaps not especially remarkable. But the 2007 school board election was the first board election since 1968 in which no black candidate appeared on the ballot, another indication of the black political demobilization over education issues.[39]

A New Superintendent and Déjà Vu All Over Again

By the time of the 2007 school board election, CMS had a new superintendent, Peter Gorman. Previously a superintendent in California, Gorman was new to the district, and choosing an outsider, an *Observer* editorial writer noted, "was the only sensible choice" because "a newcomer has a much better chance of rallying this fractured community around the public schools to aggressively tackle vital education issues."[40]

Gorman may have had the political skills to do this, but it did not take especially sensitive political antennae to discern that—as indicated by the 2007 school board election—there was much greater white political mobilization in support of the policies advocated by board members such as Kaye McGarry than there was mobilization by blacks and liberal whites in support of alternative policies. Nor did it take political acumen to discern the surging importance of national foundations with market-inspired school reform perspectives, such as the Broad Foundation, in shaping local educational efforts. Even before Gorman's arrival, CMS had recognized this importance, becoming a finalist for the Broad Prize for Urban Education as early as 2004. But under Gorman—who, as noted in chapter 1, was a 2004 graduate of the Broad Academy for Superintendents and in 2011 was a member of the Broad Center's board of directors— CMS rode the Broad wave especially well, winning the 2011 Broad Prize.[41]

Given the prevailing local political winds and the perspectives of national organizations such as the Broad Foundation, it is not surprising that Gorman made scant effort to increase racial or socioeconomic diversity in CMS schools. Rather, his efforts focused on providing racially and socioeconomically isolated schools with additional resources, such as the Strategic Staffing Initiative, which provided financial bonuses to teams of administrators, teachers, and support staff who were assigned to some of the district's high-poverty schools.[42] Similarly, his administration embraced what would become Project LIFT, an effort by local foundations to raise and funnel $55 million in resources toward a group of schools in historically black neighborhoods whose enrollment was overwhelmingly students of color and/or economically disadvantaged ones. Although the documents formalizing and specifying the nature of Project LIFT's relationship with CMS were not signed until after Gorman left CMS, it was clear from the beginning, as chapter 4 indicates, that Project LIFT's strategy for improving education did not include even a minimal effort to alleviate racial/ ethnic or socioeconomic segregation.

At the start of the 2010–2011 academic year, Gorman's last as superintendent, CMS adopted revised pupil assignment guidelines that again gave very high priority to neighborhood schools and relatively little to diversity. Charlotte's black political leadership opposed the guidelines, as did the board's two black board members and a white liberal, all three of whom voted against their adoption.[43] But with the vote coming during the summer, the revisions attracted relatively little public attention. That was not the case, however, a few months later when CMS was rocked by a controversy over school closings necessitated largely by CMS's financial difficulties, which were exacerbated by the Great Recession. Districts rarely succeed in closing schools without controversy, but the one in CMS was especially brutal. With many of the schools slated for closing located in black and/or low-income neighborhoods, the NAACP and an ad hoc group, Save Our Schools, rallied in downtown against the closings, and the head of the NAACP was arrested at one school board forum for spearheading chants by audience members demanding more time to address the board. Other school board meetings and forums were almost as contentious and featured parents from various schools arguing, demanding, and explaining why their school should be spared. When the board finally voted, schools with large percentages of students who were poor and/or of color bore the brunt of the closings. FRL-eligible students composed 80 percent or more of the students in seven of the eight schools that were permanently closed, and 69 percent in the eighth. By contrast, three schools with FRL-eligible populations of less than 40 percent that were originally slated for closing were spared by the board's vote.[44]

A NEW DECADE AND AN UNCERTAIN FUTURE

The battles and anger over the closings contributed to the political mobilization of the black community in the 2011 at-large election. As opposed to 2007, when no blacks sought an at-large seat, in 2011 five of the fourteen candidates on the ballot were black. Moreover, neither Kaye McGarry nor the other two white at-large board members sought re-election. With black turnout buoyed by the re-election campaign of black incumbent Charlotte mayor Anthony Foxx, the 2011 vote resulted in the election of two black school board candidates, one of whom became the board's chair and the other of whom became vice-chair, both without any opposition and both by a unanimous vote. Thus, in many ways the 2011 election resulted in as dramatic a shift in the demographic composition of the board and of its leadership as the 2003 election did, but in the opposite direction.

By the time the 2011 election had taken place, Gorman had left the district to take a job with the education division of Rupert Murdoch's News Corp. Thus, in the 2011–2012 academic year CMS had an interim superintendent, and the board, under its new leadership, conducted a national search for a new superintendent. Its choice was Heath Morrison, previously superintendent of Reno, Nevada, and winner of the 2012 National Superintendent of the Year award.[45] As had Smith and Gorman, Morrison hit the ground running, reaching out to many different sections of the community, promising to be a good listener, and emphasizing the need to unite a badly divided community in support of its public school system. But he did at least one thing that no previous superintendent in a generation had done as forcefully: he put the issue of race squarely on the CMS agenda by proposing that the district hire Glenn Singleton as a consultant. Singleton is president and founder of the Pacific Educational Group, whose purpose is "to transform educational systems into racially conscious and socially just environments that nurture the spirit and potential of all learners, especially black children."[46] In his work, Singleton emphasizes the need for school systems and communities to deal with institutional racism and white privilege and for whites to deal with internalized, perhaps unconscious racism. That emphasis raised predictable hackles among many whites, and as of this writing, more than a year after Morrison's proposal, it remains unclear what future role, if any, Singleton will play in the professional development of CMS staff and educators.

Whether Singleton is hired or not, issues of race and poverty will continue to have important consequences for CMS, as will the demographic composition of its schools. At the time of this writing in the spring of 2014, Mecklenburg County is experiencing greater change in the pupil assignment landscape than at any time since the 2002–2003 implementation of the race-neutral pupil assignment plan with its guarantee of attendance at a neighborhood school. One reason for the change is that CMS hopes to provide greater choice in pupil assignment with, among other things, the number of magnet schools scheduled to increase from thirty-seven in 2013–2014 to over forty in 2014–2015.[47] It remains to be seen whether these new options will alleviate segregation as magnets were traditionally designed to do, or whether they will increase resegregation as CMS's early-1990s magnet plan did.

Contributing to CMS's desire to increase magnet and choice options is the competition from charter schools, which has increased since a Republican-controlled state legislature removed the statewide cap on the number of charter schools that was imposed by the state's charter school-enabling legislation. Consequently, in the 2014–2015 school year, the number of charter schools in Mecklenburg and surrounding counties is scheduled to increase by more than

40 percent (from twenty-six to thirty-seven).[48] As chapter 5 points out, charter schools in Mecklenburg and statewide are more segregated than traditional public schools. So whatever effect CMS's increased choice options might have on segregation, there's good reason to think that the addition of new charter schools will increase the overall amount of segregation—as measured by between-school racial imbalance—in Mecklenburg County.

The increase in between-school racial imbalance likely to result from the legislature's decision to allow additional charter schools resembles the other aspects of resegregation discussed in this chapter. Little, if any, of this resegregation was caused by demographic trends and other developments about which human beings can talk but, as with the weather, cannot change. Rather, this resegregation resulted largely and primarily from choices and actions by human beings, such as that by the legislature to eliminate the statewide cap on charter schools. Of the other choices and actions, the most proximate were CMS's decisions in the 2002 pupil assignment plan to prioritize attendance at a neighborhood (home) school and not consider socioeconomic status, even though Potter's 1999 decision did not rule out such consideration. Less proximate, but also important, have been the actions (or inactions) of Charlotte's corporate class, advocacy groups, and citizens' organizations in supporting candidates and in nonelectoral efforts (e.g., organizing petition drives in neighborhoods, mobilizing attendance at board meetings, and contacting board members) to influence CMS policy. Least proximate have been decisions about the locations of new schools, residential developments, affordable housing, and roads and the other infrastructure that are necessary for economic development.

Each of these sets of decisions and choices resulted in structures that influenced CMS's agency in matters regarding desegregation. The decisions that resulted in the construction of McKee Road Elementary, McAlpine Elementary, and the Outerbelt created brick-and-mortar constraints; and Judge Potter's decision imposed towering legal constraints, at least to the pursuit of racial desegregation.[49] Nothing in his decision created such constraints to the pursuit of socioeconomic desegregation. But with the 2002 pupil assignment plan eschewing this kind of desegregation as well as racial desegregation, any attempt to pursue socioeconomic desegregation a dozen years into the operation of the 2002 plan would now occasion even more of a "pupil assignment brouhaha" than what board member Kit Cramer worried about in 2004. The possibility of such a brouhaha constitutes a political constraint that, while not as binding as legal or brick-and-mortar structures, is nonetheless a formidable one. Finally, while it is too early to ascertain with any certainty all the consequences of the legislature's lifting the cap on charter schools, it is highly unlikely that CMS's agency will be expanded by the legislative decision.

While CMS's ability to pursue desegregation may be constrained by all of the preceding conditions, they do not necessarily make such pursuit impossible. The book's concluding chapter discusses the extent to which some of these structural constraints might be addressed. However, before that discussion can occur, it's necessary to consider other aspects of the CMS desegregation/resegregation saga, which is what the next eight chapters will do.

CHAPTER 3

A Spirit of Togetherness

Desegregation and Community at West Charlotte High School

Pamela Grundy

IN SEPTEMBER 1970, a fleet of school buses descended on West Charlotte High School (WCHS), carrying students from across Mecklenburg County. No one knew what to expect. For the first three decades of its existence, WCHS had been an African American institution, the pride of the black neighborhoods that surrounded its cluster of modern buildings. But in accordance with Mecklenburg County's court-ordered desegregation plan, the school had been assigned a student body that mirrored the county's student population: 70 percent white and 30 percent black. After decades of serving African American students, WCHS was suddenly a majority white school.

The staff that met the buses had undergone an equally striking transformation. Faculties had to be desegregated as well, and most of the African American high school teachers in the district had been employed at West Charlotte. As desegregation plans progressed, administrators at Charlotte-Mecklenburg Schools informed Principal Gerson Stroud that he could keep only nineteen members of his existing staff for the 1970–1971 school year. The rest would be transferred to historically white schools. Rather than requiring experienced white teachers to move to WCHS, CMS officials gave Stroud first choice of the new, mostly young teachers that the district was in the process of hiring.[1]

Charlotte's busing plan thrust blacks and whites together on an unprecedented scale. As students and teachers struggled to adjust to new and unfamiliar situations, they also confronted many obstacles. Yet concerted efforts by a wide range of individuals across Mecklenburg County helped desegregation succeed at many schools, making CMS the most desegregated major school system in the nation for more than two decades. Despite a rocky start, West Charlotte would become the flagship school for the widely celebrated plan, serving as a national model of successful desegregation and a source of pride for the community. "Boys and girls, primarily black and white, but other ethnic and racial groups as well, went to school together, learned together, played together, fought together, cried together, and out of it all evolved a spirit of togetherness unknown in this community before," longtime WCHS teacher Mertye Rice wrote in 1982. "They dared hope and dream, and they made it work."[2]

IMPLEMENTING *SWANN* AT WEST CHARLOTTE HIGH SCHOOL

The first years of desegregation caused significant turmoil across Mecklenburg County. Decades of discrimination and stereotyping had made many North Carolinians wary of or hostile to shifts in racial relations, and many interactions reflected fear or anger. When WCHS graduate Madge Hopkins was assigned to teach at a historically white school, she found the atmosphere so alienating that she left teaching altogether for several years. Sam Haywood, principal at Olympic High School during the first years of busing, learned to monitor the morning school buses for signs of tension, and at times would take an entire busload of students straight to a separate classroom to deal with conflicts or grievances. Mertye Rice recalled that in the first years of integration at WCHS "many of the whites who came were absolutely scared out of their minds. They had heard so much about what black kids do—black people steal, black people rape, all these myths."[3]

That first year at WCHS felt "like a fog," recalled Stan Frazier, class of 1971. "I think teachers were on their tippy-toes, afraid to say the wrong thing," Frazier explained. "It was an eerie feeling. You didn't get close to a lot of people." While many students gamely tried to work together, tensions filled the halls and frequent fights broke out. The change disrupted clubs and teams, and fears of violence kept fans away from sports events. "I think that there was a general fear in the community that 'We don't want to be in an environment that's going to put the races together in masses and may cause something,'" recalled William Hamlin Jr., class of 1963.[4]

The school's future also remained in doubt. Charlotte's oldest African American high school, Second Ward, had been shut down without warning the year before full-scale busing began—a decision many African Americans believed was made because the wealthy white families that lived near Second Ward did not want their children assigned there. White families were clearly reluctant to send their children to WCHS, and a spate of transfers and withdrawals made keeping the required racial balance a constant struggle. Different groups of students were assigned to the school each year, and the shifts in population left students and teachers desperate for stability. "Can West Charlotte survive?" frustrated students asked at one point. "For four years we have gone through proposals, plans, and pupil assignments . . . How long can students be dealt like cards?"[5]

Stability finally came in the fall of 1974. Early busing plans had barely touched the city's wealthiest white neighborhoods, and this glaring inequality had intensified opposition to the plans in less well-off communities. In 1974, however, a community group brokered an agreement that spread the busing more evenly through the city. West Charlotte sat at the heart of that agreement. Realizing that the busing conflict could tear the city apart and thus short-circuit their visions of economic growth, a group of Charlotte's wealthiest and most powerful citizens agreed to send their children to WCHS.[6]

The new plan came with changes for the school. Gerson Stroud was replaced with Sam Haywood, one of the system's most respected white principals. WCHS became the site for the city's innovative "Open School" magnet program. That next summer, the school also got a facelift: six new mobile classrooms, a new paved parking lot for student cars, two new tennis courts, and a thoroughly refurbished interior. Classrooms, the school yearbook *The Lion* reported, "were painted in varying shades of pastels, and any traces of 'institutional green' were obliterated from the interiors . . . The library was considerably brightened by orange and green paint; soon after school began, carpet was installed, adding to the comfort of the studious." Gosnell White, class of 1973, noticed the difference right away. "It took integration to get the parking lots paved," he noted. "Those were gravel parking lots out there for all the years, and we had asked and asked for paved parking lots . . . And then I come back when I'm in college, we're one of the model schools and everything's paved, the office is immaculate. And I'm like, 'Well, what a difference a day makes.'"[7]

Amid the newly painted walls, students and teachers went about the hard work of making an ideal into reality. It would prove a challenging task. Even in the absence of overt hostility, old barriers were difficult to break down. Garfield Carr, who was transferred from a black school to a previously white school elsewhere in the county, explained the uncertainty with which he and his fellow students faced their new white teachers. "If you had a problem with homework, you didn't want to appear to be dumb because in some cases, that's what some of them may have thought about you," he explained. "You didn't want to give the appearance that you were. You didn't know whether to ask another student to help you because again you didn't know what they were going to think about you, or whether they would [help] or not, or [whether] what they told you was even the truth. So most of the time, when you had a break you would all tend to get with your friends—somebody we could really associate with."[8]

Such obstacles, however, were also accompanied by signs of hope. Although black children were bused far more often than their white counterparts, many African American parents were willing to make such sacrifices to give their children better opportunities. "I didn't want my children to have to be bused out of the neighborhood. I really didn't," explained Saundra Jones Davis, class of 1958, who had school-age children when CMS began its busing program. "But if that meant my children getting a better education, *yes*. Let them be bused. Somebody had to do it. The ice had to be broken somewhere. For the simple reason [that] the white schools had always had the better things."[9]

BUILDING AN INTERRACIAL COMMUNITY

Desegregation also drew strength from the many residents who were willing to work to realize a vision of an interracial society—the vision that had led Darius and Vera Swann to file the lawsuit that led to the busing plan. The Swanns' son, James, had been born in India, where the Swanns were serving as missionaries. When they wrote the CMS school board to challenge their son's assignment to an all-black school, they explained that "James has never known the meaning of racial segregation. We have been happy to watch him grow and develop with an unaffected openness to people of all races and backgrounds, and we feel it our duty as parents to ensure that this healthy development continues."[10] That vision was also shared by a number of Charlotte's white residents, who had become keenly aware of the wrongs of segregation, and were eager to begin the work of forging a more just society.

North Carolina native Bill Culp, who had been involved in the Greensboro sit-in movement, was one of a number of white teachers who jumped at the chance to work in a desegregated environment, requesting assignment to WCHS in the late 1960s. "I had grown up in a Methodist minister's home," Culp explained. "And of course the race question and the civil rights issues were very important topics in my home during the fifties and early sixties. And so I had become sensitized to questions of equality and racial harmony. And getting involved in the civil rights movement really opened my eyes a great deal ... and I think made me more sensitive and concerned about finding a way to bridge some of that gap."[11]

Building an interracial community at West Charlotte was a multifaceted endeavor, resting on a wide variety of efforts. In oral history interviews about experiences at WCHS, discussions of school spirit ranged widely, touching on individual teachers, athletic achievements, student assignment policies, a changing racial climate, and the experiences that students and teachers brought with them to the school. The great affection that WCHS inspired in its graduates came through in almost every interview. Students often described their time at WCHS as the most integrated experience of their lives, while many teachers and principals called their years at the school the high point of their careers—a time when they were able to pursue a set of ideals, and in large part succeed. They also made it clear that a variety of factors contributed to the school's accomplishments.

For Timothy Gibbs, class of 1978, West Charlotte's transition from segregation to desegregation was eased in part by the diversity of students who arrived at the school doors. WCHS enrolled students from a variety of neighborhoods around the city, mixed by income as well as race, and the combination of middle- and working-class blacks with middle- and working-class whites made it difficult to view school life in purely racial terms (this mix would be further enhanced when the school started a substantial English as a Second Language program in the 1980s). The Open School program, which focused on creative, project-based learning, also drew a particularly dynamic set of students from throughout the city. The many different groups of people, Gibbs recalled, encouraged students to associate by interest, rather than background. "One thing that I think that you'll find, and that a lot of people will tell you about West Charlotte, is there is a niche for everybody," he said. "And you don't necessarily deal with the other folks that go to the school based on race. That's not the primary determination of who your friends are. If I was interested in the arts, for instance, then there were folks that were interested in theater and dance and music. They were more likely to sort of form a clique or a group. More so than a black/white–type thing."[12]

The students who arrived at the school doors were also eager for new experiences. While some southerners continued to resist change, many others were excited by the prospect of casting off the past and embarking on new and innovative activities. "When you think about it, most of us that grew up in the seventies were rebels anyway," explained Latrelle McAllister, class of 1976. "White students as well as black students were really, probably, at a time in the culture where doing something different was okay with them. That was the norm. The norm was to do something different. We grew up in the time of the streakers." This adventurous spirit spilled over into the classroom, teacher Brian Tarr recalled. "The great thing about teaching literature at West Charlotte was that you could teach *ideas* to these students," he explained. "They loved ideas. They loved new ideas. They loved perspectives different than their own."[13]

NOT A RACIAL PARADISE

School supporters were careful to emphasize that WCHS was not an unalloyed racial paradise, and that successfully negotiating the complications of integration often required deliberate efforts from students or teachers. Even as graduates talked about the school's achievements, they offered keen analyses of the persisting patterns of conflict and interaction that spoke to a segregated and unequal past. It was one thing to want to change, to create a desegregated school or society. It was, of course, a far larger project to actually make that happen—to bring together cultures that were distinctive in many ways. "It wasn't all as idyllic as you might think," recalled Anna Nelson, class of 1980. "You might find in the cafeteria more segregation than you would hope for. You might find a little bit more segregation in some of the afterschool activities. So we weren't all perfectly—all fifty-fifty—integrated, which I think the makeup of the student body was at the time."[14]

Teachers and administrators related a variety of stories about the nuances of interracial interactions. Bill McMillan, principal from 1978 to 1981, recalled working to get more whites on the cheering squad and more African Americans in upper-level classes. Debate coach Betty Seizinger explained that she had a largely white debate team until "I realized that I had to approach the most respected black English teachers who taught tenth and eleventh grade and encourage [their students] to take debate . . . So I know that it can work, but I also know that if you don't go out there and do it yourself, it is not going to happen." Brian Tarr, who talked with such enthusiasm about the open-mindedness of his students, also noted the struggles that could accompany daily routines at such a diverse school. "It's hard work, getting along with people who are different," he said. "It's no different I guess than any other relationship. It's just real hard work. One's feelings are going to be hurt. One will make mistakes, and feel terribly guilty. There'll be successes too, but it's just hard work, and it's really minute by minute by minute."[15]

John Love Jr., class of 1980, described one of the ways that racial differences played out in even the small details of school life. "When you come from different cultures, there are different aesthetics that you respond to," he explained. "So I do remember conversations or voting things that would happen and like, say, most of the white kids would vote for one thing and most of the black kids would vote for another thing. And so it was very clear to me and to everybody else that that rift, or disagreement or separation of the ways, was just about coming from different cultures."[16] During Love's senior year, one of the points of disagreement involved the design of graduation invitations:

> It came up about the invitations and how they looked. And one of the Caucasian students said, "Well, I just think we should go with something more traditional." And my response was, "In whose tradition?" Because it was that whole thing about the assumption that this white Anglo-Saxon Protestant aesthetic is the tradition for all. And so we were sort of on it enough and savvy enough to say, "No, no, no, no, no. There are other traditions; what are you talking about?" So things like that would happen. And then everybody would take a vote and then we'd see what it was that we wanted.

Such differences, however, rarely grew into bitter conflict. Many students, in fact, cited their experiences with discussing and reconciling such disagreements as some of the most important lessons they learned at the school. "Although there was an acknowledgment probably, at least in my mind, that there were different communities, or different cliques or different groups within the high school, there was an acknowledgment that everyone needed to be included," Carrie Abramson, class of 1988, explained. "And that everyone's viewpoint was as important as anyone else's. And that it was really important to have representation from different voices. As well as just listening to different voices. That was important and that was expected. And it wasn't acceptable not to."

Barbara Ledford, principal from 1989 to 1994, described the way the school's core group of teachers helped to perpetuate this approach from year to year. "When new teachers became a new part of the West Charlotte family, or new administrators such as a principal, they more or less in a subtle way gave you an orientation as to what West Charlotte was all about," she explained. "And each of us, when you came, myself included, was familiarized through very informal ways, but very direct ways, to say: 'This is the way we do it at

West Charlotte. This is the way that we treat people at West Charlotte.' And it happened to the students too.'"[17]

FORGING A COMMUNITY

A key to the success of such interactions, as well as to other school endeavors, was the sense of community that developed at the school, an atmosphere in which students from many backgrounds could feel comfortable, rather than threatened or defensive. Such a community, interviews made clear, rested on the school's history as well as on the new ideas that students and teachers were exploring.

At first, some administrators thought that the best way to build a new community was to downplay the school's history. When Sam Haywood became principal in 1974, one of the first things he did was to clear the school lobby, taking out photos and athletic trophies that commemorated the school's accomplishments during segregation. Mertye Rice and longtime guidance counselor Marge Belton quickly set him straight. "I made some really big mistakes," Haywood later recalled. "I did a lot of things without thinking of the history. Mertye and Marge were very quick to tell me, 'Put that back. Don't do that.'"[18]

Belton, Rice, and the rest of the veteran African American staff who remained at WCHS after desegregation played an especially large role in the school's success. They set the tone for the new school culture, promoting the kind of individual, intensively caring attention that had marked the school's segregated years. "There were so, so many really kind people who just daily would come to us. 'Are you doing okay?' 'Things okay?' 'Is there anything we can do for you?'" recalled Patsy Sutherland, who came to WCHS as a novice teacher, and stayed for twenty years. The persisting strength of other traditions, such as the school's athletic teams and its legendary marching band, played roles as well.[19]

African American students, still facing the many challenges of being minorities within mainstream culture, could draw strength from West Charlotte's African American heritage—as when John Love Jr. invoked the school's tradition in his discussion of graduation invitation design. Latrelle McAllister talked about her classmates' interest in rebellion and in exploring new ideas. But her family had a long history at the school, a history whose influence became clear in a story she told about her first day at WCHS. "One of the people who had been one of my father's teachers, Ms. Marjorie Belton, was my guidance counselor," she recalled. "I was a very shy teenager. I had my father walk me to school the first day. He took my hand and placed it in Ms. Belton's hand. That was a very historic moment, but . . . the symbolism went further than that. She took his gesture of his entrusting me to her very seriously. In fact, [she] helped to mold my academic career there at West Charlotte. That was very important to me, too."[20]

White students were able to forge connections to the school's history as well. Residents of the African American community around WCHS embraced the school's new students, supporting their activities and looking out for them when they ventured off-campus. Many white students spoke eloquently about the effects that this welcoming spirit had on them and on their feelings for the school. Carrie Abramson recalled sitting at football games surrounded by fans who had graduated decades before. "It was a sense of pride in the school," she explained. "Everybody shared that and everybody smiled at each other and everybody was excited, and we all cheered together and we all said the same cheers. They knew all the same cheers we knew." That kind of experience deepened her appreciation of the school. "I was proud of the fact that people still came to the football games," she continued. "I was proud of the fact that people still came and still supported the school and the team and were so involved in what went on there."[21]

When Gosnell White, who became West Charlotte's basketball coach in 1996, talked about the school, he pointed to the extent to which school loyalty had transcended race. "When you go to West Charlotte, it doesn't matter," he explained. "It just doesn't matter what color you are. It's like you're in the community once you say, 'Hey, I graduated from West Charlotte.' I think that's the bottom line. Once you go to West Charlotte, it doesn't matter."[22]

Many of the school's African American traditions appealed to both black and white students. WCHS retained a number of specifically black traditions, especially in its music programs and cheering squads. Students of all races delighted in the marching band's distinctive sound and the cheerleaders' rhythmic moves, which set WCHS apart from most of the district's other schools. "They were the jivingist cheerleaders in the country," Anna Nelson recalled. "And I would bet my bottom penny on that. They were loose, they were fun. They were great dancers. And truly their passion showed through. They kind of mimicked the marching band, which was also very jive-oriented, very loose, a very loose dance-type choreography. A lot of dipping and bending and kind of grooving—I know those words are outdated, but at the time that was kind of the thing. And we just had great pride in all of that."[23]

White students and teachers also came to cherish their sojourn within an African American community, realizing the significance of the lessons they were learning about the world outside the sheltered enclaves where most of Charlotte's white population lived. Many of the most heartfelt statements in the WCHS interviews came from whites keenly aware of how privileged they were to have such an experience. "When I got to college I was proud of the fact that I had been to a high school where there were a lot of African Americans," Carrie Abramson explained.

> I was proud of the fact that I had been in that environment, because I met so many people who'd not been and there was a lot of racism. Overt racism—mainly language. And so having come from that environment that was integrated really helped me. It didn't necessarily help me deal with it that well, when somebody else would say something, a racial slur. But it made me feel confident in that I disagreed with them and I knew why. And I had support for that. That no, I didn't believe all people of a different color were dumb. Because I knew people of a different color who were really, really smart, probably smarter than I was, and had accomplished things I wasn't able to accomplish. And that was important.[24]

For most students, black and white, a sense of individual growth was buoyed by the pride they took in the school's status and in their fellow students' accomplishments. From the 1970s into the 1990s, WCHS benefited from a convergence of factors that helped the school stand out in many areas. The national reputation the school developed as an example of successful desegregation was periodically reinforced by visits from reporters who produced laudatory accounts of the school's achievements. As the linchpin in the district's busing plan, WCHS also benefited from careful attention to its programs and facilities. The resources and energy devoted to a variety of endeavors, ranging from the drama department to the band to the highly successful athletic teams, helped draw students and community together with a broad-based sense of their school's significance. "Our school would get to the finals of the football championship, we would win Hi-Q, we had a great debate team," recalled Anthony Foxx, class of 1989. "We just felt like there was nothing we couldn't do."[25]

FACING NEW AND OLD CHALLENGES TOGETHER

As time went on, however, WCHS also began to face some of the challenges that building an interracial community had not solved. In 1991, a reporter from the *Wall Street Journal* visited the school, and described it as "a warm picture of integrated young America." But even as the article lauded West Charlotte's success, it also pointed to some of desegregation's unfinished business—especially the persisting gap between black and white performance and a tendency to "track" more white students to advanced classes and more black students to lower-level classes. While WCHS had many high-achieving African American students, some parents and teachers became particularly concerned that the school was not devoting enough care and attention to those black students who faced greater struggles. It was becoming clear that busing had its limitations as a force for social change. "I was a part of this belief that if we could all integrate that there was just going to be a natural exchange of knowledge and resources and that sort of thing," William Hamlin Jr. explained. "But our society is very witty. And as new demands come upon us for changing, we find new ways to entrench ourselves in the old."[26]

As support for desegregation slackened across the county, and CMS began to shift away from full-scale busing, West Charlotte's African American population began to grow. School desegregation had not been matched by neighborhood desegregation, and the neighborhoods on Charlotte's west side remained almost exclusively African American. By the fall of 2000, white students made up less than a fifth of West Charlotte's student body, making WCHS one of the most segregated high schools in Mecklenburg County. A few years later, by which time the *Capacchione* litigation had resulted in CMS's implementing a race-neutral assignment plan (see chapters 1 and 2), WCHS became virtually all-black once again. In contrast to the segregated era, when WCHS drew from an African American community that included a broad range of economic classes, demographic and geographic shifts meant that the bulk of its new students came from struggling, low-income communities that had largely been left out of the city's increasing prosperity. While WCHS still turned out many successful graduates, overall test scores and graduation rates plummeted. The focus of great pride in both the segregated and desegregated eras, WCHS became a cause for hand-wringing concern, one for which a solution remained elusive (see chapter 4 for a discussion of WCHS in the present day).[27]

Four decades after the first white students arrived at West Charlotte's doors, and a decade after resegregation, the full significance of Charlotte's school desegregation history remains difficult to grasp. In many ways, the communities created by students, teachers, and parents seemed to have had limited visible effects on the world beyond school walls. After school and on the weekends, most students returned home to neighborhoods, churches, and local institutions that remained significantly segregated by race and increasingly segregated by class. Once students left WCHS, most dispersed outward, moving into multiple social, economic, and cultural circles. Many of those also remained far more segregated than WCHS had been. While Charlotte's economy boomed, far more of the benefits flowed to wealthier communities, both black and white, than to less fortunate ones.[28]

WEST CHARLOTTE'S LEGACY

At the same time, however, WCHS graduates and other Charlotte residents spoke with enthusiasm about less tangible effects that desegregation had on the city as a whole, citing both the relationships formed at desegregated schools and the transformations that a desegregated experience sparked within individuals. While ongoing racial strife tore apart civic life in many southern communities, Charlotte remained a place where people were able to talk to one another, and to work together. Many civic leaders have pointed to the success of school desegregation as a major factor in creating the political stability that fostered the city's economic growth during the last quarter of the twentieth century. The degree of success that busing achieved also created a strong and lasting constituency for school desegregation, one that would give rise to administrative and grassroots efforts to create desegregated schools well after busing ended.[29]

Maggie Ray, who had played a major role in creating the successful 1974 busing plan, and who taught biology at WCHS from 1974 to 1991, speculated that seeing the real results of desegregation would take time. "I think we have yet to reap the full benefits," she said in 2000. "And I think we have a group of young people, they're probably from thirty-five down, who went to school here who know how to act in an integrated setting. And who know that stereotypes were wrong. And that people can manage, if not in great love and peace and harmony, at least civilly, together. And my hope is that that will reap benefits. They're just now getting to be old enough to take some leadership role."[30]

But whatever the long-term effects that a once-desegregated school such as WCHS has on the society around it, the story of those efforts offers insights into both the lessons that desegregation made possible, and the kind of work required to create a successful school of any racial makeup.

Bill Culp, for example, talked about the way that issues of equity came out around the family dinner table, as he debated with daughter Carrie Abramson about the measures that WCHS administrators used to ensure that white as well as black students were elected to student government offices. "They had tried to create sort of a convoluted process to ensure that there would be a racially mixed group of students in the student government," Culp explained. "And I remember that my daughter just sort of bridled against that. She felt like it ought to just be—it ought to be just like democracy, and that if you had the votes to elect people, you should be able to elect people. [If] white students couldn't convince black students to vote for them, then there was something wrong." Culp attempted to defend the process on a number of occasions, "and I think that was a very interesting discussion. And certainly I never won that argument. On the other hand, she learned to live with the process that had been created."[31]

For William Hamlin, who sent three children to WCHS, family lessons took a different direction. One of the most stalwart members of the West Charlotte National Alumni Association, Hamlin loved the school, and while his children were attending he devoted enormous energy to school activities. Still, he perceived lingering examples of discrimination on the part of some parents and staff members—to the point where he encouraged his children to go to historically black colleges, where he thought they could concentrate on their studies without such distractions. These disappointments led Hamlin to question some of his most optimistic beliefs about desegregation. "I don't think that we're ever going to be fully integrated and maybe we shouldn't," he said at one point in the interview. But he continued to support WCHS, and the lessons he taught his children thus had many layers:[32]

> You learn to take the bitter with the sweet. You know that in a situation there's going to be some winners and there's going to be some losers. But you look at the situation: "Is it for the greater good? Is the support that we're trying to get for the greater good?" That's the summation of what I found. Even though, at some point, I may have realized that my child was not treated fairly in this particular situation, I have to draw back from it and say: "What's the greater good? Me taking it personal and saying, 'Because my child didn't get xyz, I'm not going to do xyz?' Or am I going to be an example to them and say, 'In spite of you not being given this opportunity we still are going to support [the school]. And I guarantee you, in the end, we'll all be better off.'" So that's the attitude I had to take and that's the attitude I still have today.

The ongoing combination of caring and challenge that gave WCHS life and purpose is perhaps most clearly expressed by John Love, who articulates, like so many others, an awareness of struggle combined with a strong sense of affection and achievement. "When you feel as if you belong, as if you have a reason for being there, you feel protected," he explained. "And you feel encouraged. Thriving, existing, living vibrantly. You feel encouraged to do that. That's what I think the legacy or the history of West Charlotte provided for so many people."[33]

Within the school's challenging and yet supportive atmosphere, Love was able to expand both his understanding of others and his confidence in his own beliefs. "I think I gained a more realistic sense of how the world works outside of my own community that I grew up in," he explained.

> I think I gained a sense and skills about how to deal with a variety of different people that are coming to a situation with a variety of different issues, agendas, needs, wants, desires—that whole thing. I learned the importance of remaining true to self, and remaining true to my ideals and ways of doing things and things I knew or felt were right; of questioning but not totally dismantling at every minute my moral compass, if you will. And being brave and challenging the things that need to be challenged or need to be thought about. All of that kind of stuff. I mean, the lessons were pretty huge.

CHAPTER 4

"Academic Genocide" on the West Side

West Charlotte High School in the Post-*Swann* Era

Roslyn Arlin Mickelson
Stephen Samuel Smith
Stephanie Southworth
S. Lorén Trull

> *The most appropriate way for the Court to describe what is going on academically at CMS's bottom "8" high schools is academic genocide for the at-risk, low-income children.*
> —North Carolina Superior Court Judge Howard E. Manning Jr.[1]

AT NO HIGH SCHOOL was Judge Howard Manning's strong language more applicable than at West Charlotte High School, which, at the time of his 2005 report, was CMS's lowest performing high school and had a higher percentage of low-income and black students than any of the district's other high schools. WCHS's transformation from the desegregation showcase described in chapter 3 to a school especially worthy of the judge's ire is the subject of this chapter. We begin by documenting the extent of the transformation and chronicling the reasons—those rooted in structure and those rooted in agency—for WCHS's resegregation and decline. We then consider a series of interventions designed to deal with West Charlotte's academic woes, paying particular attention to Project LIFT (Project Leadership & Investment For Transformation), an intervention modeled, in part, on the Harlem Children's Zone. As introduced in chapter 1, Project LIFT is a public/private partnership supported by $55 million in private funds that aims to provide educational and social services to students and their families in the WCHS feeder zone. Project LIFT is particularly instructive because of its scope, ambition, and distinctive public/private organization, and because, like most other CMS interventions since the turn of the millennium, its theory of educational change accepts hypersegregation by race and class as a fait accompli.

WHAT JUDGE MANNING FOUND AT WEST CHARLOTTE HIGH SCHOOL IN 2005

Disaggregating data on pass/fail rates for North Carolina's standardized End-of-Course (EOC) tests in 2004, Judge Manning's report noted that, compared to other schools, West Charlotte ranked lowest in 2004 whether one looked at the entire student population, black students, white students, or students in a school's Gifted and Talented program. Judge Manning's report also indicates that passing rates for WCHS's black students were the lowest in 2002 and 2003, as well as in 2004. The report pointed out that in 2004, West Charlotte had the highest percent black enrollment (91 percent) of all CMS high schools, the lowest white enrollment (2 percent), the highest free or reduced lunch (FRL) enrollment (61.9 percent), and the second lowest percentage of the district's students in Gifted and Talented classes (4.6 percent).[2]

Eight years after Judge Manning issued his report, WCHS's demographic isolation remained largely the same. In the 2012–2013 academic year, whites still constituted 2 percent of its enrollment; blacks, 87 percent; and other students of color, 11 percent. FRL-eligible students made up 83 percent, the second highest percentage among CMS high schools. The academic performance of West Charlotte remained largely the same as it was in 2005.

Table 4.1 presents comparative indicators of student performance in 2011–2012 for WCHS; for racially and socioeconomically diverse East Mecklenburg High School; for Myers Park, a high school attended primarily, but not exclusively, by affluent white students and one that is often ranked among the nation's top high schools; and for CMS overall. Most indicators show that compared to youths attending other CMS high schools, and especially East Mecklenburg and Myers Park, WCHS students perform poorly academically, are more likely to be suspended, and have fewer opportunities to learn (as reflected in their limited access to highly qualified teachers and advanced level classes).

TABLE 4.1   Comparative indicators of school quality and climate, WCHS and other CMS high schools, 2011–2012

Indicator	West Charlotte High School	Myers Park High School	East Mecklenburg High School	CMS (high schools only)
Students of color	98.3%	42.2%	76.1%	66%
Students receiving FRL	84.4%	33.8%	60.4%	50.4%
Short-term suspension (10 or fewer days) per 100 students	176.46	23.39	41.16	47.54
Long-term suspension (more than 10 days) per 100 students	0.55	0	0.06	0.12
EOC proficiency English I	55.8%	85.5%	85.6%	82.6%
EOC proficiency Biology	41.9%	84.5%	78.8%	84.2%
EOC proficiency Algebra I	33.7%	70.6%	72%	75.1%
EOC battery proficiency				
Whites	55.2%	>95%	91.2%	95%
Blacks	42.4%	61.2%	75.9%	71.2%
Students taking SAT	53%	78%	55%	68%
Average SAT total battery	808	1,111	995	990
Percent of total course enrollments in advanced college prep courses	2%	13%	10%	6%
Fully licensed teachers	83%	97%	94%	88%
National Board certified teachers[a]	8	39	28	12[b]

Source: North Carolina Department of Public Instruction, "NC School Report Cards," http://www.\ncschoolreportcard.org/src/search.jsp?pYear=2011-2012&pList=1&pListVal=600%3ACharlotte-Mecklenburg+Schools&GO2=GO.

Note: All three schools have IB programs.

a. Raw number unadjusted for school size.

b. District average.

Only 55.8 percent of WCHS's students passed the EOC exam in English I, 49.9 percent were proficient in biology, and 33.7 percent of the students passed their EOC Algebra I test. Within the school there was a black/white achievement gap as well, although it is relatively smaller than elsewhere in the district because all student subgroups perform poorly at WCHS. Of all the EOC tests taken, 55.2 percent of white WCHS students compared to 42.4 percent of black students performed at grade level. Although 53 percent of the students in the school took the SAT, WCHS students' average 2011–2012 SAT score was 808, almost 200 points below the districtwide average.[3] As of 2013, West Charlotte still had an International Baccalaureate (IB) program, but only 2 percent of WCHS students were enrolled in either an AP or IB course.

There is a relative dearth of human and physical resources at WCHS. Library books are older than the district average and there are fewer of them per student. There are fewer fully licensed or National Board certified teachers at WCHS than at other schools. WCHS is staffed with a generous mix of lateral entry or alternative certification instructors from Teach For America and Teach Charlotte.

WHAT ACCOUNTS FOR WEST CHARLOTTE'S TRANSFORMATION?

How different this twenty-first-century West Charlotte High School is from the national desegregation showcase of the 1970s and 1980s described in chapter 3![4] The school's transformation had a variety of causes rooted in the confluence of policy choices, demographics, and the politics of race.

One of the initial causes was the implementation of the 1992 plan that substituted a system of magnet schools for much of the mandatory busing plan that CMS had used since the mid-1970s. Among other things, the magnet plan created an IB program and science and technology partial magnets at Harding High School and an IB program at Myers Park High School. The Open Program at West Charlotte may never have officially been labeled a magnet, but it was in effect the only magnet and choice option for high school students until the implementation of the 1992 plan. The Open Program's cachet attracted motivated students from throughout CMS and also, as noted in chapter 3, helped reconcile whites from affluent Eastover to their mandatory assignment at West Charlotte. However, with the opening of the magnet program at Myers Park, which is located in southeast Charlotte, whites in that part of the city—including Eastover—had the option of applying to another prestigious program that, in addition, was much closer to their homes. Given Harding's location in a predominantly black neighborhood, its prestigious magnets may not have been all that attractive to whites, but the program siphoned motivated black students and their families away from West Charlotte. Finally, the creation of numerous elementary and middle school language immersion, science, communications, and arts magnets provided competition for the Open Programs at the elementary and middle schools that had served as the gateway to WCHS's

Open Program. By the time the magnet plan was fully implemented in 1995–1996, blacks composed 54 percent of WCHS's enrollment, compared with 46 percent the year before the plan was initiated (whereas CMS's black enrollment had increased from only 40 percent to 41 percent).[5]

Even more crucial for WCHS's transformation was the opening in the 1997–1998 school year of two new high schools, Vance in the county's northeast and Butler in the county's southeast. The two were the first new high schools to be opened in almost a decade, and their opening necessitated the redrawing of high school attendance zones throughout the system. The district's choices of how to draw the new assignment zones siphoned both white and black middle-class families from WCHS's catchment areas.

Vance was part of a high-profile, multischool Education Village that had been developed by CMS in connection with IBM, which had a major facility nearby.[6] Black school board member Arthur Griffin had opposed locating a high school there, lest it deprive West Charlotte of white neighborhoods necessary for racial balance, but amid all the fanfare about the Ed Village's high-tech accoutrements, Griffin's concerns had little traction. However, his concerns proved warranted. Upon Vance's opening in 1997, WCHS's percentage black enrollment jumped from 55 percent to 64 percent, and then increased to 68 percent the following year.

To build their faculties, the principals of Vance and Butler were allowed to hire teachers from elsewhere in CMS. They successfully recruited many of West Charlotte's highly qualified veteran teachers. While the appeal of the new schools pulled teachers away from WCHS, there was a push as well: turmoil among West Charlotte faculty triggered, in part, by a new black principal's controversial efforts to increase the number of black faculty and decrease the black/white achievement gap. Reactions to these efforts led CMS to relieve the principal of his duties mid-semester and, to calm the troubled waters among WCHS faculty, allow any teacher who wanted to leave West Charlotte to do so. Permitting this was a sharp departure from CMS's policy of limiting the number of transfers from a single school in a single year, and as a result of these twin forces, many of the best teachers left WCHS for Vance and Butler in 1997.

The 2002–2003 Family Choice Plan (FCP) exacerbated West Charlotte's demographic transformation. With its guarantee of attendance at a home school (see chapter 2), the implementation of the race-neutral assignment plan at the start of the 2002–2003 school year resulted in the school's percentage black enrollment jumping from 75 to 86 percent the very first year the FCP went into effect. Two years later, as Judge Manning's report indicated, it had increased to 91 percent. Moreover, given WCHS's location in some of Charlotte's most economically impoverished areas, the percentage of its poor students had also increased to almost 62 percent within a few years of the post-unitary assignment plan's adoption, as Judge Manning's report noted.

Within a few years of the opening of Vance and Butler High Schools and the unitary decision, WCHS's Open Program was on life support and the rest of the school was in the process of becoming a low performing, high-poverty, racially isolated dropout factory.[7] Not surprisingly, WCHS's feeder schools were also failing. Table 4.2 presents indicators of achievement among the eight schools in the current West Charlotte High School feeder pattern in 2001–2002, the year before the district began to operate as a unitary system; in 2011–2012, a decade later; and in 2012–2013, the first year that North Carolina implemented

TABLE 4.2 Comparison of school outcomes among CMS and schools in the WCHS feeder pattern before operating as a unitary school system and ten years after

School name	AT OR ABOVE GRADE LEVEL IN READING			AT OR ABOVE GRADE LEVEL IN MATH			FRL-ELIGIBLE STU-DENTS AT OR ABOVE GRADE LEVEL IN READING AND MATH		
	'01–'02	'11–'12	'12–'13[a]	'01–'02	'11–'12	'12–'13	'01–'02	'11–'12	'12–'13
CMS	76%	71%	46%	82%	82%	46%	51%	53%	18%
Allenbrook	59%	49%	22%	68%	77%	36%	45%	44%	16%
Ashley Park	64%	50%	20%	76%	76%	29%	47%	46%	13%
Bruns	80%	40%	13%	89%	54%	13%	76%	33%	<5%
Byers	N/A	46%	14%	N/A	65%	17%	N/A	39%	6%
Druid Hills	67%	39%	14%	72%	53%	11%	45%	32%	5%
Ranson	62%	53%	25%	68%	62%	21%	43%	44%	13%
Statesville Road	65%	55%	18%	83%	68%	27%	57%	49%	13%
Thomasboro	56%	45%	16%	70%	73%	28%	49%	41%	11%

Source: North Carolina Department of Public Instruction, "NC School Report Cards," http://www.ncschoolreportcard.org/src/search.jsp?pYear=2011-2012&pList=1&pListVal=600%3ACharlotte-Mecklenburg+Schools&GO2=GO.

a. In 2012–2013 North Carolina changed to standardized tests that assess the new curriculum aligned with Common Core State Standards.

its Common Core–inspired curriculum and new assessments. Table 4.2 shows that for more than a decade Project LIFT zone schools underperformed relative to CMS as a whole. The table also shows that with the implementation of the new curriculum and standardized tests in 2012–2013 students' scores plummeted across CMS.

The data in table 4.2 suggests several points that may be obvious but are still worth noting. First, any investigation of WCHS's transformation during the years discussed in this chapter needs to consider the academic preparation of the students who entered it. Data suggests that students who attend schools in WCHS's feeder pattern are not academically prepared to undertake a high school course of study. Second, this circumstance reflects the scope of the problems faced by reformers who design interventions to address the educational crisis facing West Charlotte High School, a topic to which we now turn.

A SERIES OF EQUITY INTERVENTIONS

I don't blame [Project LIFT]. I blame the whole system. I think the system we have in Charlotte, they like interventions. We love interventions, but the interventions don't get at the problem.

—Richard McElrath, CMS school board member[8]

Long before the implementation of the race-neutral, neighborhood-based Family Choice Plan in 2002, there were significant disparities among CMS schools in resources such as library books, teacher qualifications, and physical facilities. Moreover, the resource-poor schools frequently had higher percentages of poor children, homeless youth, and children of color. With the race-neutral pupil assignment plan likely to lead to further resegregation, these disparities drew more attention, especially from African Americans and white liberals. *Equity* became the CMS buzzword for alleviating, if not eliminating, such disparities, and the April 2001 school board resolution laying the basis for the race-neutral pupil assignment plan included language linking the plan's adoption to the implementation of equity throughout CMS.

In the years following the race-neutral plan's adoption, CMS implemented a wide range of interventions aimed at addressing inequities. Some equity measures involved building new schools or renovating dilapidated ones. Other initiatives included administrative changes aimed at more effective governance to boost accountability and responsiveness to parents. One such effort decentralized CMS into six geographic learning communities or administrative zones plus a seventh *achievement zone*, a non-geographically clustered administrative unit for low performing, high-poverty schools located across the six other administrative zones.[9]

More relevant here are the series of interventions aimed at providing smaller classes, better teachers, better instructional materials, and additional services to schools with high percentages of low-income children that, given the correlation between race and poverty, were typically also schools with high percentages of students of color. Targeted schools were initially called Equity Schools. Over the course of several superintendents' administrations, the label subsequently became Equity*Plus*II Schools and then FOCUS schools, the latter an acronym for Finding Opportunities: Creating Unparalleled Success. Similarly, until 2006–2007 the *differentiated staffing policy* allocated additional teachers to high-poverty schools. Beginning in 2007–2008 a *weighted student staffing model* replaced the differentiated staffing policy.[10] Then, in 2008, CMS initiated a *strategic staffing initiative* to allow teams of new staff (principal, teachers, specialists, and other administrators) to jointly transfer to seven selected high-poverty schools; the next year seven more schools were designated for strategic staffing.[11] A 2012 blog post titled "R.I.P. FOCUS Schools" by the *Charlotte Observer*'s education reporter indicates how fully these serial equity programs illustrate the "policy churn" that characterizes many aspects of contemporary education policy reform.[12] The blog pointed out that Equity had morphed into Equity*Plus*II, and then under the leadership of a new superintendent, it became FOCUS.

> A program that was once at the heart of this community's effort to cope with the consequences of high-poverty schools was quietly laid to rest at this week's Charlotte-Mecklenburg Schools budget session . . . Like so many efforts launched with great fanfare, it has been quietly nudged to the sidelines as leaders and strategies changed . . . The challenge of promoting success at schools where most students come from impoverished homes remains, of course. In just a few weeks, the board will choose [a new superintendent], and that person will no doubt bring a new set of tactics.[13]

The Equity/Equity*Plus*II/FOCUS programs included elementary and secondary schools, but CMS also developed interventions targeted solely at high schools, such as placing an IB program at West Charlotte in an attempt to draw highly motivated and high achieving students to the school and agreeing to a program in which a private foundation would give a $1,000 scholarship to every African American male who graduated from WCHS and enrolled in a college.[14]

More ambitious and systematic, however, was CMS's acceptance in 2004 of a three-year High School Challenge Grant in which the Mecklenburg County Commission offered additional funding to boost academic outcomes at West Charlotte and two other high schools. The High School Challenge Grant aimed to increase academic support (e.g., tutorial programs), improve academic rigor (e.g., replicating aspects of the Knowledge Is Power Program, or KIPP), offer student support and connectedness (e.g., extended-day schedules), enhance student management (e.g., programs to improve discipline and reduce truancy), increase high-quality leadership and staff (e.g., programs to increase teacher effectiveness and reward high performers), improve family and community involvement, and institute accountability for program management, execution, and evaluation.[15]

The High School Challenge Grant was eventually eliminated because of funding cuts, but even before then its shortcomings were manifest. Different elements of the grant's various components were implemented simultaneously at all schools without baseline data being gathered. No evaluations of program effectiveness were possible because without data on how the elements were implemented, and in the absence of baseline data, it was impossible to assess the grant's effects apart from the other reforms that CMS was implementing in the schools.[16] The difficulty in conducting a rigorous evaluation notwithstanding, it was clear by the program's third year that it wasn't living up to expectations. Despite the promise of signing bonuses and pay raises, CMS was having trouble staffing the High School Challenge schools, with the problems being most severe at West Charlotte.[17]

PROJECT LIFT

Almost a decade after the launch of the High School Challenge, West Charlotte was still significantly underperforming compared to CMS's other high schools (as table 4.1 indicates). It was this ongoing underperformance that led to Project LIFT, a partnership between CMS and private foundations that provided $55 million to improve outcomes at West Charlotte and its feeder schools over a five-year period.

Project LIFT grew out of the efforts of what was called the CMS Investment Study Group.[18] The study group's work was facilitated by the Foundation for the Carolinas, and its members were representatives of the foundations of Bank of America, Wells Fargo, Duke Power, and other local corporations; Charlotte's mayor; and the head of a local construction firm. Its advisors included the chair of CMS's school board and then superintendent Peter Gorman. One of its co-chairs was Anna Spangler Nelson, a prominent Charlotte corporate executive and daughter of C. D. Spangler, who had served on the CMS school board in the 1970s and played a key role in developing and implementing the busing plan. While in high school, Spangler Nelson was bused from her home in affluent southeast Charlotte to West Charlotte High School and lauds her experience at the school and in CMS.[19]

In its report announcing Project LIFT's creation, the study group said it wanted to focus its effort on one of CMS's feeder zones because doing so would support the "progression of students from preK through high school." It would also allow CMS "to concentrate and test evidence-based strategies" that could then be replicated elsewhere in CMS. The West Charlotte corridor was chosen because its "indicators of student achievement are the lowest in the county."[20]

Project LIFT operates as a private/public partnership designed for and implemented in the West Charlotte corridor beginning in 2012. An award-winning former CMS middle school principal, Denise Watts, serves as Project LIFT's executive director. The Project LIFT zone includes eight public schools that feed into WCHS: two K–5 elementary schools, five K–8 academies (several with preK programs), and one traditional grades 6–8 middle school with a partial pre-IB magnet within it. The Project LIFT zone serves roughly 7,250 students.[21] Its explicit goals are 90 percent of students reaching proficiency in reading and math, 90 percent of students achieving more than one year's growth in learning in one academic year, and 90 percent of West Charlotte High School students graduating. The last goal is especially ambitious considering the school's 2011–2012 cohort graduation rate of 54 percent and the reality that most students within the feeder zone face the daily challenges of living in poverty and attending hypersegregated, high-poverty, low performing schools (as table 4.2 indicates). Watts's description of how the goals of 90/90/90 arose captures Project LIFT's optimistic culture:

> As I thought about this project and as I thought about setting up metrics for how we would evaluate success year over year . . . you start looking at where you are and what could possibly be realistically attained within five years. And so, at the time, West Charlotte had a 54 percent graduation rate. So I started saying, "Okay, well, what if we went up by 5 [percent] every year?" So, we could probably end in five years at 75 percent? Who gets excited about 75 percent? . . . And I just said, "I'm not waking up in the morning for the next five years for

a 75 percent graduation rate. I'm not doing that" . . . I get excited when I can go into a school and I hear a teacher say, "90/90/90." And when that becomes a part of the culture and the DNA of this work and what we brand and what we say about LIFT, that's what gets me excited . . . So I wake up every morning and [think] "hit 90."[22]

Project LIFT relies on four main strategies (or pillars) to achieve its goals within five years. The first is building talent in the Project LIFT zone, which includes recruiting, hiring, and retaining teachers and administrators who agree with the 90/90/90 goals. The second strategy is increasing the time students are in school. The third strategy is providing improved technology for student learning, and the fourth is increasing community and parental engagement in the education of young people.[23]

These four strategies translate into a variety of nonacademic programs (e.g., dental care for students) and several evidence-based educational innovations such as year-round scheduling, expanded preK, and implementation of K–8 schools to help vulnerable youth avoid pitfalls associated with the transition from elementary to middle schools. The strategy of increased use of technology involves, for example, the distribution of twenty-two hundred XO laptops to elementary school students and the installation of smartboards in classrooms.

Project LIFT's teacher component includes Reach Extension, a program that gives responsibility for up to seventy-five students to talented teachers who mentor two or three novice or underperforming veteran teachers. Competitive Teacher Innovation Grants provide small grants to educators, and the extensive mentoring of new teachers includes their participation in professional learning communities. New teachers at Project LIFT schools also receive coaching from CMS and North Carolina's Race to the Top–funded New Teacher Support Program.[24] WCHS is a site for Teach For America and Teach Charlotte instructors, and both organizations provide additional supervision and coaching to novice educators in their programs. According to interviews, novice teacher coaching efforts are not coordinated across the programs or with CMS.

Project LIFT's design identifies parental involvement and communication as major components. To foster better communication, Project LIFT uses text messaging in addition to more traditional avenues of communication. In the first year, parents were invited to four nontraditional school meetings that included movies, a Zumba class, a health screening, and a faith-based event.[25] Project LIFT Director Watts described efforts to build community engagement:

"I would not say there is anything specific, like one resource, that we've used. I think we've used a lot of different things. I think one of the things that we're really building on this year is a lot of the Ruby Payne bridges . . . the Ruby Payne work—*Bridges Out of Poverty*—to really help parents understand about mindsets, mentality, [and the] culture of poverty versus what's valued in a different environment. So I think that would be one that we're building on this year."[26]

Project LIFT's evidence-based theory of change centers upon providing improved schooling and quality of life for students during early years of education (preK through grade 8) to better prepare students who enter West Charlotte High School to be *successful* high school students. However, the five-year window of Project LIFT's funding presents a critical dilemma to those charged with implementing and assessing Project LIFT. If Project LIFT's program follows the logic of its theory of change, resources should be invested in preK and elementary schools, not secondary schools. Such investments would demonstrate fidelity to Project LIFT's underlying model of reform but would make it virtually impossible to achieve the 90 percent graduation rate at West Charlotte High School within five years. Its leadership is keenly aware of this issue. As Anna Spangler Nelson said:

> The research would tell us that the earlier you spend the dollars, the more impact you have. Right? So it would all go to the pregnant mothers. Spend it all right there. Or the zero to five [year-olds]. So in our wish list, in our dream list, we were going to spend money on zero to four-/five-year-olds . . . [But we] have a five-year window of funding. We couldn't have an eighteen-year window for funding . . . So we had a dilemma there because we needed to show results. And . . . we needed to pay attention to the sixteen, seventeen, and eighteen—the high schoolers—because they were falling off the back of the bus just as we watched . . . And so we felt, gosh, we need to spread these funds out across the continuum.[27]

Even if the focus includes the "high schoolers," the importance of quickly gaining results remains pressing. When asked about Project LIFT's plan for West Charlotte High School, Watts replied, "the theory in year one was, what is the low-hanging fruit? What are the things that we can do in one year that will get us momentum, and traction, and credibility?" After auditing the transcripts of failing West Charlotte students, Watts realized CMS had not maximized opportunities for *credit recovery*, which soon became a key strategy for raising graduation rates among WCHS students.[28] In all subject areas, the state of North Carolina permits high schools to offer blocks of instruction that involve less than the traditional seat time required in the standard course of study. Credit recovery delivers a subset of the standard course of study tailored to the student's deficiencies and dictated by the student's skill set. The length of time in hours and the curricular components for recovering credit are not fixed. If the course requires an EOC exam, students must pass it to receive credit for the course.

Watts's insight about credit recovery led to the creation of the Project LIFT Academy. She recalls:

> So from that came this idea of doing a LIFT Academy and getting a seat-time waiver . . . this idea of the seat-time waiver so they didn't have to sit in the seat for 135 hours if they showed mastery. So we took those kids out of the West Charlotte mix, because it wasn't going to happen with them in a traditional senior-year setting, and we isolated them, and using the seat-time waiver and blended learning, assigned five excellent teachers and really got those kids working on a self-paced trajectory to make up these credits at a faster rate. So that was one strategy, the LIFT Academy.[29]

Thus, in 2013 WCHS split into two campuses: the main campus in the heart of the west side, and an off-site alternative school called Project LIFT Academy several miles away in the completely refurbished educational annex of a local church. Each campus is an official site of WCHS and has its own co-principal. Between sixty and one hundred WCHS students whose lack of academic progress puts them at risk for dropping out of school, or whose poor behavior poses a persistent risk for serial suspensions, expulsions, or distraction to other youth, attend Project LIFT Academy. Once there, enrollees receive instruction in modern, high-tech classrooms of six to ten students, often in nontraditional timeframes consistent with their unique credit recovery plan. Project LIFT Academy's extensive use of credit recovery is one innovation likely to contribute to increasing WCHS graduation rates over the course of Project LIFT's operation.

DISCUSSION AND CONCLUSION

This chapter has chronicled West Charlotte High School's transformation from a national desegregation icon to arguably a poster child for hypersegregated, high-poverty schools that fail to educate their pupils. We have shown how a confluence of CMS's policy choices, demographic shifts, and racial politics contributed to WCHS's transformation. The school system's serial programmatic responses to resegregation and their academic sequelae culminated in Project LIFT, the latest and most ambitious of CMS's equity interventions. To their credit, Project LIFT's leaders acknowledge that some aspects of the innovation will probably fail, and they emphasize that any failures will provide lessons for subsequent efforts.

As of this writing, Project LIFT is in its second year of operation. It is far too early to assess its effectiveness and, hence, its value as a reform model that can be taken to scale in CMS or the nation. Three controversial elements of this reform make an evaluation of it especially vital for the district and national education policy.

The size of the funding for this reform is the first issue. At present, Project LIFT is slated to spend $55 million on nine schools over five years. This translates to an average of $1.2 million per school each year. While this average ignores key differences in school size and the needs of elementary compared to secondary schools, by any calculation the amount of money available per school is actually relatively small and, in fact, is likely too small to have a meaningful short-term, let alone a long-term, effect. But if evaluations indicate that aspects of Project LIFT are effective, going to scale in all underperforming schools may be prohibitively expensive both in terms of financial and political capital. Political pressures from suburban constituents weary of the efforts to boost outcomes in urban schools may make it politically difficult for the school board or the county commission to fund scaling up on such a massive level. The Republican-dominated state government is highly unlikely to approve of additional funds. Perhaps CMS can turn to the private sector for continued support, but doing so raises another issue.

Project LIFT's distinctive public/private governance structure is the second matter of concern. Initially, Project LIFT board members wanted the executive director not to be a CMS employee, fearing the system's bureaucracy would stifle innovations. On the other hand, without being a CMS employee, any school leader would have limited authority or credibility with the educators he or she supervised. Eventually, the parties reached a compromise. Watts returned to CMS as superintendent of the Project LIFT Learning Community (Zone), and CMS evaluates her performance with input from the Project LIFT Board. But her salary is paid entirely with Project LIFT money. Watts noted that "CMS is the final decision maker of what goes—on paper. But if at any point the Project LIFT board decided my performance was not what they wanted it to be, then they just say, 'We're not paying the salary anymore,' and that's the end of the discussion."

Project LIFT's former internal evaluator, Christian Friend, articulated an even more fundamental concern at the heart of the public/private governance structure when he explained why he left his position with Project LIFT to return to CMS's administration. Friend lauds many of Project LIFT's efforts. But in addition to family and personal reasons for returning to CMS, he also harbored trepidations about the implications of Project LIFT's origins and administrative structure for public education. To explain these concerns, Friend described the process by which CMS typically obtains grants. The district says, "We want to go out and do this," and it finds a funder who provides resources and then receives updates about how the resources are being used. "But that's it. It's not an ongoing involvement, which is different from PL. PL is folks coming and saying, 'This is what we want to give to the district. We're going to fund it and we're going to have an ongoing involvement in creating it.'"[30]

Even though he has no doubts that everyone involved, "from top to bottom," seeks success for the students, Friend says he is:

> unclear of what the ultimate policy implications are. So, I think there are some implications around private investment in public education that, assuming the success of this initiative, people could extrapolate. And my lack of clarity around where that's headed made me a little uncomfortable . . . What I don't know is, if and when it's successful, what does the public take away from that? What do legislators take away from that and does it say, "Hey, when private dollars are used, you get a better result." And then someone makes an argument for privatization of public education, because private dollars can be more effective . . . Again, I believe everybody at that table has the best interest of the children in mind and the broader community, but when it's all said and done, what do people draw from it? . . . I can't answer that question, and my inability to answer that question made me feel like I shouldn't be there.[31]

The third and perhaps most contentious matter given the district's history is Project LIFT's acceptance of segregation in its schools. A number of interviewees noted that black and white education activists were deeply disappointed with this aspect of Project LIFT's design. Several CMS board members pointed out that since nothing in Project LIFT's strategies addressed the racial and socioeconomic hypersegregation of schools in the West Charlotte corridor, the project wasn't getting at a crucial cause of these schools' problems. These board members' fundamental critique was that Project LIFT might help for five years, but what happens when it goes away? Watts recalls being asked by a board member, "Do you really want to prove . . . that it's okay to have high concentrations of African American, poor kids in schools? Do you want to prove to Charlotte and the world that these kids can be successful? . . . That it [segregation] is okay?" Watts recalls replying, "Do I think the way we organize and assign kids to schools—do I . . . Denise Watts, believe that that's the right thing to do? Probably not, I don't. But it is a reality that we're in. And my job does not assign students, I don't write board policy, I don't figure out housing patterns—that's another board; that's the county . . . And so I'm not saying we shouldn't tackle those problems. But I'm telling you, for the next five years, I have the power and the influence to change the game for some kids and I'm not putting that opportunity to the side."[32]

A similar perspective led another board member, Richard McElrath, to vote for the agreement. Calling himself the "most outspoken" about concerns with Project LIFT's failure to address school segregation and its relationship to housing segregation and poverty, McElrath concluded, "But it's hard to vote against that [Project LIFT] because those kids . . . If somebody says, 'I'm going to put a billion dollars in here,' how can you take that away from those kids? Then you've got to say yes to that. There's no way I'm going to say no to [taking] that money, because those kids are going to profit. But it's not going to solve the problem."[33]

As McElrath's comment suggests, it would be very hard for a person of good will—much less a school board member of good will—to vote to deprive some of Charlotte's most impoverished students of the opportunities Project LIFT provides. But it's equally hard for thoughtful people to avoid addressing the issue raised by McElrath: to what extent do interventions such as Project LIFT provide a sustainable and effective approach to addressing the educational consequences of socioeconomic and racial hypersegregation? We return to this issue in the book's concluding chapter.

CHAPTER 5

Charlotte-Mecklenburg Schools in Context

Racial and Economic Imbalance at the District and State Level, 1994–2012

Charles T. Clotfelter
Helen F. Ladd
Jacob L. Vigdor

NO SCHOOL DISTRICT in the South has played a more prominent role in the nation's tortuous path to racially integrated schools than Charlotte-Mecklenburg Schools.[1] As other chapters in this volume spell out, Charlotte was the stage for a momentous Supreme Court decision, *Swann*, the Court's last unanimous desegregation ruling. CMS became famously linked to busing and racial balance by virtue of that 1971 ruling. But, four decades later, the district came to exemplify something altogether different because of its decision to dispense with the last vestiges of policies to foster racial balance in the schools, a decision made after the U.S. Court of Appeals had struck down race-sensitive school assignments.[2] Indeed, the school board's decision in 2002 to radically overhaul its student assignment policy in favor of neighborhood schools and parental choice produced marked changes in the racial compositions of many schools and a precipitous reduction in between-school racial balance and interracial contact in the public schools.

Although it stands out—for its size, its historical significance, and the rapidity of its policy transformation—Charlotte is inextricably linked to a region, a federal judicial circuit, and a state, all of which experienced changes that inevitably influenced the schools serving the city and its geographically spread-out home county. To gain a full appreciation for the changes occurring in CMS—throughout most of the period, the largest district in the state in terms of enrollment—one must understand what was happening in the other ninety-nine counties of the state of North Carolina. For one thing, the state was being engulfed by a vast demographic wave brought on by the unprecedented immigration of Hispanic families. Meanwhile, enrollments of the white majority dwindled by comparison, while the number of black families increased only modestly. The state's judicial environment also changed, ahead of the nation.

In this chapter we provide a state-level context for the racial and economic patterns and changes observed in CMS. We begin by examining the demographic patterns and trends that serve to circumscribe what racial compositions were feasible in the district's schools. We then turn to measures of racial imbalance, first as measured at the school level, and then at the level of the classroom. Measures of the latter variety make possible evaluations of within-school imbalance. Throughout, we hold up two points of reference for Charlotte: the entire state and the state's other huge school district, Wake County, home of Raleigh, the state capital. Next we apply our imbalance measure to economic status instead of racial classification. Finally, we consider how charter schools affect the racial diversity of the Charlotte schools.

DEMOGRAPHIC CONSTRAINTS

The racial and ethnic makeup of North Carolina's school population differs markedly across the state's regions. The counties in the state with the highest nonwhite proportions form a band from Charlotte to the middle of the Coastal Plain and then expand to the northeast to the Virginia state line. Most of the Piedmont region and the counties on the coast are in the middling range, having nonwhite proportions between 30 and 50 percent. By contrast, most of the counties in the Mountain region have proportions under 30 percent. For counties at either extreme, achieving a racial composition in the schools close to that of the state average is necessarily limited by community-level demography.

The state has experienced a dramatic demographic shift in recent decades, as immigration has swelled its Hispanic population and its public schools. Between 1990 and 2011 North Carolina's Hispanic population increased at a remarkable 11.3 percent per year, rising from 1.2 percent to 8.5 percent of the total state population. This surge in Hispanic population was reflected in the state's public schools. As shown in table 5.1, the share of the state's public school

TABLE 5.1 Racial/ethnic distribution of North Carolina public school students, 1994–1995 and 2011–2012

	WHITE		BLACK		HISPANIC		ASIAN		AMERICAN INDIAN	
	1994–1995	2011–2012	1994–1995	2011–2012	1994–1995	2011–2012	1994–1995	2011–2012	1994–1995	2011–2012
State of NC	65.2	52.7	30.5	30.0	1.5	13.3	1.2	2.6	1.5	1.4
Five largest counties										
Charlotte-Mecklenburg	54.2	33.5	40.4	44.2	1.6	16.8	3.4	5.0	0.4	0.5
Wake	68.9	50.1	26.7	28.8	1.6	14.6	2.6	6.2	0.2	0.4
Guilford	58.6	38.6	37.4	44.5	1.0	10.6	2.5	5.7	0.6	0.6
Cumberland	48.9	33.7	43.3	51.5	4.5	10.9	1.7	2.0	1.7	1.9
Forsyth	59.8	42.3	37.5	34.4	1.6	20.8	1.0	2.3	0.2	0.2
Other urban										
Coastal	56.4	48.7	40.9	38.8	1.6	10.7	0.9	1.4	0.2	0.4
Piedmont	59.1	44.4	37.6	35.9	1.7	16.4	1.4	2.9	0.2	0.4
Mountain	82.8	68.3	14.6	17.5	0.9	11.2	1.5	2.8	0.2	0.2
Rural										
Coastal	58.2	57.4	39.9	30.1	1.4	11.4	0.2	0.6	0.2	0.4
Piedmont	61.4	54.8	31.7	26.2	1.5	13.7	0.5	1.0	4.9	4.2
Mountain	87.9	77.7	9.6	10.3	1.1	9.9	0.8	1.5	0.6	0.7

Source: National Center for Education Statistics, Common Core of Data, 1994–1995, 2000–2001, 2005–2006, and 2010–2011; NC Department of Public Instruction, 2011–1012; authors' calculations.

Note: Percentages are weighted averages of county statistics where weights are county enrollments. Nonwhite includes black, Hispanic, American Indian, Asian, and multiracial students. For consistency with NC data prior to 2010, for 2011–2012 black and multiracial students are grouped together.

students who were Hispanic increased from 1.5 percent in 1994–1995 to 13.3 percent in 2011–2012. Over the same period, the share of white public school students fell by about the same degree, from 65.2 percent to 52.7 percent.[3] While this big shift was occurring, there was little change in the shares of the three remaining racial groups: the share for black students dropped from 30.5 to 30.0 percent; for Asian students, it increased from 1.2 to 2.6 percent; and for American Indians, it edged down from 1.5 to 1.4 percent.

In terms of racial composition of its schools, CMS, like most of the urban school districts in the state's Piedmont and Coastal regions, has a heavier concentration of black students and a smaller share of white students. Of the state's five largest districts, only Wake has a lower percentage of black students than the state as a whole. In Charlotte, as in the rest of the urban Piedmont, Hispanic enrollments have grown rapidly, their share increasing from 1.6 percent in 1994–1995 to 16.8 percent in 2011–2012 (see chapter 8 for further details). Of the largest districts, only Forsyth (home to Winston-Salem) experienced a more rapid increase.

RACIAL IMBALANCE IN GEOGRAPHICAL AND HISTORICAL PERSPECTIVE

Researchers have used a variety of measures to describe the extent of racial disparity between and within schools in a geographic area. In this chapter we focus primarily on an index of imbalance. We also present summary statistics describing the degree to which students in one racial or economic category are exposed to other groups in the schools they attend.

The *imbalance index* that we employ measures the degree to which the racial compositions of public schools in a county fail to mirror that of the county as a whole. Although indices of this sort can be calculated for school districts as easily as for counties, we chose to use counties because they are units that were created long ago and for the most part correspond to local housing markets. Moreover, 100 of the 115 school districts in the state of North Carolina are countywide districts. The comparatively few counties with more than one school district are the product of past attempts to separate students. Where multiple districts exist within a county, the decision to maintain these district boundaries is a policy choice and ought therefore to be reflected in measures of imbalance like those we develop in this chapter (see chapter 2 for a discussion of the consolidation decision in Mecklenburg County and its role in fostering desegregation in CMS). The index that we use shows the degree to which actual interracial contact in a county's schools falls short of what it could be given the county's mix of students. An index of 0.20, for example, indicates that actual interracial contact in the schools is 20 percent less than it would be if all schools in the county were perfectly balanced by race. Like the widely used index of dissimilarity, this measure ranges from 0 (signifying schools that are perfectly balanced in racial composition, and thus are not segregated) to 1 (signifying total separation of students, with no schools having more than one type of student). Thus, in the pre-1954 South, all counties and school districts had imbalance indices of 1. The imbalance index applies equally to counties no matter what their overall racial composition might be. As a relative concept, it shows the degree to which diversity in schools reflects the diversity of the county at large.[4]

Our imbalance index can be applied to any two-way categorization of students within a county. We use it, first, to measure racial imbalance, applying it not only to imbalance between white and nonwhite students, but also to white/black, white/Hispanic, and black/Hispanic imbalance. It can also be adapted to study imbalance within schools. We also use the imbalance index to examine disparities across schools within a county by income, where we use the share of students eligible for free lunch as an indicator of low income.

Table 5.2 summarizes the degree of racial imbalance in North Carolina's public schools, across the state and over time. Imbalance is measured by our 0–1 index, based on the extent of disparities in the nonwhite share across the public schools within each county. As previously noted, we use the county as the reference point for measuring disparities across schools because completely balanced schools—by racial or economic composition—are a feasible outcome and hence an appropriate standard against which to measure imbalance. Although most counties in the state contain only one school district, a few include two or more districts. For the state in 2011–2012, the index was a relatively low 0.16, suggesting that interracial contact in schools falls just 16 percent below what it would be if every public school reflected the racial composition of the county in which it is located. The state's five largest counties' districts are all countywide. Of them, CMS had the highest imbalance rate, followed by Forsyth (Winston-Salem) and Guilford (whose largest cities are Greensboro and High Point). Imbalance in Wake (which contains Raleigh) and Cumberland (Fayetteville) was lower. Among the remaining ninety-five counties of the state, white/nonwhite imbalance was highest in the rural and other urban counties in the Piedmont region. In 2011–2012, CMS stood out among

TABLE 5.2 White/nonwhite imbalance in public schools in North Carolina by state, five largest counties, and six classifications of counties, 1994-1995 to 2011-2012

	SCHOOL-LEVEL IMBALANCE INDEX			
	1994-1995	2000-2001	2005-2006	2011-2012
State of NC	0.12	0.15	0.16	0.16
Five largest counties				
Charlotte-Mecklenburg	0.12	0.20	0.33	0.33
Wake	0.06	0.09	0.12	0.13
Guilford	0.24	0.29	0.28	0.25
Cumberland	0.11	0.13	0.15	0.13
Forsyth	0.07	0.25	0.28	0.27
Other urban				
Coastal	0.11	0.14	0.14	0.14
Piedmont	0.13	0.13	0.15	0.15
Mountain	0.14	0.15	0.14	0.12
Rural				
Coastal	0.06	0.07	0.07	0.07
Piedmont	0.15	0.17	0.17	0.15
Mountain	0.07	0.08	0.08	0.08

Source: National Center for Education Statistics, Common Core of Data, 1994–1995, 2000–2001, 2005–2006, and 2010–2011; NC Department of Public Instruction, 2011–2012; authors' calculations.

Note: Average imbalance indices for the state and district groups are weighted averages of county statistics where weights are county enrollments. Nonwhite includes black, Hispanic, American Indian, Asian, and multiracial students. For consistency with NC enrollment data prior to 2010, for 2011–2012 black and multiracial students are grouped together.

the state's five large county districts, displaying the highest degree of white/ nonwhite racial imbalance between its schools.

Table 5.2 also shows how measured white/nonwhite imbalance has changed over time. For the state, it increased modestly from 1994–1995 to 2005–2006, from 0.12 to 0.16, but it has held steady since then. Among the state's largest districts, Winston-Salem/Forsyth and CMS both experienced sizable jumps in imbalance following their shifts in assignment policy in 1995 and 2002. Charlotte-Mecklenburg's index increased from 0.12 to 0.20 between 1994–1995 and 2000–2001, and to 0.33 in 2005–2006, following the 2002 revision of the student assignment policy. By comparison, Wake and Cumberland have maintained relatively low rates of imbalance, and Guilford remained relatively steady at a higher rate. In three of the state's largest districts (Guilford, Cumberland, and Winston-Salem/Forsyth), as well as the urban Mountain and rural Piedmont regions, we observe modest declines in imbalance between 2005–2006 and the present.

To explore the degree of imbalance between particular racial and ethnic groups, we calculated indices using three alternative groupings. For each index, we counted only students belonging to one of the two groups. Table 5.3 shows the resulting calculations for CMS and Wake and for the state as a whole. Black/white imbalance is more pronounced than that of whites/nonwhites. For CMS in 2011–2012, the white/black index was 0.39, compared to 0.33 for

TABLE 5.3 School-level racial imbalance in public schools in Charlotte-Mecklenburg, Wake County, and state of North Carolina: black/white, Hispanic/white, and Hispanic/black, 1994–1995 to 2011–2012

	SCHOOL-LEVEL IMBALANCE INDEX			
	1994–1995	2000–2001	2005–2006	2011–2012
Black/white				
Charlotte-Mecklenburg	0.12	0.20	0.37	0.39
Wake	0.06	0.11	0.15	0.18
State of NC	0.12	0.15	0.17	0.17
Hispanic/white				
Mecklenburg	0.04	0.22	0.35	0.40
Wake	0.03	0.06	0.10	0.12
State of NC	0.03	0.09	0.14	0.15
Hispanic/black				
Mecklenburg	0.03	0.07	0.11	0.11
Wake	0.07	0.08	0.08	0.06
State of NC	0.06	0.08	0.09	0.09

Source: National Center for Education Statistics, Common Core of Data, 1994–1995, 2000–2001, 2005–2006, and 2010–2011; NC Department of Public Instruction, 2011–2012; authors' calculations.

Note: Average imbalance indices for the state and district groups are weighted averages of county statistics where weights are county enrollments. Nonwhite includes black, Hispanic, American Indian, Asian, and multiracial students. For consistency with NC data prior to 2010, for 2011–2012 black and multiracial students are grouped together.

whites/nonwhites, as shown in table 5.2. The schools in CMS also showed a very high imbalance index between whites and Hispanic students, whereas the white/Hispanic index both for Wake and the state as a whole was slightly lower than for whites/nonwhites. In addition, the table shows the dramatic increase in separation between white and Hispanic students over time. When Hispanic students made up less than 2 percent of all CMS students, they were distributed fairly evenly throughout the schools. But as their numbers increased, their separation became as extreme as that between whites and blacks.

RACIAL IMBALANCE AT THE CLASSROOM LEVEL

Imbalance can also exist inside schools, particularly if students are separated into academic tracks and if there are racial disparities among those tracks. To determine the extent of this kind of imbalance, we used classroom-level enrollment in public schools at four grade levels: 1, 4, 7, and 10. Examining racial patterns across classrooms within schools is complicated by the fact that students at all grade levels ordinarily are taught in more than one class over the course of a day or week, ranging from pullout reading instruction and music in elementary schools to the dozens of classrooms among which high school students scurry each hour when the bell rings. Since we were most interested in interracial contact during academic instruction time, we chose to focus on the classes that most nearly approximated the basic academic instruction at each grade level. For seventh and tenth grades, we focused on language arts and English courses, since students are required to take one course in this area in every grade. We then calculated classroom-level imbalance between whites and nonwhites and separated the portion that was due to imbalance *between* schools (comparable to the rates just shown) and that due to imbalance *within* schools.

Table 5.4 summarizes our findings at the classroom level. As in the previous table, it presents data for CMS, Wake, and the state as a whole. The table shows, first, that racial imbalance was roughly the same at each grade level, but that a bigger share of it in grades 7 and 10 results from within-school imbalance, compared to elementary school. In 2010–2011, for example, within-school differences in CMS accounted for only 0.03 of the total 0.42 and 0.43 imbalance indices in grades 1 and 4, whereas the within-school portion in grade 7 was 0.09 out of 0.40, and in grade 10 it was 0.10 out of 0.42. The larger average size and smaller numbers of middle schools and high schools tend to lead to smaller racial differences *between* schools, but the greater degree of curricular differentiation in those schools introduces more opportunities for differences *within* them.

TABLE 5.4 White/nonwhite imbalance in public schools in North Carolina, Charlotte-Mecklenburg, Wake County, and state of North Carolina, between and within imbalance indices, 1994–1995 and 2010–2011

	1994–1995	2000–2001	2005–2006	2010–2011
Grade 1				
Charlotte-Mecklenburg				
Total	0.16	0.26	0.41	0.42
Between schools	0.14	0.23	0.38	0.39
Within schools	0.02	0.03	0.02	0.03
Wake				
Total	0.10	0.14	0.18	0.16
Between schools	0.08	0.11	0.14	0.13
Within schools	0.02	0.03	0.03	0.03
State of NC				
Total	0.16	0.22	0.24	0.23
Between schools	0.14	0.19	0.20	0.20
Within schools	0.02	0.03	0.03	0.04
Grade 4				
Charlotte-Mecklenburg				
Total	0.17	0.25	0.42	0.41
Between schools	0.14	0.22	0.38	0.37
Within schools	0.03	0.03	0.03	0.03
Wake				
Total	0.08	0.16	0.18	0.17
Between schools	0.06	0.11	0.14	0.15
Within schools	0.02	0.05	0.04	0.02
State of NC				
Total	0.16	0.22	0.24	0.23
Between schools	0.14	0.18	0.20	0.19
Within schools	0.02	0.04	0.04	0.04

continued

TABLE 5.4 *continued*

	1994–1995	2000–2001	2005–2006	2010–2011
Grade 7				
Charlotte-Mecklenburg				
Total	0.26	0.35	0.43	0.40
Between schools	0.11	0.19	0.33	0.31
Within schools	0.15	0.15	0.10	0.09
Wake				
Total	0.20	0.29	0.26	0.22
Between schools	0.06	0.09	0.12	0.11
Within schools	0.14	0.19	0.14	0.11
State of NC				
Total	0.19	0.25	0.25	0.23
Between schools	0.10	0.13	0.15	0.15
Within schools	0.09	0.12	0.10	0.09
Grade 10				
Charlotte-Mecklenburg				
Total	0.27	0.31	0.41	0.42
Between schools	0.11	0.15	0.29	0.32
Within schools	0.16	0.17	0.12	0.10
Wake				
Total	0.24	0.25	0.27	0.29
Between schools	0.05	0.07	0.09	0.12
Within schools	0.19	0.18	0.18	0.17
State of NC				
Total	0.22	0.23	0.26	0.24
Between schools	0.10	0.10	0.13	0.14
Within schools	0.12	0.13	0.13	0.10

Source: North Carolina Department of Public Instruction, North Carolina Education Research Data Center, School Activity Reports; National Center for Education Statistics, Common Core of Data, 1994–1995, 2000–2001, 2005–2006, and 2010–2011; authors' calculations.

Note: Average imbalance indices for the state and district groups are weighted averages of county statistics where weights are county enrollments. Nonwhite includes black, Hispanic, American Indian, Asian, and multiracial students. For consistency with NC data prior to 2010, for 2010–2011 black and multiracial students are grouped together.

Elementary schools tend to be smaller and more reflective of the neighborhoods where they are located. It is notable that within-school imbalance in the Charlotte schools is virtually identical to that for the state's schools as a whole, even though the between-school imbalance in CMS is considerably higher.

When neighborhoods are segregated by race, elementary schools will be as well if a district follows the traditional practice of drawing attendance zones that include neighborhoods geographically closest to their respective schools. For the two counties whose districts switched from racial balance plans to assignment plans based on neighborhoods, while allowing for some school choice—Mecklenburg and Forsyth—the increase in between-school imbalance in the elementary grades was especially sharp. In Mecklenburg, for example, between-school imbalance jumped from 0.14 to over 0.37 over the entire period (1994–2011) and in Forsyth, between-school imbalance jumped from 0.10 to more than 0.36. Consistent with the trends reported in table 5.2, Mecklenburg and Forsyth are the exceptions to the pattern of little statewide increase in imbalance since 2000.

Table 5.4 suggests three main conclusions regarding classroom-level imbalances: over time, within-school imbalance was steady in elementary grades, it fell in grades 7 and 10, and between-school imbalance increased. First, the district's elementary schools, like those of the state at large, had and have very little imbalance within schools. The low within-school imbalance figures (mostly 0.03) suggest that Charlotte's elementary schools do little tracking. In fact, the racial imbalance numbers achieved are about the same as if principals had assigned students at random to various teachers, since random assignment tends to produce a modest amount of variation in small samples. But for middle schools and high schools—this is the second conclusion—there was a change over time in the degree of within-school imbalance. As between-school differences in racial composition at these levels became more imbalanced over time (the third conclusion), within-school imbalances *declined*. This pattern suggests that, for middle schools and high schools, within-school imbalance acts as a substitute for between-school imbalance. As Charlotte's middle and high schools became more distinct racially, school authorities found it less important to differentiate students inside the schools. It needs to be emphasized that our calculations of within-school imbalance in middle and high schools are based on enrollments in English and language arts classes, so the imbalance measures for Hispanic students could be higher than comparable measures using other courses if language barriers increase the chance that Hispanic students will be placed in different classes than Anglo students, as chapter 8 suggests is the case for CMS's English language learners.

ECONOMIC IMBALANCE

Largely for historical and legal reasons, racial categories have dominated discussion of school imbalance. In contrast to segregation by race, segregation by economic status has never been enforced in the public schools as a matter of law. But socioeconomic inequality in educational outcomes is significant and has been increasing over the last four decades, in contrast with longer-run trends in racial educational gaps.[5] Just as racial segregation in schools is affected by family residential choices in combination with school district policies, economic segregation reflects these same forces (see chapter 7's discussion of the reciprocal nature of housing and education policy). There is one big difference, however, between racial and socioeconomic segregation: unlike race, family income is not an immutable characteristic. Thus, even in a scenario where no households moved and district policy remained constant, economic segregation might change, to the extent that there are shifts in the family income distribution.

To assess the extent of imbalance by income in North Carolina, we applied our imbalance index to two identifiable economic groups of students: those eligible for federally funded free lunch at school, and those not. The free lunch program is available to students whose families are close to the poverty level.[6] First, we excluded high schools because of the very low participation rate for free lunch among those students. Second, we added private schools. Although lack of data on racial composition prevented us from including private schools in calculating racial imbalance, we were able to include them in this analysis by assuming that the vast majority of private school students would not be eligible for this program.

The resulting economic imbalance indices are shown in table 5.5. Like those shown in other tables, the statewide index increased over the full time period, but here we do not observe a leveling off after 2005–2006, as was the case with white/nonwhite imbalance. For the state, the economic imbalance index rose steadily, from 0.11 in 1994–1995 to 0.13 in 2000–2001, to 0.15 in 2005–2006, and to 0.18 in 2010–2011. Our calculations suggest that imbalance by income is now slightly more severe than imbalance by race, using these two measures, with a statewide socioeconomic imbalance average of 0.18 in 2011, compared to the 0.17 index for white/black imbalance and the 0.16 index for white/nonwhite imbalance in 2012. Because these racial and economic indices use different sets of schools (the measure of economic segregation is based

TABLE 5.5 Economic imbalance in public schools in Charlotte-Mecklenburg, Wake County, and state of North Carolina (students eligible for free lunch/students ineligible for free lunch), 1994-1995 to 2010-2011

	SCHOOL-LEVEL IMBALANCE INDEX			
	1994-1995	2000-2001	2005-2006	2010-2011
Charlotte-Mecklenburg	0.12	0.20	0.32	0.38
Wake	0.08	0.10	0.10	0.13
State of NC	0.11	0.13	0.15	0.18

Source: National Center for Education Statistics, Common Core of Data, 1994–1995, 2000–2001, 2005–2006, and 2010–2011; National Center for Education Statistics, Private School Universe Survey (PSS), 1995–1996, 1999–2000, 2004–2005, and 2009–2010; authors' calculations.

Note: Average imbalance indices for the state and district groups are weighted averages of county statistics where weights are county enrollments. Calculations include only elementary and middle schools defined based on the majority of grades in a given school level. In the event of ties, the school is classified based on the level of the lowest grade.

on elementary and middle schools, both public and private, while the racial segregation index uses all public schools), we recalculated each using the same schools—public elementary and middle schools. The result was much the same: 0.18 for economic imbalance and 0.15 for white/nonwhite imbalance. For the state as a whole, therefore, we conclude that economic imbalance (between very low-income students and other students) is slightly more severe than racial imbalance (between white and nonwhite students).[7]

This finding underlines that imbalance by economic status deserves continued attention by school boards and state policy makers. For Mecklenburg County, the index in 1994–1995 was roughly equal to the average for the state, but thereafter it skyrocketed to 0.38 by 2010–2011. In contrast, economic imbalance in Wake County has been remarkably steady. This pattern in Wake directly reflects local policy decisions: until recent years, Wake's school assignment policy had the explicit aim of capping the percentage of any school's students who were eligible to receive subsidized lunches (see chapter 6 for a discussion of the recent political turbulence over school assignment in Wake County).

INFLUENCE OF CHARTER SCHOOLS

Like many other states, North Carolina allows charter schools to operate alongside traditional public schools, supported by public funds but relieved of numerous regulations that limit traditional public schools. Based on their enrollments in 2010–2011, we find that there was more racial imbalance among charter schools than among the state's traditional public schools, and this tendency applies to CMS as well. Compared to regular public schools, charter schools in the state were much more likely to be racially unbalanced—that is, to have fewer than 20 percent or more than 80 percent nonwhite enrollments. We compared the array of racial compositions of charter schools to that of traditional public schools. We found that 62 percent of the state's charter students attended schools with less than or equal to 30 percent nonwhite students, which is double the comparable 31 percent for the students in traditional public schools; and 17 percent of the charter students attended schools that were more than 90 percent nonwhite, which is more than twice the 8 percent for students in traditional public schools statewide. Thus, in 2010–2011 the state's charter schools were far more racially imbalanced than the traditional public schools.[8]

We performed the same exercise for the charter schools of CMS and Wake County. We divided both charter and regular public schools into ten categories defined by the percentage of nonwhite students within each school and then compared the distributions. Separate histograms of the distributions of students in charter schools and traditional public schools in the two districts are shown in figure 5.1. The horizontal axis in both histograms represents the share of nonwhite students in each category of schools, and goes from 0–10 percent on the left to 90–100 percent on the far right. The heights represent the proportions of all students in each category of school. If students were equally likely to attend schools with nonwhite proportions at all possible levels, the height of all bars would be at 10 percent. For CMS, the differences in the distributions are striking. The district's distribution implies that a disproportionate share of its charter school students had peers who were mostly white, as shown by the light gray portions at the tops of the bars at the left and far right, with relatively few students attending charter schools serving between 40 and 90 percent nonwhite students. Wake's charters were also mostly at the edges, but the distribution of regular public schools in Wake looks very different from that in CMS. In light of the tendency for charter schools to enroll disproportionately high or low percentages of nonwhite students, the expansion of charter schools statewide seems likely to increase racial imbalance in CMS, Wake County, and the state as a whole.

CONCLUSION

In its policies regarding racial disparities among its public schools, compared to other school districts of similar size, CMS has been an outlier in some respects and quite typical in others. Like virtually all districts in the South, it dragged its

FIGURE 5.1 Distribution of public school students by percentage of nonwhite students, noncharter schools, and charter schools, CMS and Wake County, 2011–2012

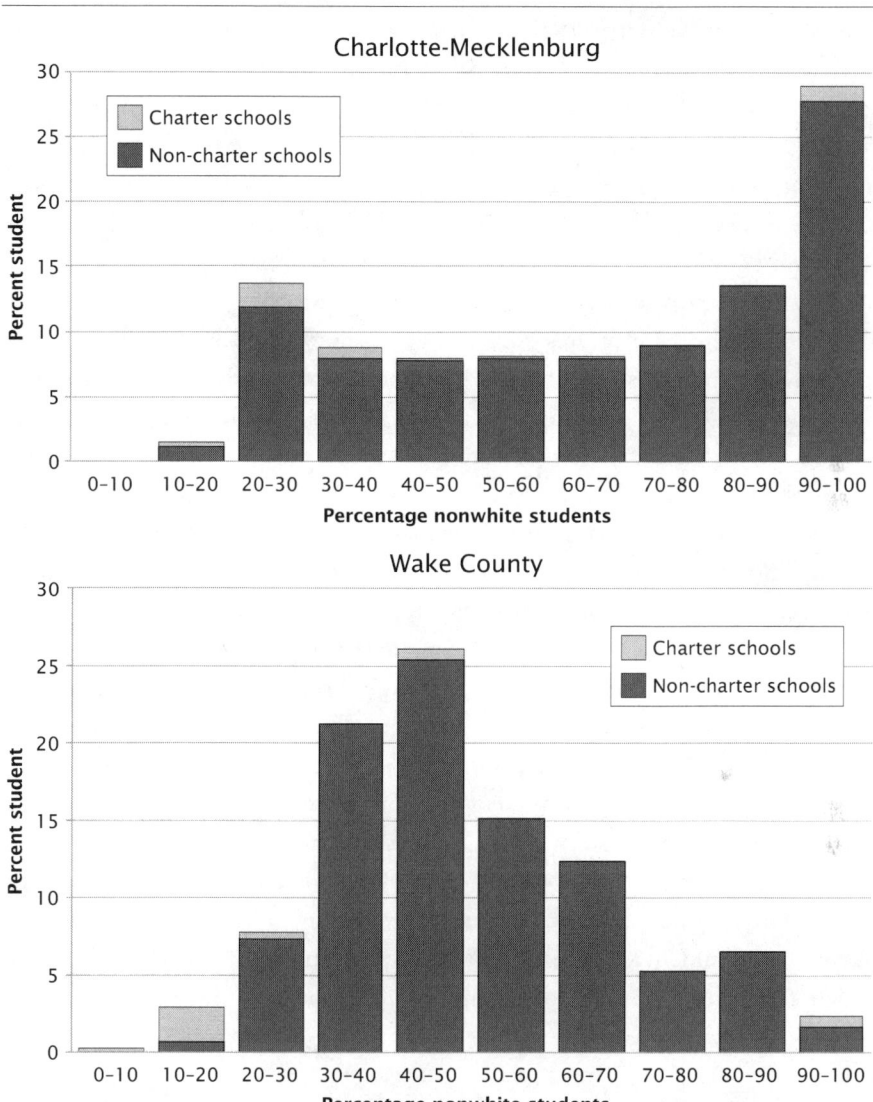

feet through the first decade after *Brown v. Board of Education*. But, when full-fledged desegregation became a reality, CMS complied in spectacular fashion, by setting up an extensive busing policy that applied to schools throughout the extraordinary geographical reach of the large, and at that time only recently merged, countywide district. There followed two decades of busing and racially balanced schools. Beginning in 1999, federal courts in the U.S. Fourth Circuit, including its Court of Appeals, foreshadowing the position the U.S. Supreme Court would later take, struck down student assignments by race in three cases: *Tuttle v. Arlington County School Board*, *Eisenberg v. Montgomery County Public Schools*, and *Capacchione v. Charlotte-Mecklenburg Schools*.[9] These rulings very likely influenced subsequent policy decisions taken by CMS, thereby contributing to a perceptible reduction in racial balance after 1994–1995, a new assignment plan based on neighborhood schools and choice in 2002, and the abandonment of explicit efforts to achieve racial balance in its schools.

This chapter traces the latter part of this history, beginning in the mid-1990s, by examining measures of racial and economic imbalance in Charlotte's schools. Our measures reflect imbalances between schools, and one measure also shows the extent to which classrooms within schools are racially imbalanced. Despite the post-1980s drift toward resegregation, in 1994–1995 CMS still displayed a remarkable degree of racial balance. Just eleven years later, however, it had the highest degree of racial imbalance among North Carolina's biggest districts. By allowing parents to choose schools closer to their neighborhoods, CMS has taken a path that makes it more typical of urban areas across the region and the country. To the extent that it remains distinct, it is because the school district serves a combination of city and suburbs in one of the nation's more racially integrated metropolitan areas. Charlotte's schools are more segregated than they once were, but children in Mecklenburg County are far from experiencing the type of profound segregation that occurs in large northeastern and midwestern cities. Nonetheless, proponents of busing for integration now look to Charlotte's in-state rival, Raleigh and the Wake County school system, as an exemplar of what is possible in an era of judicial scrutiny of race-based student assignment policies. The ultimate success of Wake's policy, which continues to encounter strong political headwinds in recent years, remains to be seen.

CHAPTER 6

A Study in Contrasts

Race, Politics, and School Assignment Policies
in Charlotte-Mecklenburg and Wake County,
North Carolina

Toby L. Parcel
Joshua A. Hendrix
Andrew J. Taylor

THE INTERPLAY BETWEEN structure and agency in relation to racial integration in Charlotte-Mecklenburg Schools can be further understood through a comparison with events in another North Carolina school district, Wake County, which contains Raleigh, the state's second largest city. Despite some historical, demographic, and political similarities, the districts' experiences with desegregation have been quite different. Both counties have grown larger and more diverse, and schools in both have resegregated. As of early 2014, schools in Wake County remain far more socioeconomically and racially diverse than those in Charlotte-Mecklenburg. This chapter's three parts explore possible reasons for the two school systems' divergent histories of school desegregation and resegregation. First, we describe the history of Wake's efforts to integrate its schools while improving students' academic performance, as well as how district policy changed after 2009. Second, we compare the two districts demographically and educationally. Third, we suggest a series of explanations for why Wake and CMS have had contrasting recent histories with respect to school assignment and resegregation.

WAKE COUNTY AND SCHOOL DESEGREGATION

Before 1976, Wake County children went to public schools in one of two different jurisdictions, the city of Raleigh and a separate district that was located in the smaller towns that ringed the capital. Despite their geographical proximity, the two systems were quite different and self-contained. Raleigh's was wealthier and its black children segregated into a small number of predominantly black schools. The county's schools were rural and had a smaller per-capita tax base, but residential patterns allowed for more natural integration. The two systems were only formally brought together by Wake's Board of Commissioners, which supplied them with much of their funding.

Serious talk of merger really began in the late 1960s as both the city and county's schools came under significant pressure to end de facto racial segregation. In 1964–1965 only seventy of Raleigh's nearly fifty-eight hundred black students and just seven of about seventy-seven hundred in the county were enrolled in predominantly white schools.[1] In 1968 the U.S. Supreme Court ruled in *Green v. County School Board of New Kent County* that districts were obligated to desegregate in a manner that eliminated identifiable white and black schools, and in *Alexander v. Holmes* the following year it determined that this desegregation should occur immediately.[2] The Johnson and Nixon administrations' Department of Health, Education, and Welfare (HEW) then moved aggressively against districts deemed segregated, including Raleigh. Following the U.S. Supreme Court's *Swann* decision in April 1971, federal district court Judge John D. Larkins Jr. rejected as inadequate a Raleigh assignment plan to better integrate the city's schools.

Other issues assisted the nascent drive to merge. Administrative simplification, the consolidation of staffing, and larger economies of scale appealed to those interested in cutting costs. It also made sense for the boards to work together on capital campaigns, as they did on a 1973 bond issuance.[3] Race, however, trumped all. Supportive white middle-class Raleigh residents did not so much worry about segregation as they feared continued white flight out of the city and the proliferation of private schools would make its public schools largely black.[4] They undergirded a very public campaign warning that without merger "only blacks" would be left in Raleigh schools and the city would be "in the same situation as Richmond or Washington."[5] County residents who favored merger saw Raleigh's superior resources as a way to accommodate population growth. Their schools had grown by a third between 1968 and 1975.[6]

In 1975, after repeated threats, HEW informed the Raleigh school system it was ineligible for nearly $1 million in funding as a result of the city's foot dragging on desegregation.[7] This pushed city education officials toward merger, and the Raleigh and Wake school boards met to decide whether to ask the county's legislative delegation to push for unification legislation during the state legislature's 1975 session.[8] The county board initially demurred, but the General Assembly enacted a merger-enabling bill in June.[9] Following additional political wrangling, the new fifty-five-thousand-student, eighty-campus Wake County Public School System was established on July 1, 1976.

The merger came about for a variety of reasons. Federal and state government pressure over racial integration and escalating population and resource imbalances between Raleigh and Wake were clearly important. Raleigh political, business, and civic leaders feared the economic effects of continued white flight. Across North Carolina and the South, other jurisdictions were responding to racial, economic, and administrative issues in public schools by bringing together city and county districts. Choices among key decision makers also played a role—including State Representative Howard Twiggs's efforts to bring the county commissioners and Raleigh and Wake school boards together, and the Wake school board's removal of a prominent merger opponent as its chair just prior to the General Assembly's vote on merger-enabling legislation.[10]

Racial integration of the new Wake County public schools was a central feature of the early years of the consolidation. This was expedited by the formation of a general consensus over school policy. Under the direction of the system's first superintendent, John A. Murphy, the school district began opening magnet schools in poorer and black neighborhoods, especially in Raleigh.[11] These schools had a particular focus—the first two contained "gifted and talented student" and "extended day" programs. A major goal was to reverse the flow of white children who were emptying from city schools and overflowing schools in suburban neighborhoods.[12] As Murphy noted in a March 1978 memo to the school board, "the magnet plays an increasingly successful role in the desegregation of public schools [because] it brings together students of different races and backgrounds . . . for educational reasons rather than for the simple exercise of mixing bodies . . . In a magnet school setting . . . racial and socioeconomic barriers [are brought down more quickly] than they are in settings where forced mixing occurs."[13] Many more magnet schools would follow.

The new jurisdiction's board also demonstrated a commitment to integration in 1981 when it established a "15/45" policy mandating that no school's racial minority population could be less than 15 percent or more than 45 percent of its entire student body. Given that black students constituted 28.2 percent of overall district enrollment at that time, such percentages would ensure racial distribution across schools.[14] Subsequent assignment policies conformed to the guidelines, and by 1999 only 21 percent of the county's black children attended a school in which a majority of students were of a minority race—as opposed to the national figure of 70 percent.[15] In 2005, it was calculated that about 15 percent of the system's one hundred twenty thousand students went to school more than five miles from their home. The aggressive magnet program accounted for four-fifths of these students, leaving roughly three thousand students "involuntarily" bused for the purpose of diversity.

Between 1985 and 1995 the system's student body grew by 41.8 percent to 81,203. An influx of new residents—mainly from the Northeast and Midwest—placed tremendous strains on facilities. In 1985, for the first time since the merger, the county's voters approved a school construction bond. Three years later residents approved $125 million in bonds to build new schools and renovate existing ones. Turnout was light, but of those who did show up at the polls, 85 percent voted yes in the referendum. Support was particularly strong in north Raleigh and Cary, two relatively affluent areas witnessing tremendous increases in population.

In 1987, the county's board of commissioners began to nudge the system to look at year-round schools as a cost-saving measure. Analysts estimated that these schools could serve up to a third more students by placing them on as many as four different calendars or "tracks." Instead of following a conventional September-to-June schedule, year-round schools are open almost permanently, with students attending for nine weeks before taking three weeks off. Year-round schooling was attractive because it would presumably alleviate the intense and constant pressure to build. These schools would also reduce operating costs, a benefit that was particularly appealing to commissioners who provided the system with about a quarter of its annual budget. The first year-round school in North Carolina opened at Kingswood Elementary in Cary in 1989. By 1995–1996 Wake had seven multitrack, year-round schools enrolling over five thousand students.

The consensus that protected the integrative assignment policy was reinforced by a unified business community that generally supported the board of education's policies. In 1983, the Raleigh Chamber of Commerce formed the Wake Education Foundation (renamed the Wake Education Partnership in

1992), a bipartisan group of prominent business executives and professionals that served to support the schools. The partnership quickly became an energetic promoter of the board's policies. It defended the assignment policy and its diversification effects, mainly because the approach had clearly not slowed the area's prodigious economic growth.

The consensus was also facilitated by a widespread belief that the county's schools and students were performing well and improving. In 1998–1999, the average SAT scores of graduating high school seniors rose for the fifth consecutive year to forty-three points above the national average. By the early 2000s, the racial and poor/rich achievement gaps had shrunk markedly, a matter viewed by many as a signature accomplishment of the 1976 merger. As a result, the county's public schools entered the millennium with significant support from a generally contented public. According to a 2000 poll by the Wake Education Partnership, 58 percent of residents agreed the school system was "improving over time."[16]

The 15/45 policy was not to last into the next century, however. Federal courts, particularly the Fourth Circuit of which North Carolina was a part, began handing down decisions that questioned the constitutionality of assigning children to schools on the basis of race.[17] In other rulings, a number of large urban school districts, including CMS, had been declared unitary and therefore no longer subject to court-ordered desegregation. Anticipating legal action against its assignment policy, the Wake school board moved to use a different strategy. Initially established for magnet schools and then quickly applied to the entire district after January 2000, the strategy involved a policy of assignment by income rather than race. The new policy set targets for schools to have no more than 40 percent of students receiving free or reduced lunch and no more than 25 percent performing below grade level. All mentions of race were stricken. Superintendent Jim Surratt called it a "momentous decision."[18]

There were practical racial effects to the change. Only around 38 percent of the county's minority students were at or above grade level and *did not* qualify for free or reduced lunch, while only 13 percent of whites performed below grade level and *did* qualify for such assistance. This, in turn, allowed for greater racial concentration in Wake's schools during the first decade of the twenty-first century. The number of schools with greater than 45 percent of their population composed of African American students more than tripled from fourteen to forty-three—very quickly after the new policy was implemented.[19] This did not adversely impact academic performance, however. Between 1998 and 2003, the percentage of African American students in grades three through eight who were reading at or above grade level rose from 57.6 to 78.3. For Hispanics, the amount increased from 66.5 to 78.2. Similar gains were made in math for both groups.[20]

THE 1990S AND EARLY 2000S: A DISSOLVING CONSENSUS ON INTEGRATION

It is not an understatement to say Wake County's population has grown dramatically since 1980. By 2000, it had reached six hundred twenty-eight thousand, having expanded by 109 percent in twenty years. The number of children under eighteen rose by about four thousand annually in the period, enough to fill four large new schools per year.

This population explosion inevitably placed tremendous strain on the system. To keep up with it, the school board needed cooperation from county commissioners who were charged by state law to provide a significant portion of funding for K–12 education. This did not always occur, particularly when the two sets of policy makers were of different political persuasions. Moreover, although voters did approve bond issuances for capital projects in 2000, 2003, and 2006—the last only very narrowly—they rejected a large $650 million proposal in June 1999 as too costly. The defeat constituted a huge blow for the board and effectively marked the beginning of meaningful opposition to its actions.

The growth was particularly pronounced in the county's western towns and suburban north Raleigh. One method the school board used to address this challenge was the reassignment of large numbers of students from growing areas to prevent overcrowding on campuses. At first, in the early 1990s, the board suggested transferring around 1,000 children a year. By 1997, this had reached 1,800 and, in the decade following 2000, often exceeded 5,000. In 2003, the board looked to other places for reassignments and moved 2,300 children in Holly Springs, a town in southwestern Wake. In 2006, it moved 9,300 students and in 2007 another 10,760. In 2008, the year before the election that resulted in the dramatic change to the school system's diversity efforts, the board suggested that over 14,000 students should switch schools.[21]

The annual reassignment was obviously unpopular among those directly affected. Children were taken out of schools and away from their friends. Parents lost social capital they accrued in their relationships with teachers, administrators, and other parents. The process that determined transfer candidates was unpredictable and opaque.[22] To many desperate parents the board seemed insensitive to their family's plight.[23] The decision to spread reassignments over a large part of the county only intensified discontent. When a neighborhood's children were targeted for transfer, parents often created organizations to fight the decision. These groups fostered a deep unhappiness with the board, one that remained long after the precipitating event had passed. They also helped fuse together what was a nascent but disparate movement to fight the board and its policies.

Year-round schools were also designed to mitigate the effects of growth. Initially, these institutions were a kind of experiment; parents had to apply to have their children attend year-round. Students were not typically assigned on the basis of residence, a process that would have permitted the district to apply its diversity rules. The result was that throughout the 1990s the students at year-round schools were disproportionally white and affluent, not least because minority parents found the unusual schedule and distant suburban locations unappealing and some middle-class white parents had recognized that year-rounds had fewer minority and low-income students.

The board responded by altering the policy so it could assign children from minority or low-income neighborhoods to year-round schools. With resources tight and the economic benefits of year-round schools increasingly appealing, twenty-one conventional schools were converted to year-round. This sea change effectively brought mandatory year-round schooling to many neighborhoods in the county's suburban communities. It was unsurprisingly met with considerable resistance from many parents. Very rapidly groups formed to protect the traditional calendar at many schools. The most active and influential—like Stop Mandatory Year-Round, WakeCARES, and Save Our Summers Wake County—were located in Apex and Cary.

A New Local Republican Party

The early 1990s also brought about a kind of revolution in Wake County politics. Despite being home to Senator Jesse Helms—a two-term Raleigh City Council member first elected in 1957 who made his name presenting editorials on local television in the 1960s—North Carolina's capital and its environs were not known for their conservatism or Republicanism. In 1994, however, the Republican Party took control of the state House for the first time in almost a century and won a majority of the state's U.S. House delegation, also capturing the seat centered in Wake. The county was now quite clearly caught up in the Republican tide that had swept much of the South. Demographically it was suited to what commentators have called the "suburban strategy"—after

Richard Nixon's 1968 effort to appeal to southerners' conservative values without talking directly about race.[24]

Even after 1994, however, Wake Republicans tended to place an emphasis on economic, not social, issues.[25] Most residents wanted low taxes, but also seemed to support strong public education and were uncomfortable with any allusions to religion or skin color, however coded or faint. This was no doubt largely attributable to the massive influx of people from outside the South. The fact that they moved mainly to places like Apex, Cary, and north Raleigh also helped suburbanize the county greatly. It became the kind of place that was making the South's politics much more like those in the rest of the country.[26]

Throughout the 1990s and 2000s many Republican-endorsed candidates— the contests are officially nonpartisan—ran for seats on Wake's school board. Toward the end of that period, these individuals were quite clearly presenting themselves more as champions of policy change and part of a broader political movement than as civic boosters and competent managers. In 2005, conservatives supported an insurgent who was challenging incumbent and fellow Republican Bill Fletcher. Although opposition on the right had been muted in the 2000 and 2003 bond campaigns, in 2006 a loose coalition led energetically by Americans for Prosperity and western Wake parents upset by the expanded use of year-round schools also fought vigorously against the $970 million proposal and nearly defeated it.[27]

These efforts helped Wake County Republicans coalesce around clear positions on public schools, such as curriculum and freedom for charter, private, and parochial institutions.[28] Others echoed positions taken by national conservative leaders on vouchers.[29] It was busing, property taxes, and the public schools' assignment policies that motivated most rank-and-file Republican and right-of-center residents of Wake, however. The tremendous influx of population meant schools were overcrowded and students regularly took instruction in trailers rather than brick-and-mortar classrooms. The socioeconomic integration policy established in 2000 was widely pilloried. Its opponents wanted children to attend schools in their own neighborhoods.

THE END OF WAKE'S DIVERSITY ASSIGNMENT POLICY

Coming into the 2009 elections, Wake County Republicans were organized, funded, and motivated enough to take on what they perceived as a liberal board and its harmful policies. Their arguments were consistent with a general political mood shaped by the emerging Tea Party.[30] They recruited energetic candidates with a unified, coordinated message. The deep recession had inten-sified people's fears for their children's economic futures, and the widespread discontent with continual reassignments and mandatory year-round schools stoked opposition further. The tremendous diversity and change in the popu-lation also likely reduced basic trust in government.[31] It should perhaps have been no surprise, therefore, when candidates endorsed by the Republican Party swept all four of the nine school board seats up for grabs that year, propelling themselves into a majority. Policy change would follow. However, just as the Republican-controlled majority was about to secure—with support from two retiring Democrats—approval for a neighborhood-based school assignment plan (formally called "controlled" choice), the October 2011 election changed things. The defeat of sitting chair Ron Margiotta and victories for Democrats in the other four seats contested in the 2011 election gave prodiversity members a slim 5–4 majority. They worked quite quickly to reverse the assignment plan it took the Republicans two contentious years to devise, and by June 2012 the county's policies were once again designed to minimize high concentrations of low performing students at each school and high concentrations of students from low-income families at each school. The policy was cemented by the 2013 school board elections, after which only one member was a registered Republican—Bill Fletcher, a moderate Republican who was now back on the board after having been ousted by conservative challengers in 2005.

It is important to recognize that the portion of the drift away from racial integration in Wake County schools that can be attributed to policy inter-vention over the past fifteen years was caused by the switch to the socioeco-nomic diversity policy established in 2000. As noted, the proportion of schools with greater than 45 percent of their student body identified as black tripled quickly after the definition of diversity was altered. It has essentially remained unchanged since then. Thus, it would be incorrect to conclude that the 2009 school board election led to major school resegregation in Wake County. How-ever, recent increased Latino immigration has also affected Wake's capacity to create integrated schools, and will play a significant role in future Wake school composition.

COMPARING WAKE AND CMS DEMOGRAPHICALLY AND EDUCATIONALLY

Table 6.1 provides data from the U.S. Census and other sources to help us compare the social and economic characteristics of the two counties. Mecklenburg County's and Wake County's populations were of similar size in 2010, with Mecklenburg being just slightly larger. But Wake is a much larger county in terms of square miles, and the population within each city is very different: in 2011 the city of Charlotte contained 81 percent more population than did the city of Raleigh. This means that more of Wake's population is spread out across a larger geographical area compared to the more centrally concentrated Mecklenburg. On average, if both counties use busing to pursue school desegregation, Wake children might be bused farther than Mecklenburg children.

The two counties also have a different history of population growth. In 1980, Charlotte-Mecklenburg's population was 34 percent higher than Wake's. By 2000, it was only about 11 percent higher, and by 2010 the difference had decreased to about 2 percent. This later surge of population growth in Wake gave it more time to establish school desegregation before that policy was challenged by growing population. In addition, Wake's population has increased rapidly more recently than has Mecklenburg's. While both counties grew notably between 2000 and 2010, Wake's 43.5 percent rate of growth outstripped Mecklenburg's 32.2 percent. And Wake continued to grow more quickly than Mecklenburg during 2010–2012. Residential segregation by race, as measured by dissimilarity indices, is more pronounced in Mecklenburg County compared with Wake, as also described in chapter 5.[32] Given the reciprocal relationship between residential and school segregation, this means that Mecklenburg would probably need more aggressive school desegregation strategies than Wake to reach the same desegregation levels. Wake is a less diverse county than Mecklenburg, which had close to a 44 percent black and Latino population in 2010 compared to Wake's 31.3 percent. Wake also has higher rates of high school and college completion, more home ownership, higher housing values, and lower rates of poverty.

Table 6.2 helps us to compare the two countywide school districts. The school districts' demographic and social characteristics mirror those of the counties as a whole: Wake has a higher percentage of white students while Mecklenburg has a higher proportion of black students. Wake's percentage of students qualifying for free and reduced lunches is lower. Wake is also the larger district in terms of numbers of students, likely reflecting, at least in part, Mecklenburg's rates of private school attendance, which are higher than Wake's at all levels of schooling. However, Wake has more home-schooled children and slightly more charter schools. Despite Wake's success in using magnet schools to desegregate, CMS actually has more magnet programs. CMS's dropout rate is higher than Wake's, its per-pupil expenditure greater. We argue that these demographic and school district characteristics are an integral part of the story motivating the two districts' divergent histories of school desegregation and resegregation.

COMPARING THE DYNAMICS OF SCHOOL DESEGREGATION AND RESEGREGATION

The dynamics of school desegregation in CMS and Wake County show key similarities. Both use countywide school districts, have been committed to improving educational outcomes generally, and demonstrated success in school desegregation and improved educational outcomes in the 1980s. Both historically have had at least nominally nonpartisan school boards that by 2000 were becoming more partisan; their school funding models also were similar, with each district dependent on county commissioners to authorize bond referenda that were then approved (or rejected) by voters.

For a number of years each district had school boards that were prodiversity. At times, both had strong superintendents who pursued policies supporting school desegregation.

Both also used busing to achieve impressive levels of school desegregation, with more recent assignment plans in both locales featuring the language of choice. Finally, both have achieved national acclaim as models of large urban districts committed to education.[33] However, the differences between the two districts are profound.

CMS and Wake County differ in the strategies they used to achieve desegregation, as well as in the timing of important historical events. Charlotte was ahead of Raleigh in terms of creating a countywide school district (1959 as opposed to 1976), and the early years of the merged districts were very different. Specifically, Wake consolidated after most of the dust from the school desegregation battles of the 1960s and early 1970s had settled. It did not have to endure the conflicts and turbulence that characterized CMS's efforts to desegregate, which may have made it comparatively easier for Wake to pursue desegregation. Thus, in contrast to CMS, the early years of Wake's desegregation efforts were marked by consensus, a supportive advocacy from the business community, and a quick adoption of desegregation strategies that worked.

In terms of outcomes, it would seem that the post–1974 period in CMS and the post–1976 period in Wake were very similar. Both districts achieved relatively rapid school desegregation as well as improved educational outcomes for

TABLE 6.1 Comparison of Mecklenburg County and Wake County population characteristics (estimates are from the 2010 U.S. Census unless otherwise indicated)

	Mecklenburg County, NC	Wake County, NC
Land area in square miles (2010)	523.84	835.22
Population (2010)	919,268	900,993
Population (2000)[a]	695,454	627,846
Population (1980)[b]	404,270	301,327
Population percent change (2000–2010)[c]	+32.2	+43.5
Population percent change (2010–2012)	+5.4	+5.7
Percentage white (2010)	60.7	70.0
Percentage African American (2010)	31.5	21.3
Percentage Hispanic/Latino (2010)	12.4	10.0
Percentage high school graduates (2007–2011)	88.6	91.8
Percentage bachelor's degree (2007–2011)	40.4	47.9
Homeownership rate (2007–2011)	61.8	66.6
Median value of owner-occupied housing units (2007–2011)	187,300	227,600
Median household income (2007–2011)	55,194	65,289
Percent below the poverty level (2007–2011)	13.6	10.1
Dissimilarity index score (white/African American, 2010)[d]	61.1	56.2
Dissimilarity index score (white/Hispanic, 2010)[e]	57.9	53.9

a. Information is from the 2000 U.S. Census.

b. Information is from the 1980 U.S. Census.

c. Information to compute this estimate comes from the 2000 U.S. Census and the 2010 U.S. Census.

d. Information is from the U.S. Census Scope (http://www.censusscope.org/). The dissimilarity index measures the relative separation or integration of groups across neighborhoods. These estimates are not available for counties, so our estimates indicate dissimilarity scores for Charlotte and Raleigh. A white/African American dissimilarity score of 56.2 for Raleigh means that 56.2% of whites would have to relocate to another neighborhood for whites and African Americans to be evenly represented across all neighborhoods.

e. Information is from U.S. Census Scope (http://www.censusscope.org/).

TABLE 6.2 Comparison of Charlotte-Mecklenburg School District and Wake County Public School System characteristics

	CMS	WCPSS
Number of schools in district (2012)[a]	159	165
Number of students in district (2012)[c]	135,000	149,508
Student body demographics: percentage white (2012)[b]	32	49
Student body demographics: percentage African American (2012)[d]	42	24
Student body demographics: percentage other (2012)[d]	23	27
Percentage of elementary school students qualifying for free lunch (2012)[c]	54	38.6
Total number of private school enrollments (2012)[d]	19,545	16,135
Number of home schools (2012)[e]	4,041	4,913
Number of charter schools (2012)[f]	12	14
Magnet programs (2012)[c]	40	31
Local per-pupil supplement (2012)[g]	2,238	2,134
High school graduation rate (2012)[c]	74	80.4
High school dropout rate (2012)[c]	3.20	2.83

a. Information comes from the district Web sites for Charlotte-Mecklenburg (http://www.cms.k12.nc.us/Pages/default.aspx) and Wake County (http://www.wcpss.net/).

b. Estimates for Charlotte-Mecklenburg are from chapter 2 and Roslyn Arlin Mickelson and Stephen Samuel Smith, "Structure and Agency in the Resegregation of the Charlotte-Mecklenburg Schools" (paper presented at the meeting of the Southern Sociological Society, Atlanta, GA, April 25–27, 2013; estimates for Wake County are from the Wake County district Web site (http://www.wcpss.net/).

c. Estimates for Charlotte-Mecklenburg are from from chapter 2 and Mickelson and Smith, "Structure and Agency"; estimates for Wake County are from the North Carolina Department of Public Instruction, Division of Financial and Business Services, "Free & Reduced Meal Application Data" (http://www.ncpublic-schools.org/fbs/resources/data/).

d. Estimates are from the North Carolina Department of Administration annual report, available at http://www.ncdnpe.org/documents/11-12CSStats.pdf.

e. Estimates are from the Division of Non-Public Education (http://www.ncdnpe.org/documents/hhh238.pdf).

f. Estimates for Charlotte-Mecklenburg are from the MeckEd Web site (http://www.mecked.org/index.php/advocacy/charter-schools/charter-data/); estimates for Wake County are from the Wake County Economic Development Web site (http://www.raleigh-wake.org/page/private-charter-and-international-schools).

g. Estimates are from the Public School Forum of NC (http://www.ncforum.org/).

children. But their strategies differed. While Wake used a system of magnets to entice white parents to place their children in urban, minority schools, CMS's primary strategy paired elementary schools with differing racial concentrations and bused between them (see chapter 2 for details). In CMS, while both races were bused, the burden fell disproportionately on blacks, a development that caused racial tension.[34] In Wake, there was busing both to and from central Raleigh; arguments that blacks bore more of the burden of busing were present, but muted compared to CMS.[35]

The 1990s were also different in the two counties. In 1991 CMS began a program of controlled choice, thus moving away from use of the paired schools. During 1996–1997, when CMS completed the depairing of elementary schools, Wake was still actively pursuing diversity in school assignments, maintaining diverse schools, and seeing improved educational outcomes. CMS also made a series of decisions to site schools in areas of strong population growth, which resulted in increased housing segregation. The location of the Charlotte-Mecklenburg I-485 Outerbelt exacerbated this trend. In contrast, while Wake also built new schools, it used year-round schools as another mechanism to contain costs and later to promote diversity. In addition, Wake's persistent use of the diversity plan provided no incentive for whites to look for segregated housing, thus discouraging residential segregation. In short, Wake was able to sustain school desegregation longer than was CMS. This combination of the sustained implementation of desegregation and the more gradual increase in minority population gave Wake more time to desegregate its public schools.

In 1999, Judge Robert Potter declared CMS unitary. His decision ended CMS's judicial mandate to further desegregate schools, and also made it impossible for proponents of desegregation to justify its pursuit by saying, "We're only doing what the courts say we must do." Moreover, as chapter 2 indicates, in the aftermath of the 1999 court order, Charlotte's business elite's commitment to diverse schools waned, while in Wake, such support remained strong. Essentially CMS lost the civic capacity to pursue school desegregation.[36] It was ironic that it was in reaction to CMS being declared unitary that Wake shifted from using race to socioeconomic status as a basis for school integration. Thus, the early years of the twenty-first century were very different in Wake as compared with CMS. Wake's policy change allowed it to continue to pursue diversity, while in CMS, which did not transition to diversifying schools based on socioeconomic status, schools resegregated more quickly.

Accompanying this change, by 2006 CMS's explicit policy moved away from emphasizing diverse schools to one that focused on providing all children with the best education possible.[37] We know that in a number of districts, ceasing to use a diversity policy, for whatever reason, has allowed racial differences in educational outcomes to increase.[38] Instead of decoupling these as in CMS, Wake continued pursing diversity *and* student achievement.

It is not entirely clear why CMS lost the civic capacity to desegregate schools. One possible reason is that Charlotte-Mecklenburg has a strong Republican history dating back to the Civil War, while Wake's is more recent. Also, Charlotte-Mecklenburg became majority-minority sooner than Wake. This reduced demographic capacity to create diverse schools may have decreased CMS's incentive to pursue school desegregation, given that the demographics of the student population were becoming more challenging. In addition, despite CMS's notable use of magnet schools, magnets were much more successful in Wake. By the time CMS really tried magnet schools, its political and civic landscape was shifting away from desegregation. The school choice models CMS more recently devised did not allow much choice because schools in newer, white areas were becoming crowded (see chapter 2 for a discussion of these trends). Thus, there were few slots available for minorities who wished to transfer there. In addition, prodevelopment arguments in Charlotte typically trumped support for desegregation.[39] Adjudicating the relative roles and weight of these various factors deserves more research, but at a minimum, they created a different policy climate for school assignment choices.

There are several additional reasons for the contrasting cases of these two districts. The first is that, unlike CMS, the integration of Wake's schools was not undertaken by court order.[40] Pressure from federal administrators and judges to mix schools by race certainly exerted considerable influence over Wake's policy makers both before and after the merger. But policies designed to bring about desegregation like magnet schools and the 15/45 plan were established without the formal supervision of a court. The broad, if tacit, support of a majority of the county's residents and business and political leaders was sufficient to bring about a degree of racial integration that prevented federal intervention. There was a natural indigenous political will and institutional infrastructure to support integration.[41] When CMS was declared unitary in 1999, the main force desegregating schools was removed and there was little to compensate for the loss of the judicial imprimatur for desegregation.

Second, the black community in Wake County appears to have been less conspicuous in education politics than its Mecklenburg counterpart.[42] To be sure, figures like Vernon Malone—who was Wake County's unified school system's first board chair—were important to the success of integration. The NAACP took a central role in the robust opposition to the Republican-majority board in 2010 and 2011, which suggests reaction to the threat of the board's antidiversity policy. However, long-term support for diversity in Wake was biracial. These apparent historical differences in civic engagement around school diversity among blacks in the two locales require additional research.

Third, Wake's politics have never been as conservative as Mecklenburg's. Its economy is based largely on government, higher education, and the professions. Charlotte's is founded on banking and the private sector—according to the 2010 U.S. Census, Mecklenburg has about 9 percent more firms than Wake, for example. These factors, moreover, likely contribute to the low level of trust in government and public institutions that exists in Charlotte, although we lack data regarding how such levels compare to Wake.[43]

All of these reasons explain why Wake public schools have not resegregated as much as CMS, although three interrelated explanations stand out. First, Wake was able to pursue desegregation longer than was CMS, and to do so within the context of improved student performance. This important combination had substantial public support, despite the outcome of the 2009 school board election. Second, CMS became majority-minority sooner than Wake public schools, which as of 2013, had just reached majority-minority status, owing largely to growth in the Latino and Asian populations in the county. Once districts become majority-minority, they are likely to focus more on student achievement than diversity in student assignment, which may allow for resegregation. Demography constitutes an aspect of structure within which agency must operate. Finally, Wake appeared historically to have greater stores of political will, a form of agency, directed toward school desegregation than did Mecklenburg. However, given Wake's changing demographics, reliance on successful desegregation and student achievement histories, as well as the agency of political will supporting desegregation, may or may not be sufficient to limit school resegregation in the future.

CHAPTER 7

Residential Choice as School Choice

The Impact of Unitary Status on Charlotte-Mecklenburg

David Liebowitz
Lindsay C. Page

IN 2007, THE U.S. SUPREME COURT barred school districts from voluntarily using racial classifications in student assignment to correct de facto segregation in *Parents Involved in Community Schools v. Seattle School District No. 1 et al.* (*PICS*).[1] The plurality opinion by Chief Justice John Roberts distinguished the voluntary choices of families to live in segregated communities from the governmentally mandated segregation of Jim Crow: "Where resegregation is a product not of state action but of private choices, it does not have constitutional implications."[2] In quoting Justice Anthony Kennedy's majority decision in *Freeman*, Roberts clearly intended to remind Kennedy—the swing vote in *PICS*—of his words from fifteen years prior: "Residential housing choices, and their attendant effects on the racial composition of schools, present an ever-changing pattern, one difficult to address through judicial remedies."[3]

The Justices in these cases view educational segregation as a product of either: (1) governmental policies and structures that explicitly assign students of different races to separate schools, in which case the state has a compelling interest to classify students by race to reassign them in an integrated fashion; or (2) individual agency and economic patterns over which the courts have no say. The plurality in *PICS* would limit the use of racial classification in student assignment policies only to instances where it is necessary to remedy the effects of past intentional discrimination. Beyond these, however, a third possibility, articulated in Justice Stephen Breyer's dissent, is that "state action," which is not explicitly racially segregative, may nonetheless lead to greater levels of residential segregation. If legal decisions and government policy actually *cause* residential segregation by changing the structure of incentives that drive private choices, then evidence of segregation resulting from state action might necessitate judicial remedy.

In this chapter, we investigate evidence of segregative private actions in the Charlotte-Mecklenburg Schools in response to the declaration of its unitary status and the subsequent change in its student assignment policy. The legal history and backdrop of this decision are detailed in chapters 2 and 10. This court-mandated shift in student assignment policy creates an opportunity to examine the impact of the declaration of unitary status on residential segregation. Specifically, we investigate whether the judicial decisions terminating the CMS desegregation policies caused families in Charlotte-Mecklenburg to respond differently to the racial makeup of neighborhoods when making residential choices (i.e., whether and where to move).

Earlier research, discussed shortly, suggests that the school desegregation orders from the 1960s and 1970s did produce changes in housing patterns. We build on a large body of prior research on the effects of desegregation decrees and declarations of unitary status to examine household residential choices. We find that although the end of the CMS desegregation policies had no impact on the overall extent of residential segregation immediately after the policy change, among those white families with school-aged children choosing to relocate from one year to the next, it did substantially increase their preference to relocate to a school attendance zone with a greater proportion of white students than their former residence. We take this result as evidence that state action, which is not explicitly segregative, nonetheless has the potential to impact residential segregation in the long run.

MOTIVATION AND CONTEXT

In *After Brown*, the seminal quantitative work on the interrelationship between the courts and educational segregation, economist (and chapter 5 coauthor) Charles T. Clotfelter identifies three indicators that court-imposed desegregation orders from the late 1960s and 1970s led to "white flight" and increased residential segregation.[4] First, in areas affected by desegregation, home values declined in the aftermath of court orders. Second, white families with school-aged children moved out of jurisdictions with desegregated schools at a faster rate than white households without children. Finally, metropolitan regions consisting of smaller districts were more likely to experience relocation of white families following desegregation orders, because smaller districts permit families to sort themselves based on race. In contrast, in districts covering entire metropolitan areas, white families were less likely to relocate—unless they were willing to enter different labor markets or commute long distances—because such moves would not ensure that their children would attend racially homogenous schools.[5]

This last result is particularly important in the CMS context, as the school district covers the entirety of Mecklenburg County—524 square miles. While some families opted for private schools, few left the county in response to the original *Swann* decision (see chapter 2 for details of this history). Thus, CMS remains a remarkably diverse district with a student population that in 2012–2013 was 42 percent black, 32 percent white, 18 percent Latino, 5 percent Asian, and 3 percent multiracial and other races (see chapter 8 for a discussion of demographic changes during the past two decades). Unlike other large metropolitan areas, many of which contain several districts serving different and racially homogenous student populations, CMS still has the potential for racially integrated schools and communities without redrawing school district boundaries.

HISTORICAL BACKGROUND

In 1970, on the eve of the *Swann* case, CMS, like many other southern districts, had made only modest progress in desegregating its schools. Clotfelter uses a segregation index to describe the extent to which children are exposed to classmates of different races relative to the proportion of nonwhite students in a district. The index ranges from 0, indicating that all schools or neighborhoods have nonwhite enrollment proportional to the overall demographics of the district, to 1, indicating complete segregation of white students and nonwhite students.[6] The index is interpretable as the fraction of nonwhite individuals who would need to move to a different neighborhood for the school district's neighborhoods to be perfectly integrated given the racial composition of the community. Figure 7.1, reproduced from Clotfelter's *After Brown* and supplemented with our own calculations, indicates that prior to the *Brown v. Board of Education* decision in 1954, CMS was entirely segregated. In 1970, the year before the Supreme Court decided *Swann*, the segregation index had only fallen to 0.63. By 1972 CMS employed a host of desegregation practices that included rezoning and

FIGURE 7.1 Segregation index in Charlotte-Mecklenburg Schools, 1950–2010

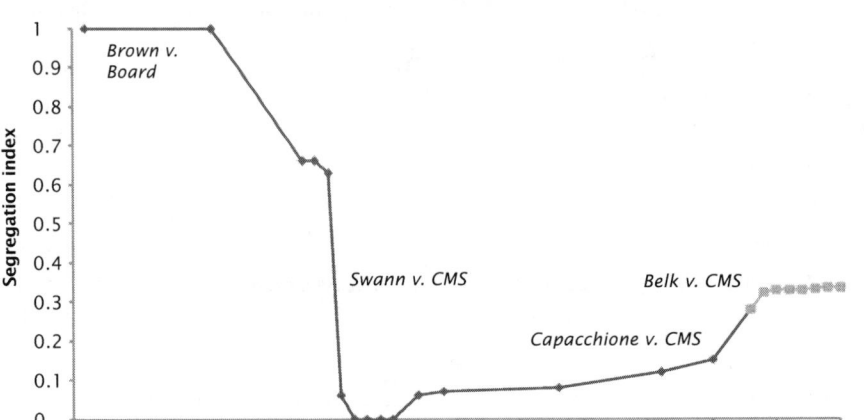

Source: Charles H. Clotfelter, *After Brown: The Rise and Retreat of School Desegregation* (Princeton, NJ: Princeton University Press, 2004); Charlotte-Mecklenburg Schools.

gerrymandering attendance zones; pairing black, inner-city students and white, suburban students to attend the same school; and busing students between city core and suburbs. As a result of these practices, CMS achieved an extremely high degree of school-level integration throughout the district, though as chapter 5 notes, this was not mirrored within classrooms. School levels of desegregation began to slightly drift toward racial imbalance beginning in the late 1980s, but overall remained high through the early 1990s until CMS replaced mandatory busing for most students with a mix of busing and controlled choice among magnet schools. School racial segregation rose gradually over the next decade before increasing sharply in the aftermath of the unitary status declaration, when CMS implemented what was essentially a neighborhood school–based assignment plan with limited choices for some families.

That the end of the race-conscious student assignment policy led to an increase in between-school racial segregation is unsurprising. Charlotte's neighborhoods were still highly segregated between 1971 and 2002, despite the school desegregation order. The Family Choice Plan (FCP), implemented in 2002, afforded parents the option to apply to other schools throughout the district but guaranteed students a seat in their neighborhood school. Under the FCP, more than three-quarters of students in the predominantly white suburbs selected their home schools, with the rest opting for magnets. In contrast, only one-quarter of inner-city residents selected their home school.[7] These patterns together led suburban schools to become oversubscribed and open primarily to families who lived in the neighborhood, with virtually no seats, and therefore no choice, available to inner-city students.[8]

Numerous studies have exploited Charlotte-Mecklenburg's declaration of unitary status and the subsequent increased levels of school segregation to explore the impacts of the change in assignment policy on a variety of outcomes. The new assignment policy has been identified as a cause of increases in school socioeconomic segregation, declines in the academic performance of both white and black students, and the sorting of more effective teachers to nonminority schools.[9] Furthermore, economist Justine Hastings and her colleagues have found that families used the options afforded through the Family Choice Plan to select schools nearer their residence that were more racially homogenous, rather than higher performing.[10] While some evidence indicates that the policy change did not widen the overall black/white test score gap in CMS, other studies find that nonwhite students rezoned to more nonwhite schools had worse academic outcomes.[11] What remains unclear is whether school segregation in CMS increased after 2002 only because families returned to schools located in already segregated neighborhoods, or because the lifting of the court order affected the residential choices of CMS families. In order to investigate this question, we examine the specific residential choices made by families before and in the immediate aftermath of the new assignment policy.

THEORETICAL FRAMEWORK

First we compare the racial composition and average achievement of the school attendance zone in which each student resides to those of the set of attendance zones into which each student might move the following year. We reason that families with school-aged children select their neighborhoods based on a combination of their own family characteristics, the associated school- and neighborhood-based amenities, and their capacity to afford a given residential area. During the period in which the desegregation orders were in place, we reason that for families choosing to live in and send their children to CMS, the school-based characteristics related to racial composition weigh only minimally in residential choice, since a family's residence does not determine the racial composition of the public school their children attend. Once a district is declared unitary, however, families can exert their school preferences through housing choice. For some families, this may entail selecting a neighborhood, and therefore a school, with a greater proportion of residents who are of the same race as their child than the proportion in their current neighborhood.

From 1971 to 2002, parents who were unwilling or unable to remove their children from CMS could not control the racial composition of the school their children attended through residential choice. In fact, as the student population grew, the district frequently redrew assignment boundaries to preserve the integrated nature of its schools. Given the metropolitan coverage of CMS, we reason that, during this period, residential choices of families with school-aged children would have been motivated by the availability, price, and quality of the housing stock; the local provision of noneducational amenities; and a wide variety of other nonobservable factors; but, importantly, only negligibly by the racial composition of the schools assigned to the neighborhood. Once the court-mandated assignment policies ended, however, families could use residential choice to select a school they perceived to be of high quality—even if one criterion was racial homogeneity of the school.

To attribute changes in family residential decisions to the unitary status declaration, we must show that Mecklenburg County residents could not have anticipated the timing of the policy change. The long, protracted court battle over desegregation clearly signaled to families the possibility of policy shifts. However, the courts were starkly divided over this case. After the District Court declared CMS to have achieved unitary status in 1999, a three-judge panel of the Fourth Circuit Court of Appeals overturned this ruling in 2000. Then, in 2001, the full Fourth Circuit, hearing the case *en banc*, overturned the 2000 decision. However, the black plaintiff-intervenors in the case quickly appealed the Fourth Circuit ruling to the Supreme Court, which only decided against hearing the case in April 2002. Given this pattern of events, we argue that it is unlikely that families would have made housing choices prior to the 2002–2003 school year that were contingent on being able to select the racial composition of their children's school.

With this historical and theoretical backdrop, we investigate the following primary question: did the unitary status declaration and the subsequent shift in student assignment policies increase the probability that families would move to a school assignment zone where the proportion of children of the same race as their own child was higher than the proportion in their current neighborhood? Building on Clotfelter, we hypothesize that white families, in particular, may be responsive to the change in school assignment policy. In 2000, median family income (in 1999 dollars) was $72,043 among whites, $39,479 among blacks, and $36,416 among Latinos in Mecklenburg County.[12] Given their more limited resources, black and Latino families, though highly mobile, would be comparatively constrained in expressing preference for wealthier, and consequently whiter, neighborhoods. As a result of both residential preferences and the financial capacity to express them through relocation, we reason that, after the declaration of unitary status, white movers would prioritize relocating to attendance zones with schools that were both higher performing and lower minority. Among those without the capacity to afford such attendance zones, we anticipate that the next most preferred option would be schools that were not necessarily better performing but still served a greater proportion of white students than their current school.

DATA AND ANALYSIS

In order to investigate residential preferences and patterns, we utilize student-level administrative data compiled by CMS for the years 1999–2009. This rich panel dataset contains information on student demographic characteristics, school identifiers, course enrollment, test performance, and—most importantly for our analysis—student race/ethnicity and student home addresses for each year of attendance. We matched each student's home address to its relevant school assignment zone.

We focus our investigation on elementary school students and assignment zones for two reasons. First, we hypothesize that families with middle- or high-school-aged children may be less responsive to the policy shift, given that they would have less time to reap the perceived benefits of a more racially homogenous setting. Second, elementary school zones are geographically much smaller and thus more sensitive to our relatively rough measures of residential integration. In separate analyses, we find that the results for older students are similar to, but more modest in magnitude than, the results for elementary school students.

Rates of Segregation

As noted, even before the declaration of unitary status, Mecklenburg County was racially and ethnically segregated from a residential standpoint. Figure 7.2 presents the racial makeup of CMS students in grades prekindergarten through 5 in each residential zone between 2000 and 2007. The darkest areas represent elementary attendance zones where greater than 80 percent of resident

FIGURE 7.2 High-concentration white and nonwhite elementary attendance zones in 2000 and 2007 (using 2001–2002 attendance zone boundaries)

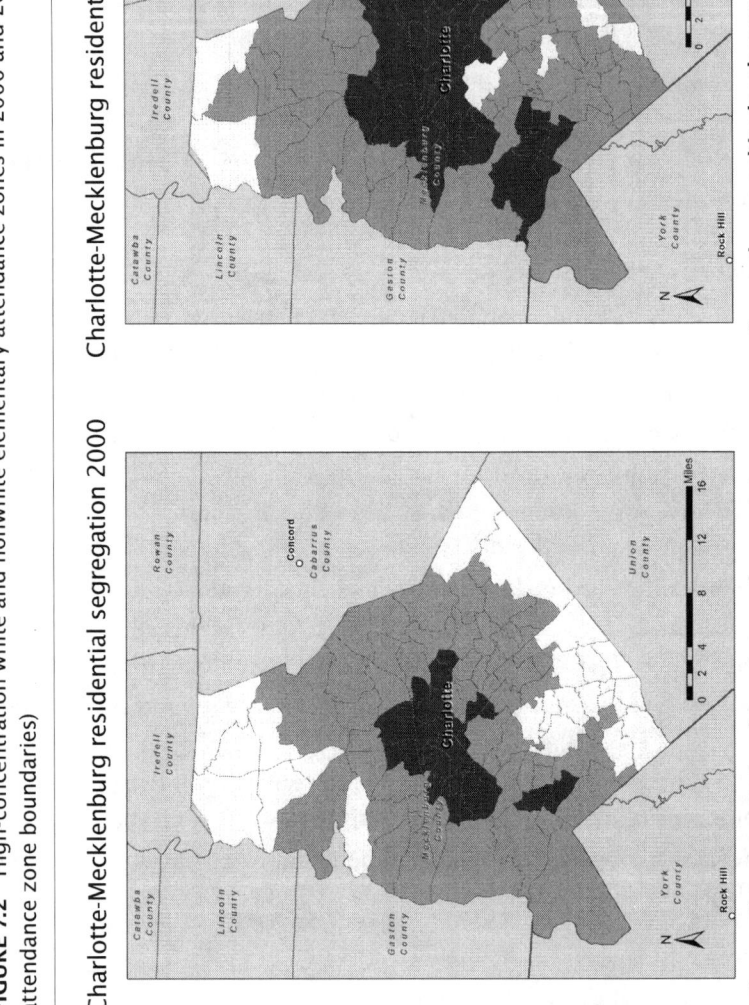

Charlotte-Mecklenburg residential segregation 2000

Charlotte-Mecklenburg residential segregation 2007

Proportion nonwhite by elementary assignment zone

Proportion nonwhite by elementary attendance zone

0–20%   20%–80%   80%–100%

Source: Charlotte-Mecklenburg Schools

students are nonwhite, while the lighter gray sections represent zones where greater than 80 percent of the resident students are white. The medium grey sections represent ranges between 20 and 80 percent nonwhite. The palest areas represent areas with fewer than 20 percent nonwhite residents. The residential segregation in these maps is striking; the geographic area of predominantly nonwhite attendance zones is large and located in the most densely inhabited central neighborhoods of the city. In 2003 through 2007, we observe growing numbers of attendance zones in which the student population is predominantly nonwhite and rapidly declining numbers of predominantly white zones.

Increases in the number of zones with high concentrations of white or nonwhite students, however, do not necessarily mean increases in patterns of segregation. The overall proportion of CMS students who were nonwhite grew from half in 1999 to two-thirds in 2009 (see chapter 8 for a detailed discussion of demographic shifts in Mecklenburg County). Therefore, even if there were no changes in overall patterns of residential segregation, we might expect to see more zones with greater than 80 percent nonwhite residents. We employ the same segregation index used by Clotfelter and discussed previously to investigate trends in the overall state of residential segregation between white children and nonwhite children in CMS between 1999 and 2009. The overall status of segregation, as measured by this index, is nearly constant over the eight years and does not appear to have been affected by the 2002 policy change.[13]

Patterns of Mobility

We additionally examine overall patterns of residential mobility over the years of our data. Specifically, we investigate, on a year-by-year basis, the share of families with elementary school children who moved across zones, who stayed in the same zone, or who left the CMS system, either because they left Mecklenburg County entirely or instead turned to a nonpublic option as table 7.1 indicates. Overall, the share of families who move is fairly stable from year to year, and while there is some fluctuation in this proportion, there are no clear trends over time or abrupt changes that appear related to the declaration of unitary status. Further, we see no trends aligned with the assignment policy change on the proportion of students who leave the district. Figure 7.3 presents disaggregated trends in cross-zone moving by race. We find that in all periods, both black and Latino families are more likely to move than their white counterparts.

TABLE 7.1 Descriptive statistics on the percent of elementary school students who leave CMS entirely, move to a new school attendance zone, or stay in the same school attendance zone from one school year to the next (1999–2009)

Year	Leave	Move	Stay	N (with leavers)
1998–1999 to 1999–2000	9.4	13.8	76.8	49,522
1999–2000 to 2000–2001	13.1	19.9	67.0	49,220
2000–2001 to 2001–2002	9.9	16.5	73.6	48,511
2001–2002 to 2002–2003	10.1	15.9	74.1	49,848
2002–2003 to 2003–2004	9.4	16.2	74.4	51,716
2003–2004 to 2004–2005	9.7	18.6	71.8	54,776
2004–2005 to 2005–2006	6.6	15.0	78.4	58,499
2005–2006 to 2006–2007	9.0	14.3	76.6	64,086
2006–2007 to 2007–2008	9.6	13.7	76.8	67,888
2007–2008 to 2008–2009	10.6	12.6	76.8	66,949

Source: Charlotte-Mecklenburg Schools

Families' Revealed Preferences

In order to understand families' preferences regarding residential choice, we examine the factors that govern a family's decision not only of *whether* but also of *where* to move.[14] Our analytic approach assumes that a family's characteristics, in a vacuum, should not influence its choice of residence. Rather, it is only how a family's characteristics intersect with the characteristics of a neighborhood of potential residence that should have an effect on whether a family selects a given attendance zone. We consider two primary factors as predictors of families' residential choices: first, an indicator of whether another attendance zone has a higher or lower proportion of white students (compared to the family's starting zone). In addition, in order to differentiate moves that reflect a preference for more racially segregated neighborhoods and ones that reflect a preference for better schools, we also introduce a critical control variable: an indicator for whether the school associated with a particular zone has average standardized math and reading achievement scores that are higher than the student's current zone of residence. Because we expect our results to vary by family race/ethnicity, we conduct and report on our analyses separately for white and nonwhite students.

FIGURE 7.3 Trends in the share of elementary school families who move to new school attendance zone by race

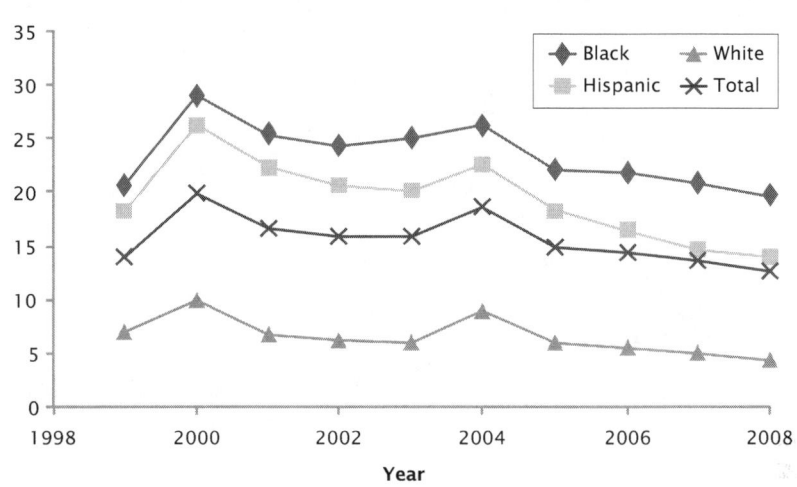

Source: Charlotte-Mecklenburg Schools

The primary results of our analyses are presented in figures 7.4 and 7.5. As illustrated in these figures, our key findings are represented in terms of odds ratios. Specifically, for each year in question, we estimate the odds of a family's deciding to move to a zone that is whiter than its starting zone relative to the odds of its choosing to move to a zone that is less white than its starting zone. In these figures, we additionally subdivide the choices that families make into those that are within school attendance zones where academic performance is higher than a family's starting zone and those that are within school attendance zones where academic performance is lower than a family's starting zone. In figure 7.4, for example, values greater than 1 indicate that white families are more likely to move to whiter neighborhoods; values that are further from 1 indicate a stronger preference.

Based on the results in figure 7.4, we find that in all years, white families who opt to move prefer to move to whiter neighborhoods than their starting ones. This preference is present even prior to the declaration of CMS's unitary status. For example, in 1999, the odds that a white family, when considering zones with lower average achievement than its starting zone, will select a new

FIGURE 7.4 Preference among white households for a school attendance zone with a greater proportion of white residents by relative academic performance of zone-assigned school (1999 to 2008)

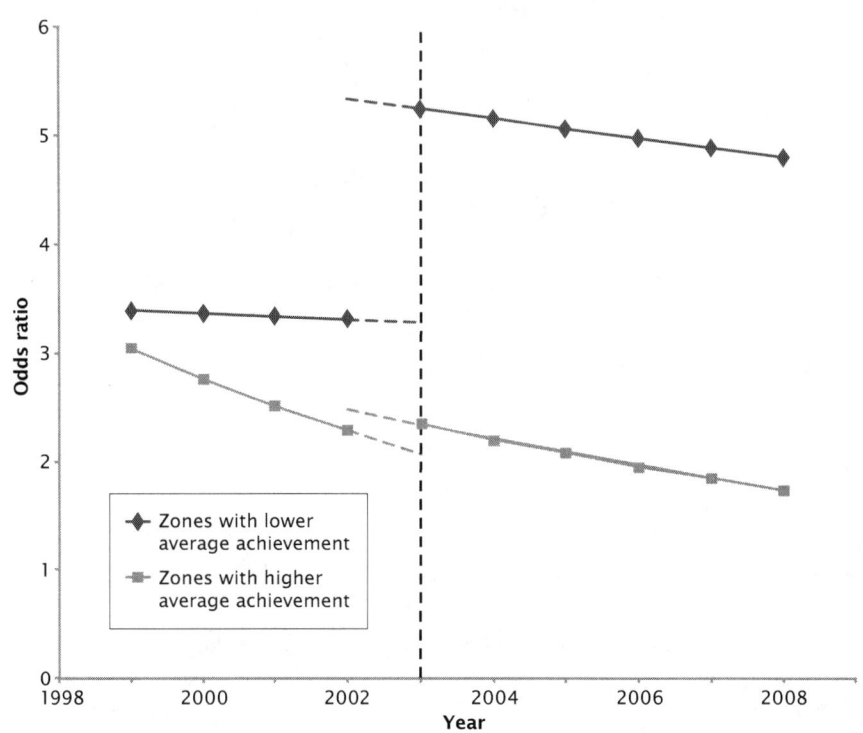

Source: Charlotte-Mecklenburg Schools

Note: Years labeled on x-axis correspond to the spring of a given academic year.

zone are over three times greater if the selected zone has a larger share of white residents than its starting zone.

Similarly, the odds that a white family, when comparing zones with higher average achievement, would select a particular zone in 1999 were over two times higher if that zone had a larger share of white residents. These predeclaration trends comport with the overall patterns of segregation in Mecklenburg County revealed in figure 7.2.

After the declaration of unitary status, we observe little change to the preferences of white families for whiter school assignment zones when considering better performing zones. However, very importantly, for white families choosing among zones with relatively lower performing schools, the relationship between the odds of a family's selecting a given zone and the racial makeup grew increasingly strong. As figure 7.4 illustrates, the odds that white families, when considering a lower performing school zone, would select a zone with a greater proportion of white residents than their starting zone jumped substantially from over three to over five.

Figure 7.5 presents an analogous set of results on the probability of non-white families making moves in a segregative direction. Specifically, for nonwhite families, the figure plots the odds ratio associated with moving to a zone that has a greater proportion of *nonwhite* students, again controlling for each zone's relative academic achievement. These results should also be interpreted relative to the benchmark value of 1, which would indicate no stronger preference for a more nonwhite zone than for a more white zone. Here, we observe a modest shift in preference of some nonwhite families also to move to

FIGURE 7.5 Preference among nonwhite households for a school attendance zone with a greater proportion of nonwhite residents by relative academic performance of zone-assigned school (1999 to 2008)

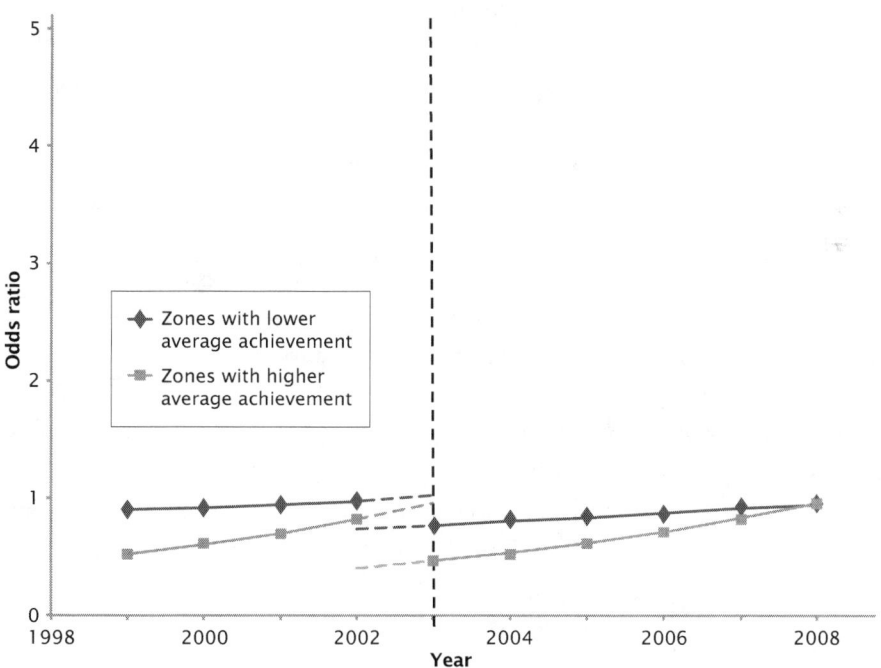

Source: Charlotte-Mecklenburg Schools

Note: Years labeled on x-axis correspond to the spring of a given academic year.

neighborhoods with larger shares of white families. Particularly when they are choosing among zones with higher average achievement, after the declaration of unitary status, the preferences of nonwhite families toward less white zones temporarily declined. This preference dissipates, however, in the years following the unitary status ruling.

Taken together, among families who choose to move within the district, we observe sharp changes in residential preferences as a direct result and in the aftermath of the CMS unitary status declaration. White families, in particular, revealed an increasingly strong preference for moving to zones that had a higher proportion of white students living in them when considering among zones that were lower performing. In contrast, we observe less dramatic shifts in the school zone preferences of nonwhite families immediately after the unitary status declaration, followed by a return to levels observed prior to the policy change.

Alternative Explanations

Though our results reveal changes in residential choices aligned to the new assignment policy, we must consider whether alternative explanations are equally plausible. It is possible that policy changes other than the unitary status declaration produced the discontinuity that we observe. A key shift in national educational policy came in January 2002 when President George W. Bush signed the No Child Left Behind Act (NCLB) into law, and states were required to release public report cards on school performance in the fall of 2003 for the 2002–2003 school year. Thus, it is possible that our results are a consequence of families taking advantage of newly available information on school composition and quality. Our results do not, however, suggest that families increasingly tended toward zones based on student achievement in the aftermath of the policy change. In fact, based on additional analyses, we find that white families were *less* likely to move to a better performing elementary or middle school zone in the aftermath of NCLB. In addition, NCLB likely had little impact on information publicly available on school-level performance in CMS. Even before NCLB, North Carolina had a strong educational accountability system based on student achievement.[15] For example, teachers could earn bonuses tied to student achievement, schools were recognized publicly according to levels of test score performance, and schools faced potential sanctions or interventions for less than adequate test performance.[16] Taken together, it is unlikely that NCLB provided CMS families with much additional information with which to assess and select among the district's schools.

While the revealed preferences of white movers were for whiter neighborhoods, we cannot eliminate the possibility that families' preferences may not be explicitly driven by race. Instead, these white families could be choosing to move to whiter zones that had other preferred amenities that were also correlated with their racial composition. While our data does not permit us to exclude the possibility that household preferences were driven by zones' socioeconomic makeup, most of the potentially observable zone differences are also likely correlated with school performance. Nevertheless, we find that including relative school zone achievement does not reduce white families' preference for whiter neighborhoods after the unitary declaration. Families' preferences for whiter school zones were actually *higher* if the zone also performed more poorly than their current residence. Minimally, we have demonstrated that white families moved in segregative directions after the unitary declaration, even if race may not have been the sole driver.

Another major threat to a valid causal interpretation is that individuals can anticipate a policy shift and respond preemptively, prior to the policy's enactment. Here, however, the tumultuous legal history in CMS suggests this is unlikely. Nonetheless, there is a concern that those families who chose to move across school attendance boundaries prior to the declaration of unitary status were different in some meaningful way from those who chose to move afterward. If this were the case, it would imply that the end of the race-conscious assignment plan did not affect individuals' residential choice, but rather induced a different set of families with different preferences to move. This might also mean that a return to the previous policy would yield no integrative benefits. We find that in all years, both black and Latino families were more likely than white families to move across school attendance zone boundaries. This may be because black and Latino families are, in general, more mobile than their white counterparts. It may also be that black and Latino families live in more densely populated, smaller school attendance zones and thus their moves may be more likely to cross zone boundaries. Indeed, when we examine the share of families who move either within or across school attendance zones, a much larger share of moves made by black and Latino families carry them across zone boundaries. Over the years considered, we observe, in general, a downward trend in the proportion of families moving across school attendance zone boundaries. This same pattern is true for white families, black families, and Latino families. We do not observe any large, discontinuous jumps in the share of families moving across zone boundaries that would threaten the validity of our substantive conclusions.

DISCUSSION

The end of the race-conscious student assignment policy in Charlotte-Meck-lenburg increased families' ability to use residential choice to exercise school choice. For white families who moved during this time period and whose housing preferences included neighborhood racial composition, the end of de-segregation made them more likely to pick a neighborhood (or school zone) with a greater proportion of white student residents. This was true for white families overall, though the effect is primarily driven by families selecting homes assigned to lower performing schools. Two equally plausible mecha-nisms may drive these patterns. One explanation is that white movers fall into two groups with distinct preferences. One set of movers prioritizes improved schooling quality as measured by student achievement on state assessments. The rate at which these families selected zones with better performing schools was unaffected by the unitary status declaration. Another set of movers priori-tizes racially isolated residential and educational settings for their children, and these families were able to exercise these preferences more easily after CMS enacted the new assignment policy. A second, competing explanation is that white movers have broadly similar preferences for neighborhoods and schools that are both whiter and academically stronger. However, within white movers, only the subset of wealthier families is able to access preferred housing stock in neighborhoods that are both whiter and assigned to stronger schools. In this explanation, there was no disruption in the relocation trends of the movers with greater financial resources on which to draw. These families continued to prefer homes that were in whiter neighborhoods and assigned to stron-ger schools. Their lower-income counterparts, however, could not buy into their most preferred neighborhood. Instead, they selected neighborhoods that, while providing them no better schooling choices, offered more racially simi-lar surroundings for their children. Unfortunately, our data lacks student-level socioeconomic information and, therefore, does not permit us to distinguish between these explanatory mechanisms.

The change in families' choices after the unitary declaration was sudden and consistent over the following five years. Nonetheless, it does not appear to have led to substantially different overall levels of segregation in the short term. This is not surprising. Although white families who moved after the declara-tion of unitary status in CMS were more likely to move in segregative ways, white families, overall, were very stable in their residential locations, with only

5 to 10 percent of those with elementary school students moving across attendance zone boundaries in a given year. Additionally, nonwhite movers were
very slightly more likely to move to whiter neighborhoods after the changed
assignment policy. These moves would serve to counterbalance some of the
segregative choices white families made during these years.

Ultimately, together with the already high starting segregation levels, mar-
ginal movers alone were insufficient to produce changes in one measure of
segregation, at least in the short run. Though we do not observe a change in
the status of segregation, the rate at which individual families make choices
over time that contribute to or limit segregation is directly connected to the
overall trend in segregation. When Jeffrey Weinstein examines the overall racial
composition of assignment zones, he finds small and insignificant changes in
neighborhood racial composition in the immediate aftermath of the unitary
status declaration, but significant, meaningful effects on segregation five years
out.[17] Our result provides evidence of immediate effects on the revealed preferences of individual households as a result of the policy change. Thus, we should
expect to observe rising values for the segregation index in the years to come.

In light of the compounding effects that we find of race-neutral plans on
residential choices, and the *PICS* decision's limits on the use of race-conscious
student assignment policies, Charlotte-Mecklenburg's schoolchildren have increasingly fewer opportunities to benefit from residential and educational integration. A large body of research discussed in the introductory and concluding
chapters to this volume points to the potentially detrimental results of this
pattern.

In this chapter, we provide evidence that state action, which is not explicitly segregative, may nonetheless have a causal impact on individual residential
choices that over time lead to greater levels of residential segregation. While the
courts and elected Board of Education did not intend for the declaration of
unitary status and subsequent adoption of the Family Choice Plan to generate
schools "segregat[ed] with the sanction of law," white families' preferences were
to live in a neighborhood that had more white students attending the assigned
school.[18] Policies in Charlotte-Mecklenburg that eliminated race as a factor in
student assignment resulted in not only less racially diverse schools, but also
in families having greater capacity to exert their preferences for less racially
diverse schools by moving in segregative ways. To be sure, race-neutral assignment policies that have disparate impacts are distinct from the stigmatizing ef-

fects of state-mandated segregation. Nevertheless, our findings suggest that the line is not clear between formalized de jure segregation and informal de facto segregation resulting from individuals' residential choices. Policy makers interested in promoting racially integrated schools and communities must consider the dynamic interplay between the legal structures they impose and the agency families exert before excluding race-conscious assignment plans as an option.

CHAPTER 8

From Black and White to Technicolor

Demographic Change in the Charlotte-Mecklenburg
Schools

Michelle Plaisance
Elizabeth Morrell
Paul McDaniel

THE LEGACY OF BLACK/WHITE race relations and racial gaps in educational outcomes often dominates discourse about the impact of school segregation for students in southern cities such as Charlotte. In this chapter, we argue
that this dichotomous perception of race-based inequity is problematic and
limiting. Recent demographic shifts across the New South, and particularly in
urban centers like Charlotte, have resulted in striking restructuring of intra-
urban spatial settlement patterns due to the influx of Latino, Asian, African, and
other immigrants. The Technicolor metaphor of our title reflects the ethnic,
racial, and linguistic complexities of the demographic shifts of the New South.
In this chapter we explicate the contours of this spatial demographic shift in
Charlotte, the consequent growth in linguistic diversity among students, and
the challenges this presents to the public school system.

We begin by describing the extent and nature of migrant population
growth in Charlotte since 1990. Not only is the *size* of this growth significant for its ongoing impact on Charlotte's schools, but the unique geographic
settlement *patterning* matters as well for its concentration in suburban settings.
The suburban settlement patterns of recent migrants have profoundly affected

neighborhood schools in middle-ring neighborhoods that were, until the past several decades, populated primarily by white students.

After setting the spatial and demographic stage for our argument, we provide a brief overview of the impacts of growing linguistic diversity on public education, the No Child Left Behind Act (NCLB), and the experiences of migrant students in U.S. schools. We then outline the specific barriers faced by non- or limited-English-proficient students within CMS, a system historically dominated by black and white students. Drawing upon the first author's experiences working within CMS in conjunction with administrative documents that describe the district's English as a Second Language (ESL) program, we offer a detailed portrayal of the procedures immigrant families encounter as they navigate the system.[1] We conclude with reflections on the likely programmatic challenges and opportunities CMS faces given the area's emerging spatial demographics. We outline the need and rationale for CMS to implement more comprehensive programs to support linguistically diverse students so that they receive not only appropriate language services, but also opportunities to acquire the knowledge, skills, and credentials that their English-speaking peers are currently more likely to receive.

CHARLOTTE AS PRE-EMERGING GATEWAY AND HISPANIC HYPERGROWTH CITY

As with other cities experiencing rapid growth in a globalizing economy, the dramatic expansion of the population and geographic area of the Charlotte Metropolitan Statistical Area (MSA) over the past several decades has contributed to significant changes in the city's social geography. Charlotte is unique for several reasons. Primary among these is the fact that the city has grown at an exceptionally rapid pace, surpassed only by Phoenix as the fastest growing major American city during the 1990s.[2] Secondly, the demographic makeup of the in-movers is remarkable for its diversity—Charlotte's newest residents hail from a multitude of locations, both domestic and international.

Charlotte's rapid growth can be attributed primarily to its status as a *globalizing city*. Globalizing cities are characterized by several features, including prominence in financial markets, socioeconomic polarization, and—importantly for our purposes in this chapter—increased ethnic diversity, often due to immigration.[3] This final characteristic has been particularly noticeable in Charlotte since 1990. Between 1990 and 2010, Mecklenburg County experienced a

410 percent growth in its Asian population, a 1,573 percent growth in its Latino population, and a 595 percent growth in its overall foreign-born population (table 8.1).[4] These remarkable numbers have earned Charlotte several designations, including "Hispanic Hypergrowth" city and "Pre-Emerging Immigrant Gateway."[5] The availability of employment opportunities and the rapid influx of immigrants into Charlotte are attributable to a confluence of several factors, including the passage of the Immigration Reform and Control Act (IRCA) of 1986, which permitted the movement of migrants across state borders in search of employment.[6]

Dramatic demographic shifts have triggered a fundamental "transformation of place" not only in Charlotte, but in other southern cities as well.[7] This "transformation" is apparent particularly in Charlotte's middle-ring neighborhoods, where an overwhelming majority of foreign migrants—Latino and otherwise—have chosen to settle. In contrast to traditional theories about social and spatial assimilation for immigrants, which contend that immigrants settle in central city locations near employment opportunities and in close proximity to coethnics, new concentrations of immigrant settlement are uneven and context-dependent.[8] In "pre-emerging gateways" such as Charlotte, immigrant settlement is often in suburban locations.[9] This pattern of suburban diversity has become increasingly apparent over time. In Charlotte, it led local historian

TABLE 8.1 Population change in Mecklenburg County, North Carolina, 1990–2010

	1990	2000	2010	Growth rate (%): 1990–2010
Total	511,433	695,454	919,628	79.8
White	364,651	445,356	465,372	29.1
Black	134,468	192,666	278,042	107.7
Asian	8,461	20,819	41,991	409.9
Latino	6,693	44,871	111,944	1,572.6
Foreign-born	17,875	68,349	124,150	594.5

Source: U.S. Department of Commerce, U.S. Bureau of the Census, 1990, 2000, and 2010 Decennial Census, and 2010 American Community Survey, retrieved from American FactFinder, http://factfinder2.census.gov. Growth rates are authors' calculations.

Note: Foreign-born population is not mutually exclusive of other population groups.

Thomas Hanchett to coin the term "salad-bowl suburbs." The availability of inexpensive, often multifamily, housing stock in middle-ring neighborhoods makes this settlement pattern possible.[10] The maps in figure 8.1 demonstrate the dramatic growth of Mecklenburg County's foreign-born population between 1990 and 2011, as well as the concentration of an increasingly diverse demographic in middle-ring suburban locations within the city.

FIGURE 8.1   Growth of foreign-born population in Mecklenburg County, 1990–2011

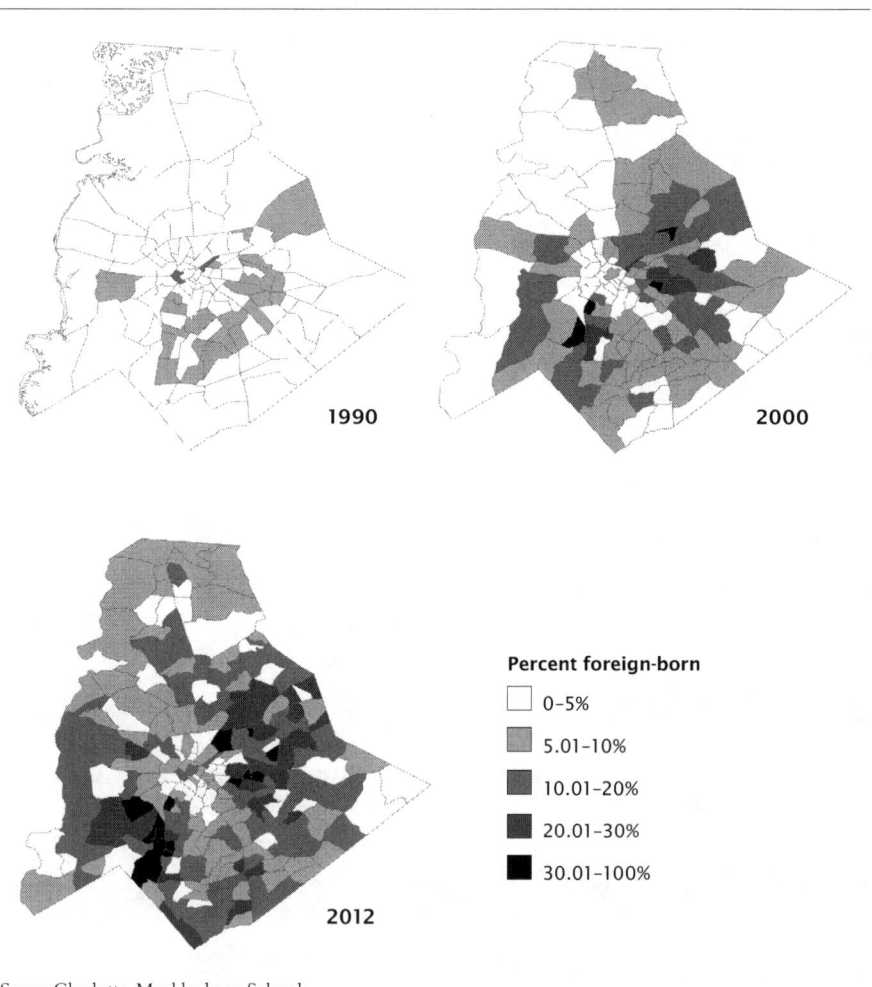

Source: Charlotte-Mecklenburg Schools

CHANGING COMPOSITION OF SCHOOL DEMOGRAPHICS IN CHARLOTTE

Charlotte's rapid immigration trajectory has had a substantial impact on the local school system. As figure 8.2 demonstrates, while enrollment of white students in CMS between 1987 and 2011 dropped from 58 percent to 33 percent and remained relatively stable for blacks, it increased for other ethnic groups. For Asian students, it increased from 2 percent to 5 percent of the total during this time period, and for Latinos it increased from close to 0 percent to 15 percent.[11] These dramatic changes in student populations during the past twenty years are most apparent in the striking growth among Latinos in the twenty-five schools with the highest Latino populations.[12] In roughly twenty years, schools that previously enrolled only a handful of Latino children (between 0.7 percent to 2.7 percent) currently have between 31 and 79 percent Latino students, most of whom are immigrants. Montclaire Elementary School

FIGURE 8.2 CMS student enrollment percent by race/ethnicity by academic year, 1987 to 2011

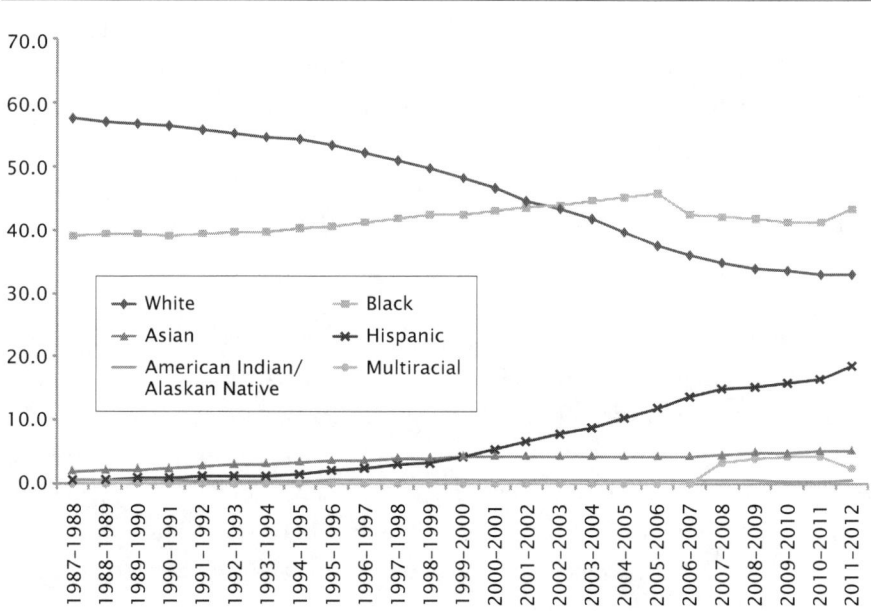

Source: U.S. Department of Education, National Center for Education Statistics, Common Core of Data (CCD), "Public Elementary/Secondary School Universe Survey," retrieved from http://nces.ed.gov/ccd/elsi/.

is the poster child for this transformation. Its population grew from 0.9 percent Latino in 1989–1990 to 78.9 percent in 2008–2009.

Equal in importance to the size of the growing Latino populations is their spacial settlement patterns.[13] The schools with the largest Latino student populations are in Charlotte's aging middle-ring suburbs—places that also have recently experienced rapid growth of immigrant populations. Notable among these schools are Montclaire Elementary and Collinswood Academy (home to a dual Spanish/English language immersion magnet program), whose Latino populations grew to 79 percent and 54 percent, respectively, as of 2009.

As of the 2010–2011 academic year, CMS reported that 20 percent of its students were international, 10.5 percent were "limited English proficient" (LEP), and 7.6 percent were enrolled in ESL programs.[14] The impact of these demographic shifts goes beyond compositional changes in the student bodies of the schools in which immigrants enroll. Neighborhood schools that witnessed growth in first- and second-generation immigrant student enrollment have also experienced challenges in addressing the language needs of these newly enrolled students. As we will demonstrate in this chapter, given the current manner in which English language learners (ELLs) are served in CMS, the schools with the largest populations of ELLs face significant hurdles in providing for the needs of these multicultural and multilingual students. Additionally, the middle-ring suburban settlement patterns of Charlotte immigrants present unique obstacles to providing comprehensive language services for them. Because of their location, many schools have yet to acquire the critical mass of non-native speakers that meets the threshold required to trigger the resources necessary to provide effective services to them.[15]

LANGUAGE DIVERSITY: A CHALLENGE OR AN OPPORTUNITY?

Most current scholarship about CMS tends to ignore Charlotte's sizeable and growing immigrant population. Previous research described segregation and unequal opportunities mainly in terms of race and socioeconomic status. To date, the educational experiences of non-native English speakers in CMS have been largely overlooked by policy makers as well as scholars.[16] Here lies the crux of our argument: CMS and its stakeholders must move beyond the historical black/white discourse to include consideration of the increasingly multicolor, or what we term the Technicolor, nature of its schools' student bodies.

The social and political context in which CMS serves its ELLs greatly influences program structures and services. As we have discussed, Charlotte has seen tremendous growth in its immigrant population; however, linguistic diversity in public schools is hardly a new phenomenon. In fact, schools in this country have always been faced with students who are non-native English speakers. What has changed over time is the public education system's reception and treatment of ELLs. Recently, accountability measures such as NCLB have brought non-native speakers into the spotlight because states, and subsequently districts, were required to implement programs to increase the achievement of these students.[17] CMS is no exception; it receives critical funding from federal programs that mandate accountability for the academic success of ELLs.

National-level research on the growing population of immigrant students in U.S. schools reveals disparate outcomes for linguistically diverse youth and the likely organizational and programmatic sources of these disparities. For example, a 2005 study of Texas ELLs found that the majority of them were placed in non-career-oriented academic tracks. Furthermore, advanced courses were not offered as "sheltered" courses (classes designed to simultaneously deliver content and language instruction). Thus, students lacking English proficiency were excluded from advanced classes despite the fact that many demonstrated aptitude for challenging coursework in their native languages.[18]

Language development is directly influenced by tracking practices.[19] Rather than placing ELLs in settings where they are able to receive the benefits of discourse with native speakers, they are often left to interact among themselves. This practice robs them of opportunities to use academic language in natural contexts with native-speaking peers, and the native speakers' lack of exposure to the talents of culturally diverse students frequently causes them to develop limiting or derogatory stereotypes. Thus, the practice further isolates ELLs socially and academically.[20]

Some ESL programs actually promote segregation and inhibit academic achievement. For many English language learners, ESL programs are a dead end. Program characteristics that are problematic for ELLs include content knowledge gaps, lack of college-bound coursework and authentic language models, and a cycle of lowered expectations that diminishes the hope and confidence of these students. Many ESL programs serve as permanent barriers to student success despite their intended purpose of providing students with temporary scaffolds for learning.[21] Next, we argue that many of these problematic elements, described in prior research, characterize CMS's ESL programs.

HOW STANDARDS-BASED REFORMS FAIL IMMIGRANT STUDENTS

The scope and structure of CMS's programs for ELLs is influenced by federal and state laws, programs, and funding streams. We focus on the federal framework in which CMS develops its programmatic responses to ELLs. The standards-based reform movements of the 1980s pressured states to improve outcomes for all students, including ELLs. This movement, culminating in NCLB, produced myriad reform measures focused on achievement and graduation rates. In 2004, the National Association of Bilingual Education issued a report that acknowledged the long-overdue need to focus on immigrants' school experiences but argued that one-size-fits-all efforts are ineffective and harmful.[22]

According to the report, NCLB's high-stakes accountability measures neglected to address the actual instruction of ELLs, as well as district-level realities including uneven distribution of resources, poor program design, and inadequate training for professionals working with linguistically diverse students. In addition, the report highlighted challenges inherent to the imposition of a system of standardized labels and categories to a characteristically diverse and fluid population of students.[23] For example, NCLB defines a subgroup of students as "limited English proficient." Yet it supplies no national criteria for placing students in this category, resulting in large variations in LEP statistics reported by states.[24] Furthermore, due to the defining characteristic of this group, achieving the ever-increasing Adequate Yearly Progress (AYP) benchmark is literally impossible, as the students who achieve proficiency are exited from the group, leaving only nonproficient students behind.[25] Perhaps the most detrimental element of NCLB for ELLs is their mandatory inclusion in high-stakes assessments from the outset of their academic tenure in the United States, despite research showing that it takes from five to seven years to acquire the academic language necessary to succeed.[26]

It is too soon to fully identify the impact of more recent federal policies, such as the Obama administration's 2009 Race to the Top initiative.[27] Under this program, CMS received funding for a wide variety of programs with objectives ranging from improving graduation rates to incorporating student growth data into the performance evaluation of teachers and principals. Like NCLB, Race to the Top emphasizes accountability and continued reliance on high-stakes, standardized testing as its primary means of defining achievement, conditions that have historically been unfavorable for ELLs.[28]

Within this context, we now describe how English language learners progress through CMS schools—how they receive instruction and language support—and the impact of the district's response to current legislation. Data for this portion of the chapter includes official CMS and North Carolina documents, policies, and procedures; the observations and experiences from author

Michelle Plaisance's ten years within CMS as an employee, school volunteer, and parent of two CMS students; as well as Plaisance's research as an ESL scholar. Five CMS ESL professionals with a combined total of forty years of experience independently read and verified the accuracy of the chapter's description of ESL services, experiences, and consequences for schools and students.

NAVIGATING THE CMS SYSTEM

All families who wish to enroll their children in CMS must register with CMS by submitting an enrollment form and providing three forms of documentation verifying residency.[29] These families, many of whom are newcomers to the area and who often lack private transportation, are required to complete the registration process at a centralized CMS facility designated as the language minority enrollment center for the entire 524 square miles of the school district.

The registration form contains a brief home language survey (HLS).[30] Research suggests that the HLS fails to identify many linguistically diverse students for one or more of several reasons: (1) the family never completes the HLS, (2) responses to the HLS are purposefully inaccurate because the family wishes for the student to avoid the stigma of being an "English language learner," (3) the family does not understand the questions, or (4) the information provided is entered into the district database incorrectly.[31] Students who indicate use of any language other than English on the HLS are labeled "language minorities" and must undergo a language proficiency assessment to determine eligibility for ESL services.

In 2008, North Carolina joined the World Class Instructional Design and Assessment (WIDA) organization, a consortium of thirty-one states focused on developing standards and assessments for ELLs.[32] All North Carolina public schools use WIDA's language proficiency assessment (W-APT), which is administered to students identified as language minorities by the HLS.[33] The LEP classification system is illustrated in figure 8.3. It presents the series of test-score–based decisions CMS makes about students' LEP status over the trajectory of their enrollment in the district. Students scoring below the state's "cut score" on the W-APT receive the LEP designation and are entitled to language services.[34] Typically, there are multiple opportunities for misidentification throughout the LEP classification process of LEP identification; however, in the case of CMS, the actual frequency of misidentification is not known, and likely not knowable, for many reasons.[35]

The LEP designation influences nearly every aspect of students' school experiences, from teacher expectations to curriculum selection. Classifying stu-

FIGURE 8.3 LEP classification process

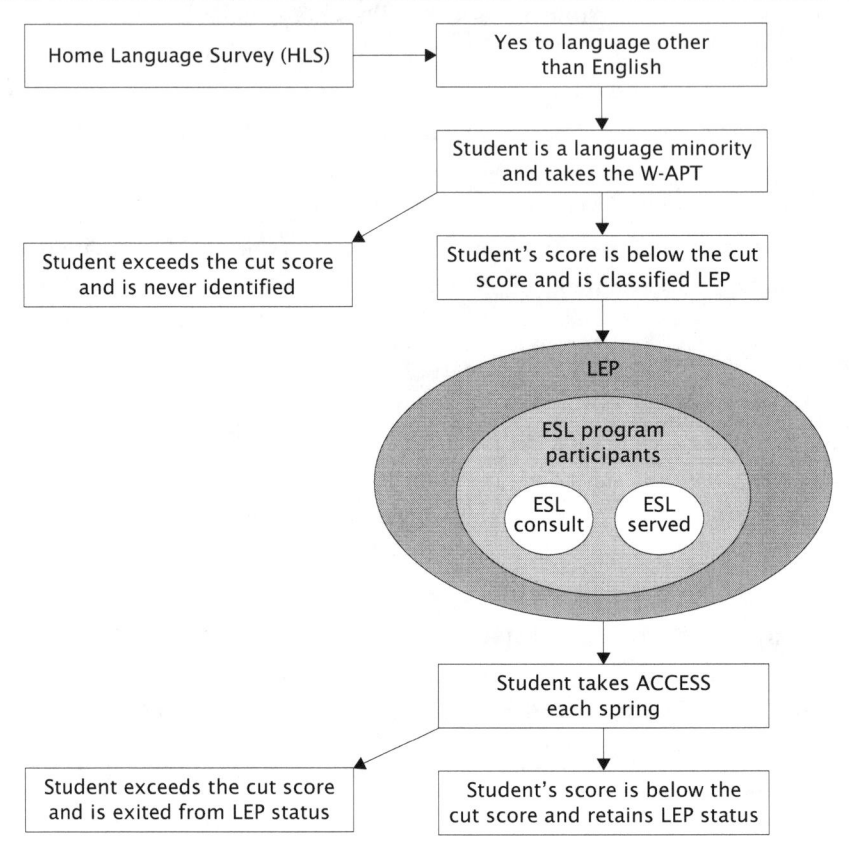

dents using any standardized assessment instrument is a difficult and inherently flawed process because what appears to be straightforward on paper becomes complicated when implemented on the ground.[36] For example, the kindergarten W–APT is administered during the first thirty days of school, an already stressful time for young students, who might become frightened when tested by an unfamiliar adult.

Additionally, the person administering the W–APT scores it as well, a practice that allows for potential subjectivity and raises issues of reliability in determining English proficiency. A final issue with the W–APT is the fact that because language proficiency is fluid and contextual, the very nature of a "cut score" is arbitrary. Meaningless differences between students who score slightly above or slightly below a cut score can thus influence placement decisions about them.[37] For these reasons, we argue that the use of the W–APT as the sole determinant of English proficiency is problematic.

Being LEP in CMS

There are times when identified English language learners do not receive language support from ESL professionals. For example, parents of ELLs may decline enrollment in the ESL program. They may wish to speed English acquisition through complete immersion or to avoid the potential stigma associated with ESL programs. Many ESL students in CMS are assigned *consultative status*, under which an ESL teacher collaborates with a student's general education teachers to monitor the student's academic progress in lieu of providing direct instruction.[38] While in theory consultations represent a form of language support, in practice they can take various forms, the quality of which ranges from regular and productive meetings between teachers to the completion of paperwork as a mere formality.

While language proficiency is one consideration for placing a student on consultative status, the experiences of author Michelle Plaisance suggest that scheduling issues and student/teacher ratios also influence this decision. Students in schools with high ESL ratios of ELLs to ESL teachers are more likely to be placed on consultative status. Staffing ratios do not appear to be closely tied to the size of the LEP student population, as there is no standard formula for the distribution of ESL-certified teachers. For example, the 2013–2014 North Carolina Title III Application shows disparate ratios, such as one half-time ESL teacher assigned to Elizabeth Lane Elementary (.5 to 47) compared to Elon Park Elementary (1 to 52).[39]

Regardless of the size of the school's ELL population, CMS lacks a districtwide formula for providing ESL services. Decisions are made by school administrators who often are juggling conflicting priorities and are unlikely to be trained in the linguistic needs of these students.[40] The unevenness of services available to ELLs in different schools, in addition to the aforementioned residential settlement patterns of Charlotte's immigrant population, results in ESL programs that vary greatly among schools.

Identified ELLs retain their status until they exceed the benchmark on a second WIDA instrument, Assessing Comprehension and Communication in English State-to-State for English Language Learners (ACCESS). The ACCESS is a standardized state assessment administered annually to LEP students. Unlike the W–APT, most of this assessment is scored by the test developer, potentially with more reliable results. However, students are assigned to tiers based on perceived proficiency, and the speaking portion of the test is still scored by the local test administrator—two practices that hold potential for measurement error.[41]

Language is context-dependent, and its assessment by a tool designed to objectify something intrinsically subjective is inappropriate. Using the results of any language assessment instrument in the same manner as traditional standardized assessments is problematic; doing so could result in disparate outcomes for equally proficient students.[42] In the case of the ACCESS, students' performance could vary greatly depending upon the tier to which they are assigned. Because the results of the ACCESS directly inform the LEP label, there is a great deal at stake for these students, both in terms of advantages (i.e., testing accommodations) and disadvantages (i.e., stigma).[43]

ESL Programs in CMS

CMS's current programs for English language learners reflect a national trend toward providing more inclusive programs for ELLs, while simultaneously supporting ESL pullout programs where students are removed from mainstream classes for specialized language instruction.[44] Research demonstrates the pullout model is less beneficial for ELLs than more inclusionary programs.[45] Students in pullout programs often miss important classroom instruction, exacerbating the gap in achievement between language minorities and native speakers. Without continued exposure to the content material delivered in the mainstream classroom at the elementary level, ELLs enter middle school with knowledge deficits, which, when coupled with the additional challenge of continued second language development, become nearly insurmountable. In addition, pullout programs often stigmatize ELLs, isolate them from their peers, and are costly due to the additional classroom space and materials required.[46]

The amount of time each student in a pullout program spends outside the classroom varies by school. These decisions are often left to the ESL teacher, who may be charged with the difficult task of creating a schedule that accommodates both general education teachers and students. The ESL central office offers general guidance regarding the number of hours or type of service students should be provided based on their English proficiency.[47] However, there is little monitoring or enforcement of these guidelines. For example, the ESL departmental guidelines include a menu of services for middle school newcomers that range from immersion in the general education classroom (presumably) with a teacher with Sheltered Instructional Observational Protocol training, to daily small-group instruction with a certified ESL teacher.[48] Yet there are no safeguards to ensure that such recommendations are followed.

While ESL pullout programs remain common throughout CMS schools, a consensus favoring more inclusive instruction has emerged among educators.[49] Administrators may encourage such models, preferring the exposure of ELLs to the content material for which they are accountable on end-of-grade assessments. However, it has only been in the last five years that the central ESL department has begun to support such models. Until then, CMS relied upon its stand-alone ESL curriculum and assessment program, which could be executed only in a pullout setting.

As a result of this ESL program inconsistency, some ESL teachers in CMS are untrained for and unsupported in the type of teaching they are asked to do.[50] Furthermore, while the implementation of inclusive models may appear as a logical solution to the problem of segregation and unequal access to curriculum, executing effective inclusive programs is an enormous challenge.[51] Collaboration between general education and ESL teachers requires joint planning time. In addition, such programs require the professional "buy-in" of all teachers assigned to collaborative teaching contexts. Achieving this goal is difficult in the face of high-stakes accountability programs. But most of all, all the ESL programs require specific, effective, and ongoing professional development for both ESL and general education teachers. CMS only began to acknowledge and address this need in its 2013–2014 budget.[52]

At the middle and secondary levels, individual principals also decide when and how ESL-certified teachers will serve students, resulting in significant variance in programs across the district.[53] Additionally, NCLB requires that teachers be "highly qualified"—as defined by criteria put forth by the Act itself.[54] This mandate resulted in an overhaul of services provided for middle and high school ELLs, because teachers formerly teaching ESL classes were suddenly required to obtain certification in an additional content area in order to maintain their "highly qualified" status.[55] School-level response to this change has been varied, with many ESL teachers being assigned to teach both native and non-native speakers in content area classrooms. This arrangement creates difficulties for ESL teachers, who often feel overwhelmed by the need to attend to the language development of ELLs as well as the content area of the curriculum.

BETWEEN- AND WITHIN-SCHOOL SEGREGATION IN TECHNICOLOR

Even in schools where English language learners are provided with appropriate services and content is delivered through more equitable programs such as sheltered instruction, ELLs may not receive the same opportunities as their English-speaking peers. The within-school segregation at the root of these disparities begins as early as elementary school, when ELLs are excluded from higher reading groups and gifted programs because they lack proficiency in English.[56] Subsequently, they are often placed in electives and remedial classes in middle and high school. This practice leaves little room in their schedules for the prerequisites necessary for Advanced Placement classes.[57]

Compounding this issue is the presence of between-school segregation and inequalities for ELLs. For example, many CMS secondary schools with high ELL populations do not offer the same quantity or selection of advanced classes as other schools, further reducing the likelihood that these students will graduate with the academic record required for admission to a four-year university.[58] Furthermore, teachers in CMS schools with high concentrations of poverty and populations of ELLs are more likely to be more transient, less likely to have advanced degrees, and lacking the same experience as teachers from schools with smaller ELL populations.[59] Thus, the *within-school* segregation we have described is compounded by *between-school* segregation based on geographic settlement patterns and access to quality schooling.

WHAT LIES AHEAD FOR ENGLISH LANGUAGE LEARNERS IN CMS?

Unlike other special needs students with powerful and organized parents, English language learners typically have few allies outside or within CMS beyond their dedicated and overextended teachers. The introduction of the Common Core State Standards and the adoption of a new series of high-stakes assessments, accompanied by the development of growth-based teacher accountability programs, do not bode well for CMS's future ELLs given the way CMS organizes and implements the services for them. Scholars agree that programs focused on accountability have not served these students well in the past.[60]

On a positive note, there is renewed attention among CMS administrators to learning environments for ELLs. For example, in 2012, CMS's superintendent created the LEP Task Force, which was composed of stakeholders within the Charlotte community.[61] This task force was charged with developing a set of recommendations for improving academic outcomes for ELLs. It offered an opportunity for a group of dedicated and knowledgeable community members to come together and share ideas and resources. While it is promising that district administrators' discourse appears to have moved beyond the usual black/white binary to recognize the educational needs of linguistically diverse students, the task force's outcome was disappointing because it primarily highlighted the "shortcomings" of linguistically diverse families rather than issues in the schools that serve them.[62]

Recommendations from initiatives like the task force are insufficient for meeting the needs of ELLs today, let alone in the future given their predicted growth trajectories. At present, CMS programs and staffing decisions tend to be driven by national and state mandates, not necessarily by the realities on the ground in CMS schools that serve ELLs. Without strong advocates on the school board or organized political allies in the community, ELLs' squeaky wheels tend not to receive the necessary programmatic grease from CMS. Yet to meet these students' needs, CMS must fundamentally change its programs so as to ensure that all students who need language development support receive appropriate services. Districtwide implementation of new evidence-based policies and programs for ELLs, equitable staffing, and professional development of teachers and support staff are necessary to merely *begin* to address the long-term educational needs of English language learners in CMS.

Furthermore, CMS must move away from defining ELLs' ability and progress using only culturally specific (and often inappropriate), standardized instruments. Although CMS remains subject to testing and accountability requirements set forth by state laws and federal funding programs, it also has access to a wealth of professionally trained staff who can develop more authentic and meaningful ways of assessing these students. Because accountability measures are likely to increase in the future, districts like CMS have an opportunity and responsibility to shape future policy by demonstrating a commitment to developing supplemental assessment programs that promote equitable outcomes for ELLs.

CONCLUSION

The complexities of the demographic changes of the New South are evident in the contours of the spatial demographic shifts Charlotte has experienced in the last twenty-five years. This chapter has chronicled the consequent growth in linguistic diversity among students and the challenges their growth presents to the public school system. CMS's response to these challenges has been undistinguished, as this chapter shows. Moreover, CMS's programmatic approach to linguistic diversity reflects a glaring normative contradiction in the larger culture. For native English speakers the acquisition of a second language is seen as a valued skill, as illustrated by the fact that there is a highly competitive lottery for entrance into CMS's five language immersion magnet programs. At the same time, the current structure of ESL services for students acquiring English as a second (or often third) language reflects a perspective that ELLs are lacking in some way, even if they demonstrate giftedness in their native language. This contradictory discourse surrounding bilingualism in Charlotte—and across the nation—is emblematic of the deficit-based models for educating ELLs that subsequently sustain group-based inequalities.[63] The current remediation-oriented programming for ELLs in CMS is at odds with evidence-based, additive approaches, such as bilingual and dual immersion programs.[64] CMS is missing an opportunity to capitalize on students' underlying language proficiency by building on ELLs' native languages. Furthermore, an additive approach that nurtures and affirms students' linguistic identities will promote culturally democratic education that is more effective and inclusive of all students—not just those whose primary language is English.[65]

The demographic composition of New South cities such as Charlotte has changed dramatically over the past several decades due to immigration and the restructuring of intrametropolitan geographies. These changes are reflected in the schools in several ways, including higher numbers of ELLs, more complex demographic mixes in the schools, and differentiated structures of current programs that increase the racial, ethnic, and linguistic isolation of students between schools and, in the case of ELLs, within them as well. As we have described in this chapter, CMS has an array of policies ostensibly targeted to the needs of ELLs; however, their implementation has not been optimal or equitable. The geographically dispersed nature of the linguistically diverse population makes meeting these students' needs under the current policies and programs nearly impossible. It is somewhat ironic that in an era of growing resegregation in CMS, given the process by which the school system allocates ELL services, the more diverse spatial geography of English language learners has the unintended consequence of making it more difficult to provide appropriate language services than if these students were more concentrated in fewer schools—that is, more segregated.

We can be fairly certain that most immigrant students and their families are here to stay in Mecklenburg County. The needs of foreign-born students, who often attend resource-poor schools in Charlotte's increasingly less afflu-ent middle-ring suburbs, differ substantially from the needs of other student groups. Rather than addressing the ethnic, racial, and linguistic complexities that accompany these demographic shifts with inadequately staffed programs that result in within- and between-school segregation of ELLs, CMS should embrace these differences and acknowledge the assets these new populations bring to our increasingly Technicolor schools and neighborhoods.[66]

CHAPTER 9

A Long Path to Success

Integration and Community Engagement at Shamrock
Gardens Elementary School

Amy Hawn Nelson

IN 1997, WHEN NORTH CAROLINA first launched its school rating system, Shamrock Gardens Elementary School had one of the lowest scores in the
state. The school looked like it had been forgotten: its grounds were overgrown
with weeds, paint peeled from its walls, and instructional materials were left over
from previous generations. Staff turnover was high, scores were dismally low, and
few people with options chose to work or send their children there. Soon after,
the school became part of the state's first efforts to take over failing schools.[1]

In 2014, by contrast, the school gardens are flourishing, the walls have fresh
paint, the library is colorful and filled with computers and new resources, and
parents are volunteering in classrooms staffed by highly effective teachers. Test
scores have risen and enrollment is increasing. All the sanctions brought on by low
academic performance have been removed, and a seven-year-old partial magnet
program focused on "gifted" education has a waiting list.[2] In 2013, the Magnet
Schools of America identified Shamrock Gardens as a school of excellence.[3]

In the present era, standardized test scores measure school success or failure.
By this metric, Shamrock has shown steady improvement, from a composite score
on North Carolina's End-of-Grade tests of 44 percent in 1998 to one of 67 percent in 2011.[4] These scores are neither above the district average nor particularly
noteworthy compared to other schools with similar student demographics—just
under 90 percent low-income and approximately 90 percent nonwhite. But on

the ground, the school's transformation has been dramatic—a new library, thriving gardens used for instruction, an active PTA, and a fully staffed school. Both white and black middle-class parents are enrolling their children there for the first time in decades, particularly those from the more affluent neighborhoods within the school boundary, thereby creating a more racially and socioeconomically diverse learning environment.[5]

Shamrock came to public notice at a time when CMS's focus was turning from busing for desegregation toward systemwide, race-neutral, performance-based accountability reforms, which included an emphasis on testing, acountability, and choice among magnet programs. This emphasis increased following the declaration of unitary status and the return to neighborhood school-based assignments in 2002. These reforms contributed to CMS's winning the Broad Prize for leadership in urban education in 2011.[6] Yet whether Shamrock benefited from these race-neutral accountability reforms remains an unanswered question. Traditional metrics of success—test scores—suggest it did not. But a broader perspective on school success that goes beyond test score metrics suggests that seeds of a success trajectory were planted a decade ago and are beginning to bear fruit.

While the district adopted the prevailing national focus on testing and prescribed curriculum and instruction at high-poverty, low performing schools, Shamrock Gardens took a different path. Although there was an emphasis on achievement measured by test scores, school administrators also focused on building a stable, experienced staff. Supporters sought to reintegrate the school—attempting to attract middle-class families living within and sometimes beyond the school attendance boundaries.

This chapter explores how Shamrock Gardens moved beyond a focus on tests to a broader, sustained school reform effort. While test scores are important, transforming school climate and school culture remains a more elusive goal for chronically underperforming schools such as Shamrock Gardens. Changing the focus in low performing schools from short-lived bumps in test scores to the kind of gradual but steady *success trajectory* that Shamrock embodies is critical for authentic school reform.

Success trajectory is a broad concept that includes a comprehensive focus on the underlying issues of school culture that lead to low academic performance. In addition to focusing on standardized test preparation (which can raise scores quickly), the Shamrock Gardens community engaged in the difficult work of transforming school culture over a period of years. Improvements included upgrading the physical environment and strengthening the underlying educational infrastructure of the school. The latter included widespread implementation of rigorous curricula, a gifted magnet program that is integrated throughout magnet and nonmagnet classrooms, small class sizes, data-informed instruction, engaged community and parent volunteers, strong leadership, and systematic teacher collaboration. These changes have been generally supported by the larger district through increased flexibility and resources. School-level improvements have led to changes in school culture and modest but steady increases in test scores, which together have slowly encouraged middle-class families to enroll in the school, creating a more diverse learning environment and broadening the available parental cultural capital. This virtuous cycle has become a success trajectory. But generating the virtuous cycle took sustained efforts over time.

Drawing upon administrative records from North Carolina and CMS, media reports, and interviews with parents, teachers, and administrators, this chapter examines the school, community, and district efforts that have taken Shamrock Gardens beyond the test score bump. Reviewing and analyzing the reform efforts from the past twenty years, I conclude that this trajectory of succcess was achieved through the combined and sustained efforts of Shamrock Gardens parents, activists, and educators.

SCHOOL ASSIGNMENT AND ENROLLMENT

CMS has long been viewed as a model urban school district.[7] As chapter 2 recounts, prior to 2002, CMS's efforts to minimize achievement gaps largely centered on court-mandated efforts to maintain desegregated schools.[8] While the historical relevance of CMS's desegregation efforts is noteworthy, levels of compliance with the desegregation mandate varied by school throughout the district. Shamrock had been built as a white school during the 1950s, but a combination of desegregation efforts and shifting neighborhood demographics turned it into a majority black school even during the height of desegregation efforts (although it remained generally within the +/−15 percent bandwidth utilized for the desegregation plan as described in chapter 2).[9] In 1993, as district support for desegregation ebbed, Shamrock reached a turning point, falling consistently out of compliance with the *Swann* guidelines. By 1996–1997, the year identified for school takeover by the state, Shamrock Gardens was 63 percent black, with 75 percent of students receiving free or reduced lunches (FRL), while CMS overall was 42 percent black with a FRL rate of 34 percent.[10]

In 1998, the district attempted to remedy the situation by assigning Plaza Midwood—a nearby, predominantly white middle-class neighborhood—to the school. But few Plaza Midwood families were willing to enroll their children in Shamrock Gardens. In subsequent years, even after CMS was declared unitary and returned to residential school assignments, Shamrock continued to enroll one of CMS's highest-poverty, highest-minority student bodies.

Starting in 2006, this pattern began to change, albeit slowly. In 2006–2007, the year the partial magnet program began, two Plaza Midwood families enrolled their children in Shamrock.[11] In 2010, ten families were enrolled in K–5. In the 2013–2014 school year, approximately nineteen families from Plaza Midwood chose their neighborhood school. Together, these students make up 15 percent of the three kindergarten classrooms. While the majority of Plaza Midwood parents continue to seek other options, each year a larger cohort of neighborhood students enrolls. In 2010–2011, 17 percent of Plaza Midwood families attended their assigned neighborhood school (Shamrock Gardens, Eastway Middle, and Garinger High School), compared to a CMS average of 75.42 percent.[12]

The main reason for the change has been the growing reputation of the partial magnet program, officially known as the Learning Immersion/Talent Development Magnet Program. This is the option Plaza Midwood families invariably choose. Shamrock Gardens is now seen as a school with a rigorous academic program and high-quality teachers, particularly for those who enroll in the magnet program. In addition, starting in 2010–2011, the school's rising performance eliminated the option for families to "opt out" of Shamrock Gardens under No Child Left Behind (2001), which made it more difficult for parents to enroll their children in other CMS schools.[13]

AUTHENTIC SCHOOL REFORM

Test score miracles are often student assignment miracles, meaning that test scores improve because the scores measure different students. Yet demographics at Shamrock have remained fairly constant. The school has remained around 85 percent to 93 percent FRL for the past decade, with a student population that is predominantly black and Latino. Since 2004 test scores have continually risen, meaning that the academic performance of low-income students of color improved because instruction improved. Even when middle-class students began to enroll, most of them were in the lower grades, where students do not take standardized tests that contribute to the school's performance composite (that situation changed in the 2013–2014 school year, when the first substantial group of middle-class students took the third-grade tests). Thus, the higher test scores of the upper grades to date suggest that authentic, school-level change underlies the improvement in Shamrock's academic outcomes.

RESEARCH DESIGN AND FINDINGS

School reform is a complex process, and multiple data sources are needed to adequately capture and disentangle converging factors in that process. To begin to capture this complexity, I conducted a mixed-methods study that combined quantitative and qualitative data. I used publicly available data to better understand the context of the school community and neighborhood and to describe long-term school and community trends. These sources included administrative data from the North Carolina Department of Public Instruction and the Charlotte-Mecklenburg Schools, the News Bank archive, and the Mecklenburg County Quality of Life Study.

To better understand the experiences of school stakeholders, particularly in regards to understanding how CMS policies and available resources constrained or enabled various actors, I conducted in-depth interviews with current and past school leaders, teachers, parents, community members, and district leaders. I started with three people from my own connections with Shamrock and three individuals recommended by current school leadership. Initial interviews introduced me to others, and through snowball sampling I conducted a total of twenty-one interviews. I used a thirteen-question protocol designed to guide but not limit discussion. Interviews ranged from 30 to 130 minutes and were recorded. After they were transcribed, two research assistants and I thematically coded them. We then compared codes to check for intercoder reliability and resolved inconsistencies through iterative discussions. All interviewees were offered the opportunity to read and critique the chapter for accuracy.

Like many other large school districts, CMS has a Web site with comprehensive administrative data. I used the Web site to confirm and provide additional background for events described by interview respondents. I also confirmed respondents' recollections using information from other publicly available sources. For example, several respondents discussed teacher retention as a key lever for change. To examine the role of teacher retention, I used school-level data from the North Carolina Department of Public Instruction, the perceptions of interviewees, data from state- and district-level reports, and targeted questions on the topic to current and past school leaders. All data sources, both quantitative and qualitative, were combined for analysis. The findings reflect my triangulated analyses of quantitative and qualitative data across all sources.

The general consensus among respondents I interviewed is that the majority of the reforms enacted at Shamrock Gardens since 1997 did little to improve student learning. Because of the absence of reform evaluations, we will never know with certainty what reforms drove or stunted the success trajectory of Shamrock Gardens. However, the findings from this study suggest that several different efforts may have come together to create a dynamic that over a ten-year period built a scaffold for the success trajectory that I will describe in the next sections.

I capture this dynamic in figures 9.1 and 9.2. Phase 1, from 1997 to 2005, is dominated by structures imposed upon the school, including accountability-based labels and mandated reform efforts. This phase resulted in a high number of interventions, high cost, and low success. Phase 2, from 2006 to 2011, was an important transition time for Shamrock Gardens, characterized by supportive structures and multiple initiatives by individual actors in the community and within the school building. This was a period of a high number of interventions and high financial costs, but continuous academic improvement. Currently,

FIGURE 9.1   Shamrock Garden's school success trajectory

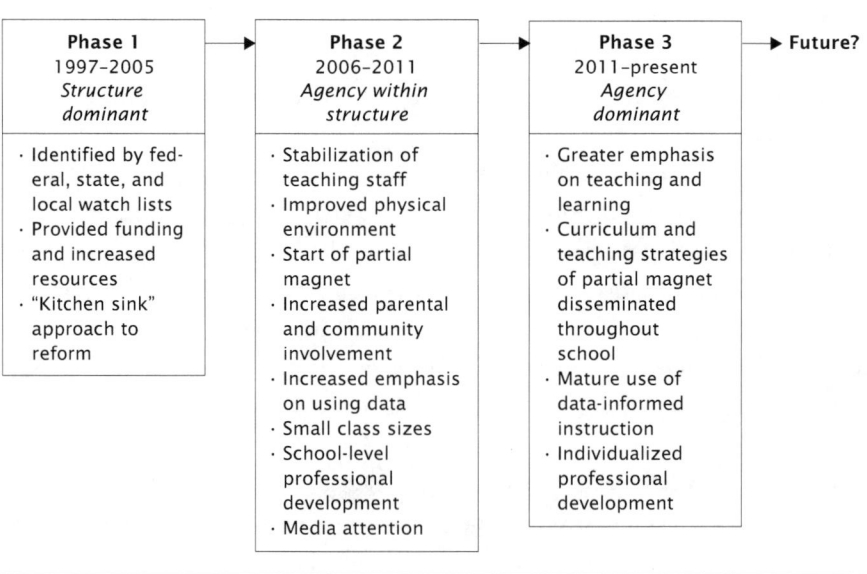

FIGURE 9.2 Shamrock Garden's school success trajectory, success and intervention quadrants by phase (see figure 9.1)

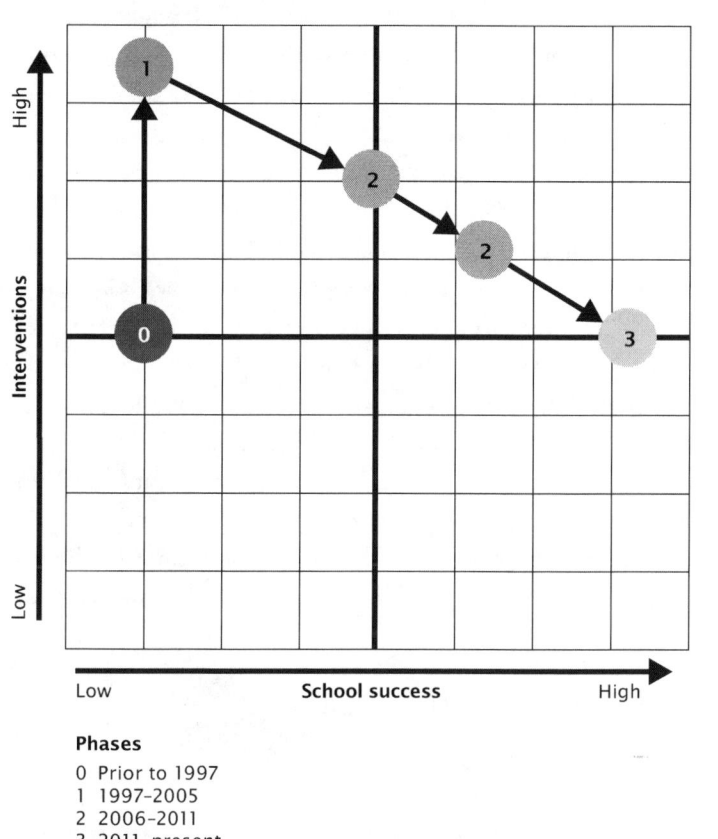

Phases
0 Prior to 1997
1 1997–2005
2 2006–2011
3 2011–present

Shamrock Gardens seems to be moving into Phase 3 of the success trajectory. The accountability-triggered structures of Phase 1 have ended and many of the supportive structures of Phase 2 are no longer in place, both because of tightening state and local budgets and because the school no longer receives the funding and district support that comes with low academic achievement. With structural improvements in place, the present period is dominated by individual initiatives and actions at the school level designed to continue to improve academic achievement with fewer interventions and lower per-pupil expenditure.

Figure 9.2 suggests the relationship among the intensity and costs of interventions and their success over time. These reforms seem to have created a tipping point in the school reform process that triggered the virtuous cycle I label the *success trajectory*. As the partial magnet matured, the curriculum materials and instructional strategies were adopted in all classrooms, which led to improved instruction and academic outcomes across the school. Simultaneously, parent volunteers brought in additional resources to support family nights, enrichment opportunities, and campus beautification. Even as district-level resources began to wane, the culture and the parent volunteers remained. Taken all together, the pieces fell into place.

The overall finding is that the synergy of actions among many actors, over time and within a supportive structure, placed Shamrock Gardens on a success trajectory. These reform efforts did not bear fruit in one year and did not originate from one person. Rather, for Shamrock Gardens, reform has taken time, sustained efforts, trust, strong leadership, adherence to basic educational principles (small class sizes, rigorous curriculum, data-informed and flexible instruction), teacher collaboration and stability, community involvement, and district-level support. End-of-Grade test scores cannot begin to adequately measure this dynamic process and while important, cannot be the sole indicator of success. The following sections elaborate on this summary of findings captured in figures 9.1 and 9.2.

EVERYTHING BUT THE KITCHEN SINK

Shamrock Gardens, like many low performing schools, was the object of numerous reform initiatives during the last twenty years. Many efforts were employed simultaneously or sequentially, the majority without any systematic formative or summative evaluation. This made it impossible to assess whether a particular reform or practice made a difference in student or teacher outcomes. Not surprisingly, interviewees commonly described reforms as ineffective due to their lack of strategic focus. Jessica Broening, a teacher at Shamrock for six years, described this history as the "reform flavor of the week," and Leta Waters, a teacher's assistant, said that "everything but the kitchen sink" had been implemented at some point. Delores Trinity, an academic facilitator at Shamrock, observed the lack of consistency: "We never do anything with fidelity and we never see it all the way through."[14] Staff members generally felt that the school was at the whim of the district and the state.

One reason for the series of reforms is that Shamrock never slipped from the central administration's radar. This is possibly because Shamrock Gardens had been a chronically low performing school. But there were other low per-forming schools in CMS. A more likely explanation is that several high-level district leaders had strong ties to Shamrock. CMS's deputy superintendent started her school leadership career at Shamrock as a principal in 1987. The longest-serving CMS school board member lives in Plaza Midwood, where he has been the pastor of a neighborhood church since 1988. His two adult chil-dren attended Shamrock for parts of their elementary school careers.

Accountability-Based Reporting and Labeling

North Carolina's standards-based accountability system, ABCs of Public Educa-tion, was implemented in 1997. Soon after, Shamrock Gardens was identified as one of the lowest performing schools in the state. In 2003, the year after NCLB went into effect, Shamrock was placed on the state's list of very low performing schools.[15] Both standards-based accountability systems resulted in Shamrock Gardens being labeled with an array of designations denoting vary-ing levels of academic failure. The labels included Title I, Equity, Equity Plus, FOCUS School, Achievement Zone, and School Improvement.[16] Such labeling resulted both in stigmas to overcome and in additional resources, training, and or funding.

Additional resources, however, did not necessarily improve the situation. Parker Loy, a teacher at Shamrock for six years, reported that one year every classroom was given a fish tank but no supplies (e.g., filters, rocks, or fish), so the fish tanks were generally used for storage. Teachers agreed that well-intended district initiatives often provided resources that were less than helpful due to lack of input from teachers about what they really needed at the classroom level to improve instruction.

Respondents differed about the effectiveness of other efforts. In 2005, a Rapid Response Team was placed at Shamrock. The Rapid Response Team effort meant two district instructional leaders were on campus daily working with teachers at each grade level. Teachers Broening, Loy, and Jasmine Sam-mons felt this was a tremendous resource, particularly in raising the bar for the quality of instruction throughout the building. Others felt that the Rapid Re-sponse Team's efforts were counterproductive. Jennifer Taylor, an instructional facilitator, was less positive: "We all just kind of felt like we were being picked at. They told us, you know, I need to be teaching exactly like the person across the hall. I was like, why did I choose this career if this is what they're expecting?"

The mandated focus on standardized tests, and the limits on the instructional freedom of teachers, at times had a negative impact on staff morale.

Teach For America

High-poverty, low performing schools like Shamrock are often difficult to staff. Interviewees described "teachers getting signing bonuses, or combat pay, for working at Shamrock," but staffing remained a challenge from the 1990s through the early 2000s. In 2004, Shamrock became a Teach For America (TFA) placement school. TFA is a national program that trains lateral-entry teachers, most of them just out of college, for the specific challenges of working in low performing, high-poverty schools. Two TFA members were placed at Shamrock in 2004, and by 2007–2008 one-third of the teaching staff was TFA, including current corps members and alumni who remained following their two-year commitment. As the school's gains made it more attractive to teachers, fewer lateral-entry teachers were needed to supplement staffing needs. In 2013, only one new corps member was placed there.

Respondents had mixed feelings toward TFA. While the greatest gains in academic achievement occurred during the height of TFA placement years, several interviewees criticized those who served their two years and left. Some interviewees credited TFA with providing strong professional development that supported efforts for data-driven instruction. Martha Holland, an active parent, said, "the common language and training has created a strong culture around student achievement." Others commented that the youthful energy and enthusiasm of TFA teachers was important at a critical time in the school's transition. However, the TFA influx occurred simultaneously with several other large changes, making it impossible to disentangle the effects of TFA from other school reform efforts.

Extended School Year

Even though school-level improvements began in 1997, Shamrock Gardens remained a low performing school. In 2005, Shamrock was identified by the state as one of three schools mandated to add ten days to their school year. All interviewees at Shamrock who were there in 2005 agreed that this was an unsuccessful mandate that served only to alienate teachers and students. Derrick Brown, a veteran administrator, stated, "We tried to negotiate some extended school hours or even Saturday school and get that done before the last day of the calendar year. But these days were added onto the end of the school year, so they didn't help with End-of-Grade tests."

Gifted Education Magnet

In 2006–2007, following a campaign by neighborhood activists, the district placed a gifted education program in Shamrock Gardens. As expected, the Learning Immersion/Talent Development partial magnet brought in high-level curriculum materials, instructional support, and a small but important parent base. I discuss the importance of the magnet for the success trajectory later in the chapter.

Freedom and Flexibility

In 2009, the principal was given "freedom and flexibility," a district initiative where leaders who had an established track record of success no longer had to adhere to certain district mandates, and key decisions could be made at the school level.[17] "All of a sudden, they were like, 'Hey! You have all the freedom to do whatever you want to now,'" veteran teacher Jasmine Sammons recalled. "And that's the year that our scores went up." All respondents agreed that the freedom and flexibility policy allowed school leaders to tailor policies at the school level that supported teaching and learning. For example, the principal was able to reallocate funding to hire specially trained literacy tutors to support small-group reading instruction. Many staff members credited this staffing change for dramatically improving student achievement.

TIF-LEAP

In 2010, Shamrock was also part of a federally funded pilot for merit-based pay, the Teacher Incentive Fund: Leadership for Educators' Advanced Performance (TIF-LEAP).[18] The program measured two student outcomes, as agreed to by the teacher and the principal, and provided teachers with performance-based bonuses if they met the stated goals. Teachers appreciated the bonuses, but felt the program did little to improve teaching and learning since the goals were not ambitious and were generally chosen so teachers could meet the benchmark and receive the bonus.

Small Class Sizes and Flexible Grouping

When asked what efforts teachers felt had the greatest impact on student achievement, the responses were unanimous—small class sizes and flexible grouping with specially trained reading tutors. Academic facilitator Delores Trinity explained, "for the kids that were below grade level, we strategically placed them in special extra pullout groups; they really improved." Teachers largely credited these changes for the rise in test scores that led to Shamrock losing its federal label of Title I School Improvement in 2009.

Priorities

A dramatic change in school priorities took place once the school emerged from NCLB sanctions. When asked about the seemingly endless sequence of reform efforts, teachers distinguished between efforts of years past and current priorities focused on strategic change. Broening said, "I feel like now we're researching more, using best practices, looking at other schools that have been successful and seeing what they're doing, instead of trying some new program that's coming out. Instead of getting rid of something and trying something new, we're trying to tweak and refine and supplement." Coming off the state watch lists seems to have had stemmed the tide of new programs and allowed school leaders and teachers to make decisions based on what they envisioned for the school, rather than waiting for directives from the district, state, and federal government.

THE RIGHT LEADER FOR THE RIGHT TIME

In the spring of 2005 CMS superintendent James Pughsley recruited Derrick Brown to be Shamrock's new principal. Brown served as principal from 2005 to 2011, and created the stability needed for Shamrock's gains during his tenure. Brown had come to CMS in 2003 after working for nearly three decades as a teacher, principal, and school superintendent in the midwest. He was aware of the challenges facing the school, primarily issues around staff morale and pervasive low academic performance. He also understood school district bureaucracy. For part of his tenure, Shamrock Gardens had the highest per-pupil expenditure of any elementary school in the district.[19] Those resources were especially valuable for keeping class size small. In 2009, the average kindergarten class size for the district and the state was nineteen students; Shamrock Gardens had an average of eleven students.[20]

Brown's strategy for improvement focused on improving staff morale, celebrating small successes, quietly encouraging change one-on-one without confrontation, and consciously supporting teachers. Former Assistant Principal Jacinta Freeman characterized his approach as:"Let's work with whom we have. They want to be here."

The focus on supporting teachers and keeping classes small paid off with a stabilized staff. In 2007 staff turnover fell below 20 percent for the first time in five years.[21] Pamela Grundy, a long-time member of the Shamrock community, observed, "Mr. Brown's goal was to build up his staff . . . to make them want to stay." Grundy, whose child was in the first Shamrock magnet kindergarten class, noted, "that first year there was a lot of turnover, but then the turnover stopped and you saw there were a lot of teachers who had started at the school and they got really good."

While interviewees described Brown as a master in the sociopolitical competencies of being a principal, he was not described as a strong instructional leader. He delegated those responsibilities to staff with complementary skill sets. Most significantly, Freeman, who served as assistant principal from 2005 to 2009, was instrumental in building a school culture focused on data and instructional alignment with standards. While Brown was described as a "very nice man" and "grandfatherly," Freeman was described as being singularly focused on results. "Ms. Freeman, you knew she was doing it for the kids and she was not there to make adults happy, which was good," Loy observed.

Data-Informed Instruction

From 2006 to 2009, Shamrock had low rates of teacher turnover and steadily improving rates of academic performance across all grade levels and all subgroups of students. However, there were more opportunities for growth, particularly in the areas of improving and norming instructional quality across classrooms. Both Brown and Freeman were trained in Data Wise processes, a Harvard-based program centered upon utilizing data to drive school improvement. Under their leadership, for the first time, teachers were expected to utilize established data processes with collaborative planning, including quarterly data days, all-day professional development in grade-level teams. Freeman admitted that there were not "particularly strong analytics behind [data days]," but such emphases were a critical starting point in training teachers to use data to drive instruction, particularly in effectively using formative assessments to utilize flexible grouping with specially trained teacher's assistants. Broening explained: "We would come together and talk about what the data was showing. We'd put charts up, sticky tabs, have these kids are at this percentage, these kids get this standard, these kids get this standard, this is what it looks like for this teacher's class . . . Our goal from those meetings was to leave with a plan of action to address what the data was saying . . . It wasn't perfect at first, [but] we got better at it."

Change in Leadership

Just before the 2010–2011 school year ended, Brown announced his decision to retire. Susan Moore, a first-time principal who had spent a decade in the district, was named as principal. Moore came to Shamrock with a strong background in curriculum and instruction. She was widely described as being a proficient curriculum specialist and coach, with strong skills in lesson delivery, lesson writing, assessment development, and professional development. Her leadership style and background as a new principal were quite a departure from Brown's, and teacher turnover reached 31 percent after her first year. But a handful of key people stayed, and a majority of respondents, particularly those teachers who stayed, believed she was the right leader for the right time.

When Moore became principal, she walked into a school that was largely seen as a turnaround story.[22] However, as she recalls, the disaggregated K–5 classroom-level data told another story. According to school-level assessment data (provided by the administrative team), students in the gifted education magnet program were performing at high levels, but students in the neighborhood program were not showing consistent growth, especially in the lower grades. She attributed the problem to the quality of teaching. Several other respondents also expressed frustration about inconsistencies in teacher quality. "Every grade level had a teacher who flew under the radar," said Alex Hernandez, a TFA teacher. "2010 was the first time I had heard of a teacher not being asked back." Professional development had seemed limited as well. "I would say I was emotionally supported," Loy stated. "But I wasn't encouraged to hone my craft."

Moore was unapologetic in describing her role as moving the school forward through improving teacher quality for all students. While Brown was at times critiqued for treating teachers too gently, and for acquiescing to parents, Freeman was at times critiqued for the opposite. "In terms of priorities, her priorities are the kids, and the teachers and parents are definitely last," Holland stated. Current staff and parents agree that her approach demanded a focus on teaching improvements that would lead to achievement for all students in the school. Since 2011, the majority of professional development has become individualized. Teachers are surveyed to identify what they need. Broening stated, "If you want to go and you want to learn about something, all you've got to do is ask. She says, 'Just go. You can go. We'll find a way.' In the past, it was excruciating. We didn't have a choice." Teachers and parents also discussed the role of classroom visits from administrators. In the past, teachers remembered less than two or three visits over the course of a year. Now, every teacher has at least one classroom visit each week. "I feel like with CMS, observations have always been, 'Oh, I gotcha.'" Broening stated. "And we are trying to get away from that. We're trying to help each other grow so we will never stop learning."

THE CHALLENGES OF A PARTIAL MAGNET

In 2006, when the magnet program started, it attracted only a few students. For this reason, in its first years the program was populated primarily by low-income students already assigned to the school. "We just identified our high flyers among our own population and challenged them more and they came through," Grundy said. The partial magnet program is credited for providing strong curriculum materials and professional development that catalyzed better instruction practices throughout Shamrock. Teachers reported widespread low academic expectations prior to the magnet's introduction. As Loy explained, "I didn't know how low the bar was until [in 2004] I went to a writing conference and saw the exemplars they were scored against, and I was like, 'Oh, crap. All these cute stories my kids are writing are not anywhere close to this.'"

Respondents agreed that the magnet program began to raise expectations. Although all teachers did not consistently support integrating magnet components into all classrooms, the wide range of academic levels mandated a transition from direct instruction to balanced literacy with flexible groupings based on skill acquisition. This did not happen only for students who applied for the magnet program. "That's the advantage of having a partial magnet," Grundy stated. "Ideally, it offers the opportunity for the kids who are already at the school who are ready for greater challenges." Loy, who became one of the early magnet program teachers, described being hesitant about the start of the magnet program. But she quickly saw the value. "There were kids in my class that were getting something that they wouldn't have gotten without it and so then I started to feel a lot better about the magnet," she said.

Several respondents explicitly discussed the role of the partial magnet as a tool for attracting middle-class families, in order to create a more diverse school within a naturally diverse school boundary. When asked about what success looked like, several parent and community respondents included the word *integrated* in their response. They clearly stated that failure would look like a segregated school within a school. Still, the arrival of growing numbers of middle-class students brought both possibilities and challenges. Chandler Gibson, an active PTA parent and CMS staff member, recounted efforts that began in 2010 to support all classrooms within a grade level. While the effort improved the schooling experiences of both magnet and nonmagnet students, they also revealed disparities. "Several parents ran Friday afternoon clubs," she explained. "We rotated between classrooms. And that was really eye opening, just seeing the differences between—it wasn't equal."

Respondents noted that, as in many academically challenged schools, the strongest teachers had frequently been moved into the grades that took state tests (grades 3–5), and weaker teachers often ended up in the lower grades. "From what I saw, if you were a teacher who couldn't handle classroom management and high expectations, you were moved to K–2," Jones said. "If you could, you were moved to 3–5." But meeting the expectations of middle-class magnet parents required strong teachers in all magnet classes. As of the fall of 2011, several respondents described a sharp division in the lower grades: the magnet classrooms with strong teachers, and the nonmagnet classrooms without them. "K–2 was a mess," Loy stated. "The only kids that were learning in K–2 were the magnet kids."

Several respondents also suggested that any middle-class white student who enrolled in the school was quickly moved into the magnet, whether or not there was space. In 2010, after some initial shuffling, all of the Plaza Midwood kindergartners were placed in the magnet program. In 2011–2012, when 14 percent of the school was white, the majority of those students were in the magnet program.[23] Sally Monroe, a middle-class Plaza Midwood resident, recalled that her child was initially placed in a nonmagnet classroom. She met twice with school administrators to express concerns about what she considered poor instruction and handling of discipline. A few weeks into the school year, classes were rearranged, and her child was moved to the magnet classroom. "That was very good for us," she said. "Now, if I take off my parent hat and ask, 'What happened to the kids that got moved out of magnet classes to make room for my child?' I think it was based on testing, but I also know that the school wants more Plaza Midwood parents . . . so I can't say this is how it happened."

Still, all respondents noted conscious efforts to counteract this unintended consequence of a partial magnet. Current staff members and parents reiterated the importance of the two programs becoming integral parts of Shamrock. Moore discussed the growth that she saw in reducing the disparity between classrooms. "In my [grade-level] team, I finally have a teacher whose performance rivals the magnet and she's in the neighborhood program. Her kids did just as well. And literally, when we got the data, I sat in my office and I cried. Because they did it." Current staff members also describe more consistency in teacher quality and effectiveness across grade levels.

THE SHAMROCK WAY

Shamrock Gardens' deeply caring environment emerged as a theme in every interview. Moore described it as the "Shamrock way" and "the way we treat people at Shamrock." Dawn Simon, a Plaza Midwood parent, described this as simple acts throughout the school. "If I'm at Shamrock walking down the hallway and a kid is coming through the door at the same time, they will wait until I go through the door." Respondents provided similar illustrations of the positive school climate. "It was always a school where you just felt everybody really cared about the kids," observed longtime volunteer Louisa Menke.

Many teachers talked about beginning their careers at Shamrock, and the importance of the Shamrock way in making them feel comfortable and supported as new teachers. "My first day I walked in and [a staff member] came and hugged me and was like, 'We're so glad you're here,'" Loy recounted. Then the assistant principal asked all the first-year teachers to stand up. "They [the veteran teachers] were like, 'Remember when it was your first year?'" Loy continued. "'Let's take them under our wing.'"

All school leaders interviewed discussed the importance of nurturing this culture. "Your teachers need to be happy and feel like they're accomplishing things," Brown stated. "If you want to have a good climate at your school and if you want to keep people that are good, it just has to be a happy situation." The Shamrock way appears to be an important part of the turnaround formula, particularly in creating a strong, positive culture where staff, parents, and students felt supported and empowered.

COMMUNITY INVESTMENT

Shamrock Gardens' main building was built in the 1950s, and suffered for many years from a lack of adequate maintenance. Respondents who recalled earlier eras talked at length about the poor state of the building—mold and mildew in rooms, windows painted shut, HVAC issues, leaky roofs, and more. While the main building is still dated, the overall physical condition of the campus has improved. Several respondents believe that many of those changes came about because of an active base of middle-class parents who demanded a suitable learning environment, and had the time and resources to help bring it about.

When the PTA reconstituted in 2006–2007, the grounds were a priority. "We got the PTA started and we worked on the grounds, because they were kind of a mess," Grundy said. "We fixed up the teacher lounge and we had beautification days." Eventually those efforts grew into an extensive system of raised beds that included specialized areas for growing vegetables, studying butterflies, and examining the effects of ozone on plants. The PTA also started parent involvement programs, such as a set of grade-level parent dinners paid for by a foundation grant. These dinners and family nights have evolved to well-attended family-oriented themed programs that draw participants across race, class, and linguistic backgrounds. Programs include an art night, fitness night, and Wii nights—where rooms are set up with borrowed Nintendo Wii consoles—and after dinner, everyone dances. The PTA distributes all materials in English and Spanish, and supports an active Hispanic Parent Club.

This part of the Shamrock turnaround story is rife with individuals taking initiative within a supportive structural context. Early efforts were largely spearheaded by Grundy and a small group of other magnet parents, who developed strong relationships with school leadership, teachers, and district officials, while also applying for grants and publicizing the school's endeavors.[24] These efforts improved the situation on the ground and kept Shamrock in the forefront of district and community attention through positive media coverage. From 1998 to 2013, there were 1,119 stories about Shamrock Gardens in the local media, compared to 626 stories for an elementary school with similar demographics and improvement challenges. "We just tried to show that we were putting the resources to good use and giving a sense that this was a school that was really worth investing in because it would pay off," Grundy said. Staff members also felt empowered to drive change. In 2010–2011, the school's technology and media center specialist wrote a grant for a nationwide competition that won a major media center makeover funded by Target stores. Respondents were clear that individual instances of seizing the initiative within the school community have been consistent levers for change, in part because the school's leadership welcomed and encouraged their efforts.

DISCUSSION AND CONCLUSION

School reformers generally have strong opinions about the importance of school-level policy levers to accomplish change, but the evidence of such reforms' efficacy is mixed. A 2013 Institute of Educational Sciences (IES) evaluation of ninety randomized control trials revealed that 88 percent of interventions produced weak or no positive effects.[25] While there has been a tremendous amount of funding devoted to determining how to turn around a low performing school, the IES meta-analysis shows that when it comes to improving educational outcomes, particularly in high-poverty schools, we have few strong evidence-based models to implement widely. With the number of high-poverty schools increasing nationwide, the need to better understand successful reform mechanisms for them is paramount.[26]

As mentioned earlier, the general consensus among interviewees is that most of the reforms enacted at Shamrock Gardens since 1997 did little to improve student learning. Yet the findings suggest that several different efforts combined to create a dynamic that over a ten-year period built a scaffold for the development of a *success trajectory*. Shamrock Gardens' success trajectory has three phases. As depicted earlier in figure 9.1, Shamrock Gardens is now moving into Phase 3. With structural improvements in place, the present period is dominated by individual initiatives and actions at the school level designed to continue to improve academic achievement with fewer interventions and lower per-pupil expenditure. Figure 9.2, shown earlier in the chapter, suggests the relationship among the intensity and costs of interventions and their success over time. Importantly, even as district-level resources started to wane, the culture and the parent volunteers remained. Taken all together, the pieces fell into place. Again, these reform efforts did not bear fruit in one year and did not originate from one person. Rather, for Shamrock Gardens, reform took time, sustained efforts, trust (i.e., the Shamrock way), strong leadership, adherence to basic educational principles, teacher collaboration and stability, community involvement, and district-level support. End-of-Grade test scores cannot begin to adequately measure this dynamic process and cannot be the sole indicator of success.

While the story of Shamrock provides a strong case study of sustained school reform within a large urban district, an important unanswered question remains: what will Phase 4 look like? More importantly, Shamrock Gardens' story also raises the question of whether its success can be taken to scale across CMS. Shamrock is somewhat unique in that it is a small school (comprising typically fewer than five hundred students) and located in a naturally diverse school boundary area. However, the individual pieces of the success trajectory are not elusive, and findings suggest that with sufficient district support, the scaffold for reform efforts can be replicated. Given the likely continuation of the demographic shifts in student populations, the normative and political climate in the district, and the legal framework in which CMS leaders will make their decisions about the district's future, Shamrock Gardens' success trajectory provides an important case study of an approach to urban education improvement that is feasible.

CHAPTER 10

The Law's Delay

Pursuing School Diversity and Equity in *Leandro*'s Shadow

Mark Dorosin

Luke Largess

WHAT ARE THE LEGAL PROSPECTS for promoting integrated public schools? In North Carolina, the answer to that question is more promising under state law than under federal law, which once commanded public schools to desegregate. This chapter looks at parallel developments in federal and state law and explains why the North Carolina constitution offers more promise to those fighting for integration.

The past half-century has seen dramatic changes in the federal courts' approach to school segregation. In the aftermath of *Brown's* far-reaching but slow-to-implement pronouncement in 1954 that segregated schools were inherently unequal, there was a surge in federal court orders ending segregation during the late 1960s and early 1970s. However, since then, there has been a steady federal retreat from efforts to achieve integration, with some conservative judges going so far as to declare that court-ordered or voluntary desegregation is as unconstitutional as *de jure* segregation. Thus, the federal courts that once pried open doors to desegregate schools and classrooms now severely restrict good faith efforts by school districts to combat the racial and socioeconomic isolation of students of color. But for a nod from the Supreme Court and the Obama administration to the continuing value of diversity, we have now come nearly full circle into a new epoch of "separate but equal" schooling.[1] That shift in the federal law has left school districts like Charlotte-Mecklenburg in the situation of having to address the consequences of school segregation mainly by devoting additional resources to dramatically separate, racially isolated schools in their poorest neighborhoods.[2]

The legal question facing school districts and advocates of integrated public schools is whether there are any judicial remedies that *allow* school districts like CMS to integrate schools voluntarily, let alone compel them to address an issue that the public appears to have largely turned from. This chapter looks at a series of decisions under the North Carolina constitution over the last twenty years that have offered some hope as the federal judiciary abdicated its role of protecting the rights of poor, minority students to equal protection in the pursuit of educational opportunity.

THE FEDERAL COURTS AND THE DESEGREGATION OF CMS

The legal and community struggle to desegregate CMS involved perhaps the most important Supreme Court school decision after *Brown v. Board of Education*. The 1971 ruling in *Swann v. Charlotte-Mecklenburg Board of Education* decisively affirmed the power of the federal district courts to impose desegregation plans upon recalcitrant school districts.[3] A unanimous Court recognized that the district courts had broad authority to fashion effective remedies to end school segregation and "repair the denial of a constitutional right."[4] The Court approved of a range of remedies ordered by the Charlotte federal judge, James McMillan, including the redrawing of attendance areas, the pairing of racially imbalanced schools, and—most famously—the use of mandatory "bus transportation as one tool of school desegregation."[5]

Twenty years later, CMS moved toward a voluntary integration plan that incorporated racial guidelines in assignment to magnet schools located mostly in black neighborhoods and bused black students involuntarily to suburban schools. A group of white parents challenged this use of race in this magnet program, which had never been approved by the federal court.[6] The lawyers for the original black plaintiffs challenged the lawsuit as a collateral attack on the court order in *Swann*, and a federal district court judge who had opposed *Swann* as a private citizen, Robert Potter, reopened that case and ordered a trial on whether CMS was unitary—that is, had eliminated the "vestiges" of a segregated school system.[7]

By the time *Swann* was reopened, the legal landscape of school desegregation had been reshaped dramatically by *Board of Ed. of Oklahoma City v. Dowell* and *Freeman v. Pitts*.[8] In these cases, the Supreme Court emphasized a return to local control and lowered the legal burden on school districts seeking to be removed from court supervision. The Court declared that districts would not be held responsible for resegregation of schools caused by voluntary demographic changes in communities; "white flight" was beyond the reach of the courts.[9] These cases defined the legal issues for the CMS unitary status litigation. Following a lengthy trial that riveted the community, the district court judge, relying on *Dowell* and *Freeman,* ruled that CMS had eliminated vestiges of its segregated system "to the extent practicable" and was now unitary.[10] That decision was hotly contested. A Fourth Circuit panel reversed the district court judge 2–1, but the *en banc* court voted 6–5 to reinstate the trial court decision.[11]

Having been declared unitary, and reluctant about relying expressly on race in assigning students to promote diversity, CMS implemented a new race-neutral student assignment plan in 2002 that focused on parental choice and gave priority to neighborhood schools. Given the persistent racial and socioeconomic segregation of Charlotte's neighborhoods, the public schools resegregated dramatically by both race and class (as previous chapters in this volume have shown). Predominantly white schools in outlying neighborhoods soon became overcapacity, while inner-city schools became overwhelmingly black and Latino and undercapacity.[12]

THE STATE COURTS CREATE AN OPPORTUNITY TO ADDRESS SEGREGATED SCHOOLS

At roughly the same time that the white families challenged the CMS magnet plan, a group of parents and students and the school boards from five mostly rural and very poor counties filed *Leandro v. State (Leandro I).* They challenged the statewide system for school funding as violating their right to an adequate education under the state constitution.[13] An intermediate appellate court voted to dismiss the case, asserting that the state constitution guaranteed only that all children have equal access to schools—it did not address the quality of those schools.[14]

The state supreme court rejected this interpretation of the state constitution, ruling that "the right to education provided in the state constitution is a right to a *sound basic education.* An education that does not serve the purpose of preparing students to participate and compete in the society in which they live and work is devoid of substance and is constitutionally inadequate."[15] The court defined the components of a sound basic education as follows:

- Sufficient ability to read, write, and speak English, and sufficient knowledge of math and science to function effectively in society

- Sufficient knowledge of geography, history, and basic economic and political systems to enable informed choices about critical issues
- Sufficient academic and vocational skills to successfully engage in post-secondary education or vocational training and to compete on an equal basis in further education or employment opportunities[16]

While holding that the state constitution created a right to a sound basic education and defining its parameters, the court rejected the claim that unequal state funding among school districts was unconstitutional. Noting that express constitutional language allows local governments to supplement state education expenditures with local funds, the court said that "there can be nothing unconstitutional in their doing so or in any inequality of opportunity occurring in the result."[17] The constitution establishes a floor of minimum standards, but imposes no ceiling on local government spending on education, despite the dramatic funding inequities and related educational impacts.[18] The case was then returned to the trial court for further proceedings on whether those school districts were providing the constitutional minimum.

At trial, much of the evidence focused on rural Hoke County, including student performance on state-mandated standardized tests. In the first of three lengthy memorandum opinions, the trial court opined that the state's teacher certification standards, funding formula, and curriculum were constitutionally sound, but held that student outcomes demonstrated that the state was failing to provide these students a sound basic education.[19] The second opinion asserted that the right to a sound basic education may require access to "early childhood prekindergarten education."[20] The third opinion held definitively "that there are at-risk children in Hoke County and throughout North Carolina who are . . . not obtaining a sound basic education."[21]

In April 2002, a year after the Fourth Circuit *en banc* decision in *Swann*, the trial court ruled that North Carolina had violated its constitutional obligation to provide a sound basic education to schoolchildren, including prekindergarten. The judge held that the constitution required that "every classroom be staffed with a competent, certified, well-trained teacher, that every school be led by a well-trained competent principal, and that every school be provided, in the most cost-effective manner, the resources necessary to support the effective instructional program with that school so that the educational needs of all children, including at-risk children, to have the equal opportunity to obtain a sound basic education, can be met."[22]

The state appealed, and in 2004, nearly ten years after the case began, the North Carolina Supreme Court unanimously affirmed. In this ruling (known as *Leandro II*), the court first held that the trial court appropriately had considered evidence concerning school "inputs," educational components provided by the state and the local boards, and "outputs," measures of student achievement and performance. Inputs included providing adequate curriculum, teachers and administrators, and funding. Outputs were test scores, graduation and dropout rates, and data on employment potential and postsecondary education achievement. From this comprehensive review, the trial court properly concluded that the state had violated its constitutional duty to provide children the opportunity for a sound basic education.[23]

As to funding, the court reaffirmed its conclusion in *Leandro I* that despite inequities caused by local government supplements, North Carolina is required only to provide sufficient funding for all students to receive a sound basic education. The court agreed with the trial judge that the state was failing to utilize available resources in Hoke County and that it was obligated to "assess its education-related allocation to the county's schools so as to correct any deficiencies that presently prevent the county from offering its students" a sound basic education.[24] It also reaffirmed that the state, as the entity that created the local school boards and authorized them to act on its behalf, bore the ultimate responsibility for any local board's failure to provide such an education.

The court also endorsed the lower court's findings related to the critical value of early childhood education and the state's duty toward at-risk children, but reversed the lower court's order mandating the provision of preK. Citing both the constitutional separation of powers, and the responsibility and experience of the legislative and executive branches in overseeing the public schools, the court declared that those branches be given the opportunity to determine the most effective remedy for addressing the needs of at-risk preschoolers.[25]

LEANDRO AND RESEGREGATION

While the opinion avoided direct discussion of resegregation and emphasized that the constitutional right at issue belongs to all students, it identified the importance of teaching at-risk students, "who, due to circumstances such as an unstable home life, poor socioeconomic background, and other factors," face particular challenges to securing the opportunity for a sound basic education. The court went on to define an at-risk student as having any of these characteristics: being a member of a low-income family, participating in a free or reduced lunch program, having parents with limited education, possessing limited English proficiency, being a member of a racial or ethnic minority, or being part of a single-parent household.[26] The court found that the state had a special responsibility to these students, and that the evidence of its constitutional failure not only to serve these students, but to even adequately identify them or the hurdles they confronted, was clear and compelling.[27] Having violated its constitutional duty to provide a sound basic education, the state, the court said, had an affirmative obligation to develop remedial measures. The court reiterated that the legislative and executive branches should have "an unimpeded chance" to do so, subject to the court's continued oversight and review.[28]

In the wake of *Leandro II*, the state began to implement a series of measures designed to address its remedial duties. These included funding initiatives—the Disadvantaged Student Supplemental Fund, increased allocation to the Low-Wealth Schools Fund, expanded and additional funding for the state's prekindergarten programs, and various programs to enhance recruitment and retention of strong teachers and administrators.[29] The trial court continued to hold hearings and issue memoranda on the state's progress or lack thereof as to test score results, dropout, retention and graduation rates, and other measures.[30]

CMS AND *LEANDRO*

By 2005, CMS and other urban districts had intervened in *Leandro*, arguing that they had disproportionate numbers of at-risk students compared to rural districts and had needs that the court must also consider. After *Leandro II,* the trial court focused on CMS in its review of the state's progress in remedying constitutional violations. In May 2005, the trial court issued "Report from the Court: The High School Problem," a blistering analysis of the failure of the state's secondary schools.[31] Although the trial court looked at high schools across the state, it singled out for opprobrium high schools in CMS, finding the "composite scores jumped out like a 'sore thumb.'"[32] Eight of the district's seventeen high schools had End-of-Course (EOC) test pass rates of less than 60 percent, and only one over 80 percent. By comparison, Wake County, the state's other large urban district, had twelve out of sixteen schools with passing rates over 80 percent.[33] In a section of the report subtitled "CMS High Schools—A System with Too Many High Schools in Crisis," the court found "a chilling picture" of the district's performance data when disaggregated by race: 77 percent of white students passed their EOC standardized tests in 2004, compared to only 40 percent of African American students. The court found little or no progress in addressing this achievement gap over the preceding three years.[34]

Even the four highest performing schools—Butler (75 percent passing rate), Myers Park (75 percent), North Mecklenburg (72 percent), and Providence (85 percent)—all showed racial achievement gaps of at least 22 percent. And in all schools except Providence, black students' performance was below the 60 percent benchmark. Conversely, with the exception of West Charlotte, even at the lowest performing schools white students' passage rates exceeded 60 percent.[35]

The court avoided any ruling on or even mention of one glaring piece of this data—the racial and socioeconomic segregation of the schools. In the 2003–2004 school year, CMS was approximately 42 percent white and 45 percent black, and 46 percent of students qualified for FRL.[36] As table 10.1 indicates, the four lowest performing high schools were racially identifiable minority schools with high percentages of FRL-eligible students, while the four high performing schools reflected the inverse relationship between school-level racial composition and concentrated poverty.[37]

TABLE 10.1 Percent nonwhite and percent free or reduced lunch in four lowest and four highest performing CMS high schools, 2003-2004

	Percent nonwhite	Percent free or reduced lunch
Four lowest performing high schools		
West Charlotte	98	62
Garinger	90	57
Phillip O. Berry	88	58
E.E. Waddell	81	46
Four highest performing high schools		
Butler	27	14
Myers Park	34	18
North Mecklenburg	34	13
Providence	18	14

Source: Judge Howard E. Manning, *Report from the Court: The High School Problem,* North Carolina General Court of Justice, Superior Court Division, 95 CVS 1158: *Hoke County Board of Education et al., Plaintiffs and Asheville City Board of Education et al., Plaintiff-Intervenors v State of North Carolina; State Board of Education, Defendants,* May 24, 2005, 22–23.

The court minced no words in its assessment of these statistics or of the testimony of CMS administrators. "Unfortunately, the Court found no comfort in the testimony presented by the CMS employees . . . for turning the high schools around and achieving decent academic performance of its at-risk student population (*the majority of whom are black*)."[38] The court declared that "what is going on academically at CMS's bottom '8' high schools is *academic genocide* for the at-risk, low income children."[39]

Despite this strong indictment of the district, the dramatic evidence of racial and socioeconomic isolation in the schools identified, and the recognition in *Leandro II* of both racial and low-income subgroups as being at-risk and demanding special attention, the court avoided comment on the impact of CMS's student assignment plans on the district's ability to comply with *Leandro's* orders to provide an education consistent with the requirements of the North Carolina Constitution.

The court's failure to address the racial and socioeconomic segregation of CMS schools under the *Leandro* paradigm was especially troubling, given that it had the express opportunity to do so. In February 2005, a group of CMS parents and the Charlotte branch of the NAACP moved to intervene in *Leandro* and to add CMS as a *defendant* along with the state and the state board of education. The parents' and NAACP's complaint focused on the changes in CMS since the district had been declared unitary and the new race-neutral pupil assignment plan had been implemented. The complaint alleged that CMS knew its transition to "neighborhood" schools would create high-poverty, racially isolated schools because of persistent residential racial and socioeconomic segregation. The complaint also detailed the significant academic and administrative shortcomings of those schools, saying that CMS's student assignment policy concentrated those shortcomings into a cluster of schools with high enrollments of students of color—and that they could not be meaningfully addressed merely by additional financial resources. Calling on the state and the court to ensure that students attending these schools receive a sound basic education, the complaint asked the court to compel the defendants to implement "a revised, systemwide student assignment plan that will end the large socioeconomic divisions that currently characterize the CMS district."[40] In addition, the complaint alleged that the then-current assignment plan violated the state constitution's guarantee of equal protection because it failed to provide the necessary fiscal, human, or education resources to ensure that the students in the district's high-poverty schools receive a sound basic education.[41]

Joining a lawsuit already in progress is different from filing a new case. The court has broad discretion in determining whether to allow parties to join the case and the scope of the issues that the intervening party may pursue. In August 2005, the court allowed the new Charlotte plaintiffs to join the *Leandro* litigation but would not permit consideration of any claims regarding student assignment. The new parties would be permitted to litigate only the questions of adequate funding and other resource allocation. The court would not take on CMS's responsibility in creating schools with high concentrations of at-risk students. Nor would it consider whether there was any causal link between assignment and school-level outcomes (from test scores to the ability to attract and retain high-quality teachers and administrators). The court would review only whether the district, having created the high-poverty, racially isolated schools, was committing adequate resources to provide a sound basic education to students in those schools.[42]

While the court has continued to hold periodic hearings on the state's remedial efforts, the progress of the case has become glacial, leading many to wonder whether and how the litigation will effectively conclude. With the exception of hearings related to changes in the state's preK program in 2011, most of the hearings since 2006 have involved data reporting and review, not adversarial hearings like those held in 2001 and 2002. Moreover, the CMS-specific litigation was indefinitely stayed in 2006 to allow for the ongoing exchange of longitudinal data related to student achievement, dropout and graduation, and teacher quality and performance metrics, and for outside analysis of that data.[43]

One goal of the Charlotte plaintiffs' intervention in the *Leandro* litigation was to establish the impact of racial and socioeconomic segregation in schools on students' ability to receive a sound basic education, and to emphasize that addressing demographic isolation is a necessary component of creating constitutionally compliant education. Additionally, the express language of *Leandro II* defining the subcategories of at-risk students to include racial and ethnic minorities, along with the finding that the state is obligated to identify and address the needs of such students, seemed to invite litigation of the issue of resegregation through *Leandro*'s principles.

All of these developments may seem as discouraging as federal court indifference to resegregation. Significantly, however, the superior court's decision to deny the intervening Charlotte plaintiffs' request to proceed on their student assignment claim was not a substantive ruling that *Leandro* does not reach such issues as a matter of law.[44] This means the impact of a segregative student assignment plan—and the concomitant creation of high-poverty, racially isolated schools—on whether students are receiving a sound basic education is an issue that can still be independently litigated.

The relationship between the *Leandro* court's focus on providing a sound basic education and the impact of racial and socioeconomic isolation on the state's ability to provide such an education is further reinforced by the High Schools Problem report. The pattern reflected among CMS high schools just described is consistent throughout the report. Forty of the forty-four lowest performing high schools identified in the report were racially segregated, predominantly nonwhite schools, many by very high percentages. The reverse was also true: forty-three of the forty-four highest performing schools were racially isolated, predominantly white schools, many also by very high percentages. The relationship of socioeconomic factors to achievement also was stark. Thirty of the forty-four low performing high schools were majority low income. Only one of the forty-four high performing schools was majority low income.[45]

The challenge of ensuring that every child in North Carolina receives a sound basic education is an enormous one; identifying and addressing the particular needs of at-risk children, as required by *Leandro II*, compounds both the scope and the stake of that challenge. The state must effectively utilize every possible measure available to meet its constitutional obligation. Doing so necessarily includes student assignment, particularly when the educational consequences of creating racially and socioeconomically isolated schools are so clear and when race, ethnicity, and low wealth have been acknowledged by the courts as at-risk demographic categories. While there may be remedial measures available that do not involve student assignment and school-level demographics, an abundance of evidence indicates that the impact of those measures are blunted by the structural limitations of a segregated system.[46]

The *Leandro* cases have been characterized as limited to issues of school funding, and consequently any remedial measures must be similarly limited, and district-level issues—like student or faculty assignment—are either beyond the scope of the constitutional right or the court's remedial power. The limiting construction of the two decisions ignores both the nature of the state constitutional right of North Carolina students to a sound basic education and the state courts' language describing the parameters of that right. While adequate funding is clearly a component of the state's constitutional obligation, particularly for low-wealth districts, *Leandro II* established that the state has an additional responsibility to ensure that educational funding and resources are utilized locally in a manner that effectively provides all of the components of a sound basic education. And while those components—highly qualified teachers and administrators, and effective instructional programs—depend on funding, they also require engagement on a range of challenges that includes the racial and socioeconomic segregation of schools. A limited focus on funding cannot ignore the well-documented impacts of racially isolated, high-poverty schools and the extraordinary level of additional funding needed to recruit and retain highly qualified teachers or provide the curricular support that *Leandro* demands.[47]

Given that the state's constitutional mandate is to ensure that every child receives a sound basic education, and given that student assignment policies that establish and maintain racial or socioeconomic isolation create nearly insuperable impediments to fulfilling that mandate, the *Leandro* decisions empower the courts to directly address assignment policies in guaranteeing that educational resources are used and deployed in a constitutionally compliant manner.

For example, in 2010 the CMS school board embraced the district's post-unitary resegregative trend when, looking for federal Race to the Top grant money, it voted to close ten schools—the majority of them inner-city, hyper-segregated by race, and high poverty—and move middle-schoolers into experimental K–8 schools.[48] Of the twenty-five thousand students affected by the closings, only about 5 percent were white.[49] Especially controversial was the fact that the students from the poor, hypersegregated middle schools closed in this plan were reassigned to similarly poor, hypersegregated elementary schools that were remade overnight into K–8 schools—the only nonmagnet K–8 schools in CMS. While these decisions were ostensibly made to address underutilization of the closed schools, at several school sites CMS had to acquire and repurpose trailers to supplement buildings that were beyond capacity once they were remade into K–8. Moreover, middle school students in the new K–8 programs have limited, if any, access to extracurricular activities like band or sports, though such activities are readily available on-site to all other middle schools in the district.[50]

THE ABILITY TO IMPLEMENT VOLUNTARY MEASURES TO INTEGRATE

In the midst of CMS's return to segregated schools and the failed effort to address those issues through *Leandro*, the U.S. Supreme Court issued a decision that would shape the future of school diversity litigation in the federal courts.

The Court's divided opinions in *Parents Involved in Community Schools v. Seattle School District No. 1 (PICS),* reaffirmed the constitutional value of promoting racial diversity in public K–12 education, but significantly restricted what school districts could do to accomplish diversity with student assignment.[51] Ironically, in overruling a school-district-implemented voluntary student integration plan, the *PICS* court ignored the Court's almost universal adherence to the principle of local control of schools.[52]

PICS involved two different cases and school districts—Seattle and Jefferson County, Kentucky (Louisville). Both districts implemented voluntary student assignment plans that included consideration of race as one of several factors used to assign students and promote school diversity. The Seattle school district had never been subject to a judicial desegregation order. Jefferson County, like CMS, had been under court order for decades but had been declared unitary in 2000.[53]

The Court issued a fractured opinion finding that these voluntary integration plans violated the Constitution. A majority of the Justices, in an opinion by Justice Anthony Kennedy, agreed that promoting diversity and eliminating racially isolated schools was a legitimate and compelling interest for school boards, and that they could adopt voluntary assignment plans to further that interest. The plans adopted in Seattle and Louisville, however, were not sufficiently limited to survive strict judicial scrutiny.[54] Chief Justice John Roberts, joined by Justices Antonin Scalia, Clarence Thomas, and Samuel Alito, argued vehemently that racial integration and student diversity are not a compelling interest in K–12 schools.[55]

Although Justice Kennedy's opinion agreed that particular aspects of the Seattle and Louisville plans required that they be struck down, he stressed that the holding did not ban districts from considering racial segregation in their schools or developing policies to promote diverse schools. Any voluntary integration plan had to avoid the specific race-based classification or assignment of a particular student to be constitutional: "If school authorities are concerned that the student-body composition of certain schools interferes with the objective of offering equal education opportunities to all of their students, they are free to devise *race-conscious measures* to address the problem in a general way and without treating each student in a different fashion solely on the basis of a systematic individual typing by race."[56] Justice Kennedy then described some of these race-conscious measures that schools could utilize to further integration in a constitutionally permitted manner. These measures included siting of new schools, drawing attendance zones that take account of aggregate neighborhood demographics, targeted recruiting of students and teachers, and allocating resources to support special programs. Additionally, the opinion endorsed tracking various school metrics (e.g., enrollment, performance, graduation and dropout rates) by race, thereby enabling administrators to evaluate the racial impacts or effectiveness of its policies.[57]

Four years after *PICS*, the Obama administration's Departments of Justice and Education jointly issued a long-awaited *Guidance on the Voluntary Use of Race to Achieve Racial Diversity and Avoid Racial Isolation in Elementary and Secondary Schools (Guidance).*[58] The *Guidance* provided several specific examples for school districts interested in pursuing racial diversity, but as an initial matter stressed the importance for a district to establish how and why the adoption of any voluntary integration plan meets its educational mission and goals.[59] Notably, the Introduction section of the *Guidance* provides a succinct summary of the impacts of racial isolation on students and schools "where schools lack a diverse student body or are racially isolated . . . they may fail to provide the full panoply of benefits that K–12 school can offer. The academic achievement of students at racially isolated schools often lags behind that of their peers at more diverse schools. Racially isolated schools often have fewer effective teachers, higher teacher turnover rates, less rigorous curricular resources, and inferior facilities and other educational resources."[60] The *Guidance* also acknowledged that students consigned to racially isolated schools missed critical opportunities to interact with and learn from others with different backgrounds.

In describing alternatives for pursuing voluntary integration, the *Guidance* suggests the following hierarchy: first, race-neutral policies that rely on factors other than race to promote diversity; second, race-conscious policies that expressly consider race, but only in a generalized context; and third, policies that consider the race of an individual student, but do so in a very limited and narrow manner.[61] Among the race-neutral metrics for improving diversity are student socioeconomic status, parental education level, neighborhood socioeconomic status, and student familial status (i.e., single-parent household).[62] Of course, the likelihood or extent of any of these measures improving racial diversity in schools depends on how closely correlated they are to race in the particular school district.

Comprehensive data collection and analysis are critical in determining whether or how effectively any of the race-neutral approaches achieve the intended level of diversity. If they do not, such data helps provide the policy imperative for turning to race-conscious methods. Examples of race-conscious policies endorsed by the *Guidance* include those that are based on the overall racial composition of neighborhoods or of existing schools or school attendance areas. The *Guidance* explains that these race-neutral or race-conscious policies, or some combination of the two, can be applied to decisions involving facility and program siting, grade alignment and feeder patterns, attendance zone creation, enrollment policies, admission to competitive schools or programs, and student transfers.

CMS ADOPTS GUIDELINE FOR STUDENT ASSIGNMENT

Over a year before the *Guidance* was issued, in August 2010, the CMS board adopted new, post-*PICS* student assignment guidelines.[63] The guidelines contain a generalized acknowledgment of the importance of diversity, but list diversity below home (neighborhood) schools, magnet schools, and stability in a feeder system of elementary, middle, and high schools. The guidelines call home schools the "foundation" of the instructional model and the "first priority" in assigning students.

In the guidelines' explicitly stated "prioritized decision-making rubric," diversity is the third consideration—after the founding principle of home schools and the corollary goal of "stability and predictability." The home school goal weighs three factors: travel distance from home, keeping neighborhoods intact, and creating a neighborhood feeder system through high school. The stability and predictability guideline is a variant of that home school emphasis—an attempt to assure families that a feeder system will not change. Only after weighing those concerns is consideration given to "creating a relative balance of economically disadvantaged students (EDS), with the understanding that there is currently a predictive link between poverty levels and achievement gaps."[64] Given the patterns of residential segregation and the deprioritizing of diversity, CMS's capacity to promote diversity is considerably limited.

The promise of *Leandro I* and *Leandro II* is their requirement that the state prevent educational deficiencies that the CMS guidelines on diversity openly acknowledge—the same educational deficiencies affecting racially isolated, high-poverty schools that are highlighted in the post-*PICS Guidance* and reflected in *Leandro* (e.g., lack of effective teachers, limited curricular and other educational resources, inferior facilities). This synergy demonstrates that many of the methodologies laid out in the *Guidance* for creating diverse schools can, and in fact must, also form the basis for developing *Leandro*-compliant remedies for the educational consequences that unfairly impact students in these segregated schools.

THE PROSPECT BRIGHTENS FOR EXPANDING *LEANDRO*

The issue of the appropriate scope of the *Leandro* holdings, as well as the scope of any potential remedies, has been the subject of additional state court litigation since *Leandro II*. While federal courts in North Carolina have shown a reluctance to interpret the state constitutional right to education more broadly, a recent state supreme court decision provides an expanded although still limited view of the sweep of *Leandro*.[65] *King v. Beaufort County Board of Education* considered the impact of school disciplinary policies in the *Leandro* context. In that case, the student asserted that her long-term suspension from school, without the possibility of assignment to an alternative school, deprived her of the right to a sound basic education. Recognizing that wholesale exclusion from any educational programs potentially violates the constitutional rights of students, the court held that unlimited discretion for school officials to "maintain safe and orderly schools" could not be reconciled with its prior *Leandro* rulings.[66] Accordingly, before school districts can wholly exclude students from school, they are constitutionally required to "articulate an important or significant reason for denying a student access to alternative education."[67] Although the court ruled that *Leandro* did not create a constitutional right to placement in alternative schools, it did recognize that school disciplinary policies may directly impact and ultimately deprive a student of the right to a sound basic education.

The *King* decision is critical step forward for advocates determined to address the continuing impacts of racial disparities in access to a sound basic education. Although not specifically enumerated in the list of educational inputs or outputs examined in *Leandro II*, school policies regarding student discipline, suspension, and expulsion, as well as the significant racial inequities in the application of such policies, can be shown to substantially limit "access to educational opportunities," particularly for at-risk demographics.[68] Following *King*, disparities in student disciplinary policies, like segregative student assignment policies, have become another avenue for advocates to pursue through the *Leandro* paradigm.

Finally, although they have not specifically addressed the breadth of rights recognized in the *Leandro* cases, it is worth noting that North Carolina courts have reaffirmed that there exists a private right of action to bring direct claim under the education provisions of the state constitution and that the state cannot assert it is immune to such claims. These cases provide the procedural foundation for new challenges to the denial or deprivation of the right to a sound basic education.[69]

CONCLUSION

Despite Justice Kennedy's opinion in *PICS* and the identification of the permissible means to promote integration provided by the Departments of Justice and Education's joint, post-*PICS Guidance*, the federal courts' narrowing view of the role of race in schools offers relatively little hope for challenging school resegregation in CMS or in other North Carolina school districts. At most, the courts will *allow* school districts to consider race in some limited manner in creating assignment plans generally, but will not *require* a district to do so. At the same time, risk-averse school boards are reluctant to even consider student diversity as an educational priority. The precepts of *Leandro* and the state courts might provide a more promising avenue to challenge resegregation. But so far the focus of that case has been on school resources and the impact on student outcomes, a separate but equal approach, and another indication that achieving integration has become less important for districts and more challenging for advocates. Like Hamlet, this, then, is our burden—to take action, and to no longer allow "the law's delay" to prevent us from fulfilling the constitutional promises of educational equity and racially diverse schools.[70]

CHAPTER 11

Obligation and Opportunity

Charlotte-Mecklenburg Schools Face the Future

Stephen Samuel Smith
Roslyn Arlin Mickelson
Amy Hawn Nelson

> *The vision is to ensure that the Charlotte-Mecklenburg School System becomes the premier urban, integrated system in the nation in which all students acquire the knowledge, skills, and values necessary to live rich and full lives as productive and enlightened members of society.*
>
> —CMS vision statement, September 1991[1]

> *Charlotte-Mecklenburg Schools provides all students the best education available anywhere, preparing every child to lead a rich and productive life.*
>
> —CMS vision statement, March 2014 [2]

HOWEVER GRANDIOSE AND LOFTY Charlotte–Mecklenburg Schools' 1991 vision statement might appear, there was a time when it was not an implausible one for CMS. Three decades ago, CMS's desegregation plan was considered one of the nation's best, and it was reasonable to view CMS as a desegregation showcase. The district received national acclaim for its school desegregation accomplishments, illustrated by the experience of West Charlotte High School. But that same high school in 2014 is a vivid indication of why today CMS does not make the slightest pretense of aspiring to that goal. West Charlotte and its feeder schools are now hypersegregated and the focus of a policy intervention, Project LIFT, which, while noteworthy in many respects, accepts hypersegregation as a given and makes no effort to alleviate it. While CMS may not be as segregated as some large urban school systems, the district is far from being a desegregation showcase.

Before proceeding, we want to make our perspective clear. We regret CMS's resegregation. Our regret is born of thirty years of research and experience in the district. We acknowledge and salute the very hard work and individual accomplishments of thousands of current and retired CMS educators. Roslyn Arlin Mickelson and Stephen Samuel Smith's children, and Amy Hawn Nelson herself, attended desegregated CMS schools and benefited from that experience. But much more important to our perspective than such personal experience in CMS is the immense scholarly evidence showing desegregation's academic and nonacademic benefits, both nationally and in CMS itself. Included in that growing corpus of social science research are several studies exploiting the natural experiment provided by data comparing CMS before and after it was declared unitary. These studies find direct links between resegregation and a host of negative outcomes. CMS's current uphill struggles to improve segregated schools in conjunction with this new research are testaments to the power of concentrated poverty and racial segregation to undermine even the most brilliant and dedicated teaching and clever reforms. We deeply regret that CMS is so much an embodiment of the social science record and the judicial principle that separate is not equal.

Earlier chapters explored the causes and consequences of CMS's transformation. Summarizing the core causes and theoretically framing them in the dynamic interplay of structure and agency is the first goal of this chapter. The second is to use the earlier chapters as a springboard to identify possible future trajectories of CMS's desegregation saga. The third is to discuss the relevance of CMS's experience to other school districts and national educational reform efforts.

HOW AND WHY CMS RESEGREGATED

CMS's resegregation resulted from the complex interplay of structure and agency over time, in particular as decisions and choices (i.e., agency) made at one time became the conditions (i.e., structures) that constrained decisions and choices in future years. Of these decisions, the most salient are those by the federal courts in *Swann*. Just as federal district court Judge James McMillan's 1969 decision in the original *Swann* litigation laid the basis for Charlotte's desegregation successes, federal district court Judge Robert Potter's 1999 decision in the reopened case presented high obstacles to desegregation, at least by the means that CMS was using at that time.

But important as court decisions might be, they have not been the whole story nationally or in CMS in explaining the course that desegregation and resegregation have taken. No significant school desegregation occurred in the South in the decade following the Supreme Court's *Brown v. Board of Education* decision. Iconic as that decision is, it was not until the upsurge of the civil rights movement in the 1960s changed the country's political landscape that significant school desegregation occurred.[3] Similarly, important as Judge McMillan's decision was, his wisdom in letting the community develop a desegregation plan (rather than his mandating a particular plan) facilitated desegregation in Charlotte and helped it avoid the kind of turmoil that engulfed Boston's contemporaneous desegregation efforts.[4]

Another indication that court decisions are not the whole story is that even before the 1999 trial—while CMS was still legally required to pursue desegregation—the district drifted toward resegregation. Key causes of that drift involved the relationship between desegregation and development, and Charlotte's corporate class's perceptions and actions concerning that development. CMS's school desegregation success contributed to economic development by helping Charlotte become—and market itself as—a paradigmatic New South city whose race relations were progressive, tranquil, and not mired in the swamp of Jim Crow. As chapter 2 indicates, in the battle for mobile capital, Charlotte's corporate class got a lot more mileage from touting Charlotte as "The City That Made It [school desegregation] Work" than it could have by boasting that, like Atlanta, it was a city "too busy to hate." Moreover, the corporate class's support for the busing plan was part of the political alliance with black political leaders that facilitated the electoral success of prodevelopment candidates and bond referenda. But once Charlotte began shaking off the muck of Jim Crow and development had taken off, school desegregation became no more necessary for local development or connectivity with the global economy than it was for the development of Atlanta—a city whose schools remained heavily segregated—or the contemporary development of New York, Chicago, or the many other cities whose schools are also heavily segregated. Thus, in conflicts between desegregation and development, the latter typically won.[5]

Resegregation increased in CMS because of various other factors, including decisions about pupil assignment. Among these decisions—as chapters 2 and 4 indicate—were the 1992 switch from districtwide mandatory busing to voluntary participation in magnet schools and choices about where to site, how to staff, and whether to redraw attendance boundaries of new schools to incorporate racially and economically diverse neighborhoods in a school's catchment area.

The post-*Swann* era especially indicates how agency led to structures whose effects cascaded. Not only did Judge Potter's decision create legal conditions that discouraged the majority on the school board from continuing to pursue any form of diversity, but the adoption of the race-neutral pupil assignment plan facilitated—as chapter 7 shows—whites moving into neighborhoods with a higher percentage of whites than their previous neighborhoods, thereby creating further obstacles to educational diversity, given the priority that the 2002 race-neutral plan accorded attending a neighborhood school.

A different aspect of the interplay between structure and agency leads to second-generation segregation, and its results are evident in both the *Swann* and post-*Swann* eras. Grouping and tracking decisions early in children's school careers influence available options and perceived choices in subsequent years that, in turn, shape students' achievement and attainment. Educators' actions are integral components of race- and socioeconomic-status-correlated grouping and tracking decisions such as identifying a child as gifted and talented, labeling a child as having special needs, designating a child as an English language learner (as chapter 8 illustrates), and guiding students to take or avoid certain classes. These decisions have consequences throughout the rest of a student's educational career, including college. Ironically, as chapter 5's authors note, levels of tracking in CMS have declined as segregation at the school building level has increased in the last decade.[6] It appears that as Charlotte's schools become more distinct racially, policies that differentiate students inside the school building are less common, and segregation due to tracking has declined.[7]

National and state-level forces also contributed to resegregation in CMS. The continued existence of these factors allows us to consider them in the next section's discussion of the barriers to the pursuit of educational diversity.

DOES THE FUTURE HOLD MORE OF THE SAME?

At all levels of the nested structures within which CMS makes choices and implements them, there are significant barriers to the district's reversing resegregation and pursuing increased diversity.

National and State Barriers

At the federal and state levels, the barriers seem very formidable. No Child Left Behind, as noted earlier in the book, proved no friend to desegregation or school improvement even though diverse schools likely would have made achieving Adequate Yearly Progress much easier.[8] Nothing in the law privileged or rewarded diversity, while fatal flaws in its design and implementation resulted in well-publicized "school failures" that fed into the ongoing national narrative about flawed public education.[9] Nor has the twenty-first century's other major federal education policy, Race to the Top, done much to deal with resegregation. To be sure, President Obama's proposed 2015 budget includes a Race to the Top Opportunity initiative that will support innovative programs that advance diversity and increase opportunity for underserved youth. But it's difficult to see that initiative as more than a drop in the bucket compared to the overall education program that has essentially ignored desegregation and diversity. As Gary Orfield has written, the Obama administration has "virtually ignored segregation, offered no strategies to deal with the rapid resegregation of many suburban communities, and embraced unrestricted choice, expansion of a highly segregated charter school system, and even more pressure on teachers as its basic educational strategies."[10]

The situation in the federal courts would also appear unpromising. In addition to facing the 1999 ruling declaring CMS unitary and the Supreme Court decisions upon which that ruling drew, any effort to pursue diversity must deal with the Supreme Court's 2007 decision in *Parents Involved in Community Schools v. Seattle School District No. 1* (*PICS*).[11] In that case, the Supreme Court declared unconstitutional Seattle and Louisville's voluntary efforts to increase the diversity of their schools, and that case is often viewed as limiting similar efforts in other districts.

State-level considerations would also seem to point in the same direction. North Carolina may be considered a purple state in presidential elections, but the Republicans presently control the governor's office and both houses of the legislature, allowing them to pursue draconian policies that have limited funding for education, attacked teacher tenure, and removed incentives for teachers to earn advanced degrees. The same factors that make North Carolina a purple state in presidential elections may allow the election of Democratic governors in the future. But the gerrymandering of legislative districts that followed the 2010 census created significant structural barriers to the Democrats regaining control of either house of the state legislature. Moreover, even if Democrats were to regain control, it's unlikely that there will be any significant effort to limit the growth of charter schools, which in North Carolina—as chapter 5 notes—are more segregated than traditional public schools, just as they are nationally. After all—perhaps because of Race to the Top's encouragement of charter schools—the legislation removing the cap on charter schools was signed by a Democratic governor and, moreover, passed with heavy Democratic support. In the state's courts, the *Leandro* litigation does offer some promise, but as chapter 10 indicates, so far that case has focused on school resources and their impact on student achievement, rather than on trying to improve achievement by addressing socioeconomic and racial hypersegregation.

In addition to factors at the state and federal level, local conditions, structures, perceptions, and events—the main focus of this book—would also seem to militate against any reversal of CMS's resegregation, as the following discussion indicates.

Local Demographic Considerations

Of the local conditions and structures that are relevant to any discussion of desegregation and diversity's future in CMS, Mecklenburg County's demographic conditions are especially salient. The significance of the county's demographics is evident when they are compared with those of Wake County, whose public schools, unlike CMS and as discussed in chapter 6, continue to pursue desegregation. The comparison of the two counties presented in table 11.1 indicates that, compared with Wake, Mecklenburg has a higher poverty rate, a lower

TABLE 11.1 Comparison of demographic characteristics of Mecklenburg and Wake Counties

	BLACK		WHITE		POVERTY RATE	
	County	School system	County	School system	County	School system
Mecklenburg	31.5%	42%	60.7%	32%	13.6%	54%
Wake	21.3%	24%	70%	49%	10.1%	38.6%
Mecklenburg to Wake ratio	1.48	1.75	0.87	0.65	1.35	1.40

Source: Tables 6.1 and 6.2 of this volume.

percentage of whites, and a larger percentage of African Americans. Moreover, the demographic differences between the two counties' school systems are even greater than those between the counties themselves.

These demographic differences point to why CMS faces greater challenges in pursuing diversity. As chapter 8 indicates, diversity in CMS must be considered from numerous aspects, several of which have historically been and remain extremely important to policy makers. The first aspect is economic diversity, which is much harder for CMS to achieve with a poverty rate that is 54 percent (compared with 39 percent in the Wake public schools). Not only do poor students tend, on average, to have lower academic achievement rates than nonpoor students, but there is now important evidence that the income gap in achievement is greater than the black/white gap.[12] Moreover, the overlap between race and poverty can result in a situation where there is considerable integration of two groups of students of color—such as that between blacks and Latinos in contemporary CMS—but these students are concentrated in high-poverty schools.[13]

The second aspect involves white enrollment. Education policy makers frequently attach considerable importance to retaining whites in public schools because of whites' often greater political clout, income, wealth, and the type of cultural capital helpful for student achievement. But some whites' reluctance to attend schools with large percentages of students of color, especially low-income African Americans, creates a situation—if the system-wide percentage of whites becomes too low—in which there are not enough whites to populate many of a district's schools with a percentage white enrollment that other whites consider acceptable. As chapter 7 indicates, whites who changed residences after the implementation of the race-neutral pupil assignment plan preferred moving to attendance zones of schools with a higher percentage white enrollment than their previous school even if the new school was a low performing one. Addressing many whites' reluctance to attend schools with large percentages of low-income students of color poses problems for any efforts to staunch or reverse CMS's resegregation.

Political Will Within the CMS Leadership

Less obvious but also very important is how differently human agency has played out in the two counties and school systems. As chapter 6 indicates, the triumph of conservative candidates in the 2009 Wake County school board elections posed a severe threat to Wake public schools' capacity to pursue desegregation.

But there remained sufficient political will and community sentiment to continue desegregation, and the results of the 2011 and 2013 school board elections changed the board's membership enough to allow the district to continue its diversity policies.

In 2011, CMS's board membership also changed significantly. In the previous eight years, as chapter 2 indicates, CMS paid scant attention to resegregation. It adopted guiding principles for pupil assignment (in which diversity ranked low) that were opposed by the board's two black board members and a white liberal. These years were also characterized by black demobilization around education issues, as illustrated by the fact that the school board had only two black members, the lowest number since 1995. However, in 2011 many blacks were angered by school closings and energized by a popular black mayoral candidate, and the 2011 school board election saw large-scale black political mobilization. With no incumbents seeking any of the three seats on the ballot, that mobilization contributed heavily to the election of two black candidates, Ericka Ellis-Stewart, an educational activist and CMS parent, and Mary McCray, a retired teacher and former president of the Charlotte-Mecklenburg Association of Educators. Still on the board (because their seats were not on the 2011 ballot) were the two aforementioned black board members and the white liberal who had voted against the current pupil assignment guidelines. With these five members constituting a majority of the nine-person board, the 2011 election raised the possibility of CMS's addressing resegregation. This possibility seemed even stronger after the board chose Heath Morrison as superintendent, who quickly put the issue of race on the front burner by proposing that CMS hire consultant Glenn Singleton, known for his emphasis on combating racism and white privilege (see chapter 2).

But unlike the 2011 election in Wake, the 2011 election in Mecklenburg has had—at least as of spring 2014—no apparent effect on policies involving desegregation. A big reason for the difference is that in 2011 (and 2013) in Wake, desegregation advocates were trying to hold off recent challenge to policies that had been in effect for a decade. By contrast, any CMS effort to pursue desegregation after the 2011 election would have required reversing a policy that had been in effect for a decade. As board member Thomas Tate has said about the possibility of such a reversal: "It was my impression that we as a district took the most conservative reading of the Potter decision and as a result, where we might have had things we could have done initially, we didn't do them. And then the further we got away from it, the harder it was going to be to undo things, and that's what I'm talking about."[14]

In other words, the "brouhaha" and instability that board member Kit Cramer feared in 2003 might result from any attempt to revisit pupil assignment (see chapter 2) would, in Tate's view, be even greater now. Board member Ericka Ellis-Stewart voiced similar thoughts. When campaigning in 2011, she noted the importance of Charlotte's struggle to desegregate and has been urging the board to revisit the guiding principles of pupil assignment. But there has been, she explains,

> a hesitancy on the part of the board . . . And I think there is a hesitancy because—I think it's going to be hard work to revisit the assignment plan, whether you're doing it because you value diversity or . . . because you want to have a plan that is not as piecemeal and as band-aided together as what we currently have. No matter what your intent is, it's going to be hard work. And it will be an emotional time for the community. People get very concerned when you start talking about student assignment. And typically it does boil down to race, ethnicity, and economics. But a lot of time the conversation doesn't focus on that specifically.
>
> I don't see a political will at this point to make diversity, particularly around economics in the schools and how that ties back to academic success, to make that a priority in a fashion that would mean we would no longer have schools with high poverty. I think the push at this time is really around how do we educate students in spite of their personal poverty, but also in spite of the fact that they are in a school that has 80+ percent to receive FRL.[15]

Nor is desegregation by socioeconomic status or race a priority for the CMS administration at the time of this writing in spring 2014. When asked about the possibility of CMS revisiting the pupil assignment plan with a view toward ameliorating large-scale socioeconomic and racial segregation, Superintendent Morrison replied "it's not really an area I've delved into yet because our current board has not requested that we revisit student assignment at this time . . . that's not something I've looked a lot at because it's not been something that we've been asked to do."[16]

Morrison is certainly correct: the school board is primarily responsible for pupil assignment. But perhaps Morrison's inaction on this issue is less about board responsibility and more about his learning a valuable lesson in 2013 about community backlash when he proposed that CMS hire Singleton to address issues of race in the district (see chapter 2). Morrison's time in Charlotte appears to have taught him to exercise caution around certain topics, including politically volatile attempts to revisit pupil assignment.

The Corporate Class, African Americans, and White Liberals

Paralleling the district's reluctance to address resegregation has been a lack of pressure to do so from the corporate class, the African American community, and white liberals. The lack of pressure from the corporate class is hardly surprising. As noted earlier in this chapter, there is currently little economic incentive for the corporate class to push the issue, and many of its current members lack the roots in Charlotte and its desegregation experience that the previous generation of corporate chieftains had. As Ericka Ellis-Stewart observed: "In the last twenty or twenty-five years our corporate community in Charlotte has shifted from folks who live here, they are based here, they have a true concern about the Charlotte community, to folks who, you know, the headquarters is here but their heart isn't here."[17] Similarly, reflecting on the broader contemporary political climate in Charlotte compared to the late 1960s when he brought the *Swann* litigation, attorney Julius Chambers observed "I don't see the business community as involved as they had been and I guess . . . the business community thinks that we made all the advances that we need to make in that connection."[18]

During the era of the *Swann* litigation, Charlotte's corporate class faced pressure from African Americans and white liberals to support CMS's desegregation efforts. However, that pressure has diminished. To be sure, longtime supporters of school desegregation and diversity, such as members of Charlotte's NAACP and League of Women Voters, continue to talk about their importance. But much of contemporary liberal Charlotteans' educational advocacy focuses on combating the testing fetish and high-stakes accountability systems that typify public education, and what they see as the Republican-controlled state government's attacks on teacher tenure, education funding, and other aspects of public education.

A major reason for this decreased emphasis on desegregation is the structural changes in African American communities over the past four decades, in particular generational changes, the growth of a middle class, and increasing black suburbanization. In talking about the lack of pressure for integration from middle-class black Charlotteans, Ellis-Stewart noted that desegregation is "less of an issue because they have the means to create other avenues for their children. But I have had conversations with many, whether their kids were in public school or not, about the issues of educating black children and the success of black children in public schools and just all of those topics. And they 'get' the issue, many have concern about the issue, but I have not seen a public desire to lift that up as a call to action."[19]

Similar sentiments are expressed by Arthur Griffin, an African American who attended a segregated school, was chair of CMS's school board, and cast the lone vote against the adoption of the race neutral-pupil assignment plan. He noted how a thirty-something, middle-class African American mother with whom he was acquainted would characteristically think:

> "And what's in the best interest of my babies?" She wasn't thinking about Charlotte's babies, okay? . . . the forty-year-old group has her kind of mentality, which is "how do I help me and my immediate neighbor and maybe not necessarily the broader community?" . . . I'm not painting every young person, but . . . a lot of young African Americans are basically saying, "you know, well, the school system is not doing whatever it needs to do, so why can't we create a charter school or support vouchers or support tax credits or some other alternative and I'll feel good because I'm helping these two kids (my kids)" . . . young African Americans, I don't feel they have a sense that "I can make a difference out there because I'm over here, but I can make a difference right here by creating a charter school, getting on the board of directors of a charter school, so that I can help this group."[20]

GLIMMERS OF HOPE

Given the many obstacles to CMS's reversing resegregation and pursuing diversity, it may seem futile to discuss the possibility of the school district's doing so. But such a discussion is imperative because accepting school resegregation means that Charlotte is forsaking the many benefits that, as chapter 1 indicates, accrue to students who experience a desegregated and diverse education. Setting aside moral or ethical considerations for the moment, among those benefits are: higher academic achievement, increased cross-racial friendships, fewer contacts with the police and courts, increased graduation rates, and higher lifetime incomes. The last three especially benefit the larger public in terms of decreased government expenditures and increased government revenues. These fiscal advantages are especially relevant in this era of tight budgets. The best available studies indicate that the financial costs of programs that significantly reduce educational segregation and improve education are dwarfed by the fiscal benefits to the public.[21] Thus, accepting CMS's resegregation means forsaking these many public benefits, too.

To be sure, CMS efforts to reverse resegregation and increase diversity would benefit from changes in any of the nested structures within which such efforts would occur. Perhaps a recent city council decision allowing the construction of subsidized housing in the far south of the county augurs increased approval and construction of much more affordable housing throughout the county.[22] Perhaps North Carolina will limit the growth of segregated charter schools and significantly increase funding for all aspects of public education rather than channel public dollars toward voucher programs. Perhaps Obama's recent Race to the Top Opportunity initiative is a signal that his administration will provide more financial and technical support to school districts pursuing diversity and lower its emphasis on high-stakes accountability systems.[23] Perhaps the economy will surge, the social safety net will be strengthened, and poverty rates will plummet. Some of these "perhapses" would obviously be more beneficial or possible than others. But CMS would be foolish to count on any of them happening. So in discussing the possibilities of the school district's reversing resegregation and pursuing diversity, we assume no significant change in any of the nested structures within which CMS makes its policy choices.

Public Opinion

Local public opinion is one reason why we think it's fruitful, rather than futile, to discuss the possibility of CMS's reversing resegregation and pursuing diversity. Local public opinion and its effect on school board elections are central to any efforts by a school system to pursue diversity, as indicated by recent events in Wake County in which there has been longstanding community support for the school district's diversity efforts. As noted, when a newly elected majority of Wake board members tried to reverse that school system's longstanding diversity efforts, subsequent elections resulted in the dismantling of that majority and the continuation of these efforts.

Throughout the *Swann* era in Mecklenburg and even in the first two elections *after* the 1999 court order declaring CMS unitary, elections also resulted in a school board with a majority strongly committed to diversity. As chapter 2 indicates, it was only in 2003—after the race-neutral pupil assignment plan went into effect and resegregation jumped sharply—that the prodesegregation board lost this majority. However, as noted earlier, the 2011 election saw the board's composition again change dramatically and raised the possibility of CMS trying to reverse at least some of its resegregation. Nonetheless, our interview data suggests a paucity of political will among educational decision makers to do so.

That lack of political will perceived by our interviewees notwithstanding, the best available survey data indicates that public opinion in Mecklenburg County is currently no less supportive of diversity than it was more than a decade ago when CMS was much more integrated and school board members who strongly supported diversity were elected and re-elected. This data comes from seven surveys commissioned by the Charlotte-Mecklenburg Education Foundation (CMEF) from 1995 to 2001 and one survey conducted by the University of North Carolina's Urban Institute (UI) in 2013.[24] From 1995 to 1997, the CMEF survey asked about support for "assigning children to neighborhood schools." From 1998 to 2001, it asked about support for "assigning children to neighborhood schools even if it means that a number of schools will become racially segregated." This longer question was also asked on the UI survey.[25]

As Figure 11.1 indicates, support for neighborhood schools was lower among blacks than among whites.[26] More interesting is the decline in support by both groups for neighborhood schools when the caveat about racial segregation is added. But most interesting is how little difference there is between 2001 and 2013 for both groups' support for neighborhood schools if such schools would result in racial segregation. Indeed, to the extent there are differences,

FIGURE 11.1   Support for assigning children to neighborhood schools

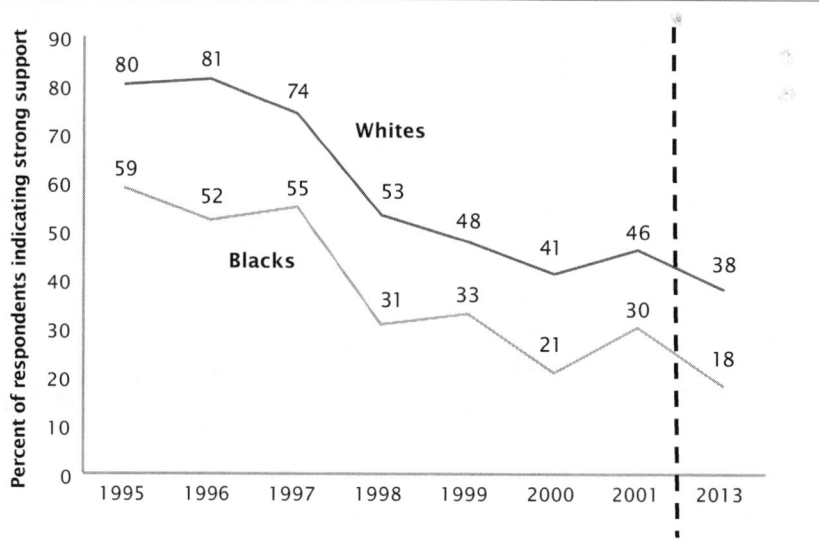

Note: Question changed in 1998 and subsequent years. See text for details.

in 2013 both groups indicate less support for neighborhood schools if such schools would result in racial segregation. Moreover, it appears that support for neighborhood schools is lower in Charlotte than it is nationally, though differences in the way the questions are worded makes it impossible to know for certain.[27]

Table 11.2 provides more detailed comparisons between 2001 and 2013, which also indicate striking similarities across the decade.[28] In 2013, support for neighborhood schools declined and opposition to them grew stronger among blacks. Among black respondents, there was support for neighborhood school assignments even if they are racially and socioeconomically segregated in 2001 and 2013, but opposition to it was also greater. Similarly, in both years a large majority of blacks expressed strong support for ensuring that low–income and

TABLE 11.2 Percent support for creating socioeconomically and racially diverse schools in CMS among Mecklenburg County residents by race, 2001 and 2013

| | BLACK | | | | | |
| | 2001 | | | 2013 | | |
	Strongly support	Neutral	Do not support	Strongly support	Neutral	Do not support
Response range	10–8	7–4	3–1	10–8	7–4	3–1
Do you support assigning children to their neighborhood schools, even if it means a number of schools will become racially segregated?	30	29	40	18	29	52
Do you support assigning children to their neighborhood schools, even if it results in the concentration of low-income children in a few schools?	31	30	35	30	30	40
Do you support ensuring that low-income students are not concentrated in a few schools?	68	18	7	59	22	19
Do you support ensuring that minority students are not concentrated in a few schools?	65	20	10	56	26	19

minority students are not concentrated in a few schools, although replies of "Strongly support" declined slightly. White respondents offered somewhat contradictory responses in both years. A plurality supported neighborhood school assignments even if they lead to more racial and socioeconomic segregation, although responses of "Strongly support" for that position declined in 2013. At the same time, pluralities of white respondents in both surveys supported ensuring that minority and low-income students are not concentrated in a few schools. In fact, by 2013 support for this approach to school assignment grew among whites.

TABLE 11.2 *continued*

	WHITE					
	2001			*2013*		
	Strongly support	Neutral	Do not support	Strongly support	Neutral	Do not support
Response range	10–8	7–4	3–1	10–8	7–4	3–1
Do you support assigning children to their neighborhood schools, even if it means a number of schools will become racially segregated?	46	34	16	38	32	29
Do you support assigning children to their neighborhood schools, even if it results in the concentration of low-income children in a few schools?	42	38	16	43	29	28
Do you support ensuring that low-income students are not concentrated in a few schools?	44	35	15	47	29	23
Do you support ensuring that minority students are not concentrated in a few schools?	43	37	15	48	29	23

Source: Charlotte-Mecklenburg Education Foundation, 2001; University of North Carolina at Charlotte, Urban Institute Annual Survey, 2013.

Note: Percentages in rows by year by race do not always add to 100 because of rounding errors or "Don't Know" responses not shown.

The gist of all these comparisons suggests stability in blacks and whites' public views on school diversity. The normative climate for integrated education in CMS does not appear to have changed markedly from what it was more than a decade ago, a time when the CMS school board embraced diversity and the voters supported board candidates who held these positions and subsequently led the board in implementing them. In calling attention to this stability in public opinion, we are not trying to minimize the paucity of political will or of advocacy for desegregation that we've noted earlier. However, if CMS were to exercise leadership and education advocates were to put diversity on the front burner, this stability suggests that such efforts would receive more support than the current lack of will and advocacy would seemingly indicate. Moreover, history suggests that CMS's electoral structure is congenial to the kinds of school board members most likely to exercise that kind of leadership.

Electoral Structures

The way in which school board members get elected is important. It is one of the reasons why the board's prodesegregation majority remained intact after Potter's decision and wasn't dismantled until the new pupil assignment plan was implemented and black mobilization around education decreased. Three board members are elected at-large, and six are elected from single-member districts.[29] Ever since this system of representation was implemented in 1995, two of the districts have always elected a black representative, and a third district has always elected a white liberal. On most crucial desegregation-related issues, members from these three districts have voted together. As a result, board decisions on desegregation-related issues have largely hinged on the views of representatives elected to the three at-large seats.

Since this system went into effect, there have been five elections for the three at-large seats: 1995, 1999, 2003, 2007, and 2011. In 2003, black turnout was low; in 2007, no black candidates were even on the ballot. The predictable result was the victory of candidates for whom reversing resegregation and increasing diversity were not a high priority, one consequence of which were ongoing pupil assignment guidelines in which the home-school guarantee trumped all other criteria by a large margin. But the elections of 1995, 1999, and 2011 were different. In 1999 and 2011, two of the at-large seats were won by African Americans.[30] In 1995 an African American won one of the at-large seats and a white liberal known for her strong support of diversity won the other.

None of these five elections should be seen as a referendum on desegregation. In all of them—including the one in 1999 just two months after Potter's decision—many other factors were at work.[31] Moreover, the past is not necessarily prologue. But since the same electoral structures remain in place, the history of at-large elections in Charlotte provides strong suggestive evidence that if African Americans and their white allies are politically mobilized, they stand an excellent chance of constituting the school board's majority, and if they have the political will, to begin reversing resegregation and pursuing diversity.

Brick-and-Mortar Structures

Without minimizing the extent to which brick-and-mortar structures such as the location of schools in outlying areas undermined desegregation during the *Swann* era, there are reasons for thinking that some of these structures may now facilitate it. Those reasons hinge on African Americans being less concentrated than previously in historically black neighborhoods. In explaining why residential diversity increased in Charlotte between 2000 and 2010, Edward Glaeser and Jacob Vigdor call attention to the "familiar story of black entry into suburban neighborhoods," noting that "the proportion of Mecklenburg County census tracts with fewer than 5 percent black residents declined from 46 percent to 39 percent between 2000 and 2010."[32] That "familiar story" helps explain why many of CMS's recently constructed schools in outlying areas have relatively large black enrollments. For example, all five of the most recently opened elementary schools for which enrollment data is available as of this writing are located outside the I-485 Outerbelt.[33] In three of these schools in 2013–2014, African Americans were the largest racial group, with enrollments ranging from 46 to 71 percent of the student population, and in a fourth of these schools African Americans were 32 percent of the student population (blacks were 40 percent of the district's systemwide elementary school enrollment). Consequently, the location of new schools in outlying areas is not necessarily the barrier to diversity that it was in the *Swann* era, and in some cases their location may even facilitate it.

WHAT IS TO BE DONE?

CMS has a choice between two roads. It can continue as it has for the past fifteen years, making minimal effort to alleviate resegregation, and hoping that somehow interventions designed to mitigate its academic consequences—perhaps along the lines of Project LIFT—will be successful, can be sustained, and can be brought to scale. Or CMS can take the other road and try to reverse resegregation and facilitate diversity.

Socioeconomic and Racial Diversity

There are four reasons why, in our view, most initial efforts should focus on socioeconomic diversity, the first of which is the legal constraints imposed by *PICS*. The second, also mentioned previously, is the growing evidence that the income gap in achievement is greater than the black/white gap (which has previously received the most attention). Third, socioeconomic diversity is likely to be more acceptable politically, and fourth, the experience of the eighty-plus districts currently using socioeconomic diversity provides a wealth of contemporary and accessible experience upon which to draw.[34]

Despite the overlap between race and poverty, socioeconomic diversity is no guarantee of racial diversity. Thus, the latter at some point almost certainly needs to be considered, which leads to a discussion of *PICS*. Although the Supreme Court struck down two school districts' voluntary desegregation plans and imposed limits on how racial diversity can be pursued, there are, so to speak, limits on those limits. The Court was bitterly divided on the case and struck down Seattle and Louisville's plans by only a 5–4 vote. But while finding that Seattle and Louisville's use of individual students' race was unconstitutional, one of the justices in the majority, Justice Anthony Kennedy, affirmed the importance of diverse schools and said that race-conscious pupil assignment plans could pass constitutional muster if they took other approaches:

> In the administration of public schools by the state and local authorities it is permissible to consider the racial makeup of schools and to adopt general policies to encourage a diverse student body, one aspect of which is its racial composition . . . If school authorities are concerned that the student-body compositions of certain schools interfere with the objective of offering an equal educational opportunity to all of their students, they are free to devise race-conscious measures to address the problem in a general way and without treating each student in different fashion solely on the basis of a systematic, individual typing by race.
>
> School boards may pursue the goal of bringing together students of diverse backgrounds and races through other means, including strategic site selection of new schools; drawing attendance zones with general recognition of the demographics of neighborhoods; allocating resources for special programs; recruiting students and faculty in a targeted fashion; and tracking enrollments, performance, and other statistics by race.[35]

Given its hostility to desegregation, affirmative action, and similar race-conscious policies, it is unsurprising that, in the immediate aftermath of *PICS*, the Bush administration sent a letter to local school districts inaccurately characterizing the decision as forbidding any consideration of race in pupil assignment. More surprising is that it took the Obama administration almost three years to correct the situation. Nonetheless, in its December 2011 *Guidance on the Voluntary Use of Race to Achieve Diversity and Avoid Isolation in Elementary and Secondary Schools*, the Obama administration emphasized the importance of first checking the possibility of race-neutral policies, but it then indicated a wide range of situations in which various kinds of "race-conscious" policies could also be employed. In this context, the *Guidance* listed facility and program siting, grade alignment and feeder patterns, attendance zone creation, enrollment policies, admission to competitive schools or programs, and student transfers.[36]

First Steps

Whether the goal is greater socioeconomic and/or greater racial diversity, we see efforts toward that goal as falling into two broad categories. The first involves six steps that are modest and largely consistent with the present guiding principles for pupil assignment. The second hinges upon revamping CMS's principles and much of the current pupil assignment plan.

The first step of the former category is to address second-generation segregation due to tracking. Detracking initiatives pose technical, normative, and political hurdles, but successful detracking is feasible, has been done successfully elsewhere, and can be done in CMS. It will require school-based leadership to confront and remedy the educational consequences of disparate placement decisions, difficult conversations addressing the harms of tracking, professional development for classroom educators to facilitate instruction for heterogeneous classrooms, preparations so all students are ready to learn in untracked classrooms, and a fair amount of effort helping *all* families understand the benefits of detracking for their own children.[37] The latter is especially true of families who presently think they benefit the most from tracking.[38] Eliminating second-generation segregation will have limited impact on within-school diversity in hypersegregated schools, but in the majority of CMS schools detracking will create some diversity and augment achievement for all students. Any school improvement strategies or equity reforms designed to close race and socioeconomic achievement gaps that do not also detrack curricula and instruction are akin to trying to warm a room in winter with a window left wide open.

A second step is to site new schools in locations that facilitate diversity. Budget constraints sometimes severely affect CMS land acquisition decisions.[39] We don't question the existence of these constraints, nor do we mean to disrespect the many people who are working hard to make Project LIFT succeed. But the comparison between the difficulties of sustaining that initiative and the long-term and continuous academic benefits of diverse education lead us make the following suggestion: the bottom-line-conscious business executives who fund Project LIFT would do well to consider whether they could get a better and safer long-term return on their "investment" if they helped fund the purchase of school sites in locations that facilitate diversity than they can get from funding interventions that fail to address racial and socioeconomic hypersegregation.

A third modest step is to take advantage of the openings of new schools by drawing attendance boundaries in a way that facilitates diversity. The same might be said for the closings of schools. Indeed, we suspect that the 2010 school closings that occasioned so much public resentment might have proven less contentious had the students displaced by them been reassigned to low-poverty schools.

The fourth involves the use of *partial* magnets. The use of magnets to facilitate diversity has recently attracted a lot of attention, as evidenced by a February 2014 *New York Times* article, "Magnet Schools Find a Renewed Embrace in Cities."[40] As the article notes, magnet schools have historically been used to attract whites to inner-city schools and provide students in these neighborhoods with educational options they would not otherwise have. However, the issue of magnets is a complicated one. *Full* magnets in or near diverse neighborhoods can often decrease diversity and/or weaken nearby schools by siphoning educationally active parents from these other schools. By contrast, partial magnets are generally more effective because they facilitate strengthening neighborhood schools rather than "creaming" families from attendance areas, as full magnets are apt to do. Partial magnets must avoid physically segregating magnet students from nonmagnet students. The effects of partial magnets are especially beneficial for schools in or near diverse neighborhoods because they can help stabilize the neighborhoods and keep educationally active parents from moving or seeking schools elsewhere in a district. Moreover, due to the smaller geographic boundary of partial magnets, there are reduced transportation costs compared to full magnets, so there is a strong fiscal argument as well.

However, to fulfill their potential, partial magnets must avoid becoming a school-within-a-school. That can be avoided—as illustrated by the discussion of Shamrock Gardens Elementary School in chapter 9—by conscious policies to ensure equitably distributed community involvement, high-quality teaching, and rigorous instruction in magnet and nonmagnet classrooms. Also important is developing a schoolwide collaborative culture by involving teachers in both programs in joint planning sessions and professional development activities to maximize the instructional benefit of the partial magnet curricular focus throughout the school.[41]

The fifth modest step involves recalibrating priorities in the present reassignment policies. At the October 22, 2013, board meeting, CMS specified the rubric it would use to evaluate community requests for changes in attendance zone boundaries. The rubric was based on guiding principles for pupil assignment that were adopted during the Gorman administration. The principles gave the highest priority to assigning students to their home schools, which the principles call "the foundation of our academic instruction delivery model."[42] Thus, of the total of twelve points that were distributed among the four elements in the rubric, the criteria associated with assignment to a home school received a total of six points. The likely long-term stability of any changes received one point, the extent to which the change facilitates economic diversity received two points, and the effective use of capital resources received three points. Asked how the weights in the rubric were established, staff replied that it "was a value judgment." Without any change to the guiding principles for pupil assignment, a recalibration of the points given elements in the rubric could accord diversity more priority than it currently has when communities request reassignment. Such changes would, of course, affect only the relatively small number of neighborhoods that request reassignment, but they could pave the way for more ambitious changes.

Generating a diverse student body through the five prior strategies we've suggested is not enough. After bringing students together in the same space, it is necessary to promote authentic inclusion through meaningful social and academic interactions. Thus, the sixth step zeroes in on schools' core activities. It extends multicultural education beyond the formal curricula and Cinco de Mayo and Black History celebrations. CMS leaders can pursue deliberate strategies that transform the social relations of the classroom, the playgrounds, the professional staff, and school/parent/community partnerships.[43] Doing so will generate authentic inclusion across race, linguistic, and socioeconomic differences.

Success in implementing these steps would presumably increase public receptivity to more ambitious ones. A wealth of data from public opinion surveys and in-depth interviews indicates that families and students who have had firsthand experience with desegregation are more supportive of it than people who have not.[44]

More Ambitious Steps

In addition to the steps just suggested, more ambitious changes would involve revisiting and revising the 2010 guiding principles for pupil assignment. In considering that possibility, it's worth remembering that these principles' adoption hardly reflected a popular mandate. They were adopted by a 5–3 vote of the board, a reflection of divisions in the CMS leadership and the community.

It would be presumptuous for us to try to delineate the specifics of new pupil assignment guidelines, but the possible contours of such guidelines might come from CMS's history and the Future School Planning Task Force that CMS convened in 1997.[45] Comprising thirty-three citizens (and thus called the C33) with a wide range of perspectives on education and politics, the task force was an attempt by CMS to develop community consensus around pupil assignment issues and minimize, if not preempt, political and legal challenges to district policy. In some ways, the committee must be considered a failure. Within a month after its report was issued, William Capacchione filed the lawsuit that led to the reopening of *Swann* and all the legal and political turmoil that accompanied and followed its reopening.

However, the C33's approach to pupil assignment remains useful because the four criteria for pupil assignment that it identified—stability, proximity, utilization, and diversity—are basically the same as those in CMS's current pupil assignment guidelines. But unlike those guidelines, the C33's report did not prioritize any of the four criteria, but instead set guidelines for achieving each, realizing that the school board would have to balance the often-conflicting criteria to make new school siting and assignment decisions. There is a lot to be said for CMS's assignment guidelines doing the same thing and not binding individual decisions the way the current guidelines do.

For more than a decade, the pupil assignment pendulum has swung far toward proximity and the notion that the home school is "the foundation of our academic instruction delivery model." Based on the literature on schooling processes and outcomes, it is unclear why a neighborhood school should be a foundation of an academic instruction model more than a diverse school, and it's well-nigh time for the pendulum to swing back toward diversity.

Just as it would be presumptuous for us to delineate the specifics of a revamped set of pupil assignment guidelines, it is beyond our ability to specify the mix of strategies used to fulfill these guidelines because that mix would probably include, at a minimum, a complex combination of neighborhood schools, partial magnets, full magnets, paired schools, redrawn attendance zones, a new site selection policy, and even regional approaches—all of which consider a range of underlying indicators rather than single or race-based metrics. Developing such a plan requires access to data, software, and planning capabilities that we make no pretense of having. But there are institutions and organizations, such as the Haas Institute at the University of California at Berkeley, that do have all those resources and are available to help local districts develop legal and effective pupil assignment plans that facilitate diversity.[46]

In fact, about a decade ago, one such institute let it be known to board members that it was available to help CMS develop an assignment plan that was consistent with the district's changed legal situation and that would also promote diversity. But as a board member confided to Mickelson, CMS turned down that invitation "on the advice of their [legal] counsel." In other words, CMS did not want to run the risk of additional litigation. It is difficult to know the magnitude of that risk or the amount of money and energy CMS would have had to expend to deal with the litigation had it taken place. But it's not difficult to know that it's incumbent on CMS to weigh the risk of being sued with the risk of not fulfilling its vision of providing "all students the best education available anywhere." Given diversity's benefits and how low diversity has been on CMS's list of priorities, CMS's scale for weighing those risks has been woefully out of balance.

Developing Social Purpose Politics

Efforts to increase diversity would benefit greatly from the development of what Clarence Stone has called *social purpose politics*. In his studies on school reform, Stone—probably contemporary political science's most influential urbanist—has emphasized the importance of social purpose politics, or the ability of interested parties to go beyond a "narrow understanding of their stake in the education system . . . [and] come together around a larger vision of what is at issue." That coming together, in turn, contributes to mobilization "in support of a communitywide cause."[47] By all accounts, Charlotte's busing plan was just such a cause, and the success of its implementation bespeaks the existence of social purpose politics. Very little of that kind of politics characterizes Charlotte's educational landscape today.

But the prevalence of social purpose politics in the early years of the *Swann* era and its paucity in the early years of the post–*Swann* era cannot be attributed simply to the passage of time. In the same years it was so absent in Charlotte, it was on ample display in one of Charlotte's suburbs—Rock Hill, South Carolina. Moreover, social purpose politics was present in the very issue, school desegregation, from which it was absent in Charlotte. Despite the many differences between the two places, the comparison is instructive because at the same time CMS was resegregating, the Rock Hill School District (RHSD) was aggressively pursuing desegregation despite a lawsuit whose plaintiffs were represented by the same legal team who had represented the white plaintiffs in the reopened *Swann* litigation.[48] But in RHSD, these attorneys and their clients did not prevail. Rather, they agreed to a compromise settlement prior to trial.

In the aftermath of that settlement, RHSD opened a third high school and used that opening to draw attendance boundaries for its three high schools aimed at redressing longstanding and locally well-known racial and socioeconomic disparities between the district's two existing high schools, Northwestern and Rock Hill. The details of the assignment plan were worked out in a citizens committee facilitated by Associate Superintendent Lynn Moody. Her comments about the committee's deliberations indicate how social purpose politics developed:

> I never thought we would get close enough to take it [a recommendation on assignment] to the board. They [committee members] were so diverse in their thinking, in what they truly believed. We would go back to our ground rules about, *Are we doing this for all children or just for our neighborhood?* See, just the way the committee was set up . . . by their schools . . . They all came with their individual agendas. I'm going to protect Sullivan; I'm going to take care of Oakdale; I'm going to take care of Old Pointe . . . They saw themselves as a representative to fight for that community, to the people who lived in that community, not to come up with something that was comprehensive for all children. But yet when they set their ground rules—we had a lot of conversation, we went back to it and back to it—and they challenged each other: *Who are you talking about? Do you really believe in all children? Well, then why are you saying that?* I think it was a soul searching of each other, a real challenge of each other . . . I don't think any

one of them would say they didn't have to do some compromising (authors' emphasis).[49]

The citizen who chaired that committee had initially wanted everyone going to the closest school. He recalled, "but then [when] we started doing the data and looking at it, it didn't work. It was too far out of balance. And again, where I came from, and how I was raised, I just didn't feel that was right.[50] Where he "came from" was very different from where he is now. Currently a successful building contractor, during his school days, the family "didn't have a lot of money" and he and his siblings were "on free lunch." So, he explained, "I know the struggles that a lot of the people have . . . so I have been on that side of the tracks, and I have not forgotten where I came from."[51]

That kind of empathy and social purpose politics are not easily bottled and distributed to other districts, even ones as nearby as Charlotte. But CMS is not entirely devoid of calls for that kind of empathy or the largeness of mind to which Moody's comment draw attention. One especially magisterial call came in an op-ed piece by a local minister urging support for a bond package shortly after CMS was declared unitary in 2000. Entitled "School Bonds Will Reveal If Charlotte Has a Soul," the article evokes the importance of empathy and reads like a textbook example of social purpose politics. "This issue asks us to feel the pain of every part of our city and calls us to exercise 'soul,' our capacity to be related to the whole," it said, concluding by asking Charlotteans "to look beyond the welfare of their part alone to the welfare of the whole and support the bonds."[52]

That referendum easily passed, perhaps an indication that Charlotte has some of the soul the clergyman exhorted it to have. But it's hard to find much soul in the past decade's discussions about pupil assignment either in the community at large or on the risk-averse school board. In thinking about how social purpose politics might be developed here, it's worth noting—as Julius Chambers pointed out when interviewed for this book—that religious leaders played an important role in developing support for Charlotte's initial desegregation efforts and how a similar effort from them is now needed.[53]

Recent efforts at the state level by the Forward Together Moral Movement (organized by the North Carolina NAACP) and the Presbyterian Church appear to be a small step in encouraging clergy support for educational reform.[54] While resegregation of schools is not a core component of the clergy's message to North Carolina policy makers, this slight shift in discourse at the state level could be a positive sign of a previously dormant base to advocate for change at the local level. Given the important role religious institutions play in the city's life, enlisting their efforts to help develop social purpose politics would be an important first step.

Clergy and community leaders played a pivotal role in building social purpose politics around school assignment policies in the desegregation battles of decades past. With this in mind, another important step could be to cultivate a small but growing group of community activists who are focused on efforts to reintegrate schools in naturally diverse areas, such as East Charlotte, where schools often do not reflect the diversity of the communities in which they are located. It has been this kind of grassroots effort, supported by CMS, that helped Shamrock Gardens succeed (as described in chapter 9). Members of this group are developing a network of educational activists in Charlotte and believe that efforts to build diverse schools from the ground up are as important as building them from the top down. Such efforts include promoting policies that support naturally diverse areas and expanding the use of partial magnets, but also spreading the simple message that if you believe in the importance of diversity, then you should send your child to a diverse school. Although it's too early to know whether the group's efforts will be successful, early indications are promising.[55]

A BELLWETHER ONCE AGAIN?

CMS has been a bellwether twice in the nation's desegregation history. The *Swann* litigation paved the way for desegregation in many other districts, and CMS's experience provided a model of how a busing plan can successfully be implemented. For the same reason that CMS was a desegregation icon during the *Swann* era, the 1999 decision lifting the original *Swann* order—despite CMS's desire to remain under it—was a nationally recognized signal of how strongly committed activist conservative federal judges were to abandoning judicial efforts to fulfill *Brown*'s promises. These days, nobody can claim that CMS is now a desegregation or diversity bellwether of any kind.

Some might dismiss such resegregation, saying CMS is now a bellwether of another kind, a national leader in urban education as indicated by its receipt of the Broad Prize. We know that thousands of CMS personnel and students sweated blood to boost test scores and meet the Broad Foundation's expectations. Such hard work certainly deserves to be rewarded. But the Broad Foundation's approach to education reflects, as explained in chapter 1, the wave of foundation-funded and market-driven school reform strategies that is sweeping over public education and jeopardizing the *public* in public education. There's a terrible disparity between the vigor with which CMS is swimming along with that tide and how mercilessly it is allowing itself to be buffeted by the resegregation wave also sweeping over public education.

Given the strong evidence that school desegregation and diversity improve academic achievement, increase graduation rates, raise lifetime incomes, improve intergroup relations, decrease involvement with the criminal justice system, and are more cost-effective than programs that funnel additional resources to high-poverty schools, it's ironic that the bottom-line-conscious business executives, such as Eli Broad, who are so eager to improve public education don't establish prizes for districts that reverse resegregation and pursue diversity. Perhaps some members of Charlotte's corporate class who know CMS's desegregation history, and may even have been part of it, might do so themselves.

Even if that were to happen, for CMS to swim against the resegregation tide will take courage and political will. But the effort offers the promise of improving educational outcomes and saving money. It could also be an example to other districts, perhaps even allowing CMS to once again be a bellwether.

Lest we be seen as too enthusiastic about CMS's bygone desegregation accomplishments, we want to emphasize that we're fully aware that the *Swann* era was not one rapturous kumbaya moment after another. It was replete with tension and conflict, and many of *Swann*'s promises were no more fulfilled than *Brown*'s. But CMS was doing better than most districts in fulfilling those promises, and it was paving the way for others to fulfill them, too.

Yes, it's crucial—as CMS's current vision statement indicates—that the district seek to provide all students with the best education available anywhere and prepare them to lead rich and productive lives. In the era when CMS aspired to be the nation's premier integrated urban district, it didn't see a conflict between those goals and integration. It saw all of them as intimately related. They still are. In fact, diverse schools are integral to providing the kind of education that will properly prepare CMS graduates to step into the globalizing city and multiethnic nation that awaits them. Moreover, CMS's aspiration of being the nation's premier integrated urban district was never solely about viewing integration as a strategy for improving educational outcomes. It was also about two additional lofty goals. The first was CMS's obligation to help itself, its students, and the community fulfill the moral imperative of racial and social justice. It has the same obligation today. As noted by a longtime CMS employee currently working in a school in which over 90 percent of the students are economically disadvantaged and over 96 percent are either African American or Hispanic: "Regardless of your political beliefs or beyond what you believe is best for your child, is it acceptable to you that CMS and many other school districts across the country have been resegregated? What does this say about us as a people? What type of future are we forging when we know beyond a shadow of a doubt that segregated education is detrimental education?"[56]

The second goal was the opportunity to reap the benefits of diversity. Having experienced firsthand many aspects of the *Swann* era, we—the three editors of this book—are fully aware that the era was plagued by numerous conflicts, tensions, and problems, as chapters 2 and 3 make clear. Yet chapter 3 also makes clear how students benefited from attending the school, sometimes in life-changing ways. The chapter's account resonates with others, such as the study by Amy Stuart Wells and her colleagues of 1980 graduates of West Charlotte and five high schools located in other cities. Noting how a white female graduate of West Charlotte said, "You cannot suddenly teach someone how to get along with someone [who's] different from them. You can't learn that from a book," Wells and her colleagues continue:

> Day-to-day high school experiences with members of other racial groups left many of these graduates with a fundamentally altered way of seeing the world that they feel cannot be fully transmitted to those who have not shared those experiences. A white woman who graduated from [a different high school] and played on several predominantly black athletic teams there concluded, "I think I learned something there that you can't teach anybody, just learned about people and acceptance of life things that I don't think you teach, you just have to have lived that kind of environment, you just know it.[57]

The obligation to fulfill desegregation's moral imperative and the opportunity to reap diversity's benefits are goals as lofty, worthy, and cardinal in 2014 as they were in 1970. For all the reasons discussed in this chapter, today's obstacles may be greater than they were a half-century ago. But what is the alternative? This book's opening pages took note of President Reagan's denunciation of busing as a "failed social experiment" as well as of the silent Charlotte crowd's implicit rebuke of the president and the *Charlotte Observer*'s explicit one, both of which were based on CMS's experience. But there's an even more telling rebuke based on the national experience. If busing for desegregation is considered a "social experiment," there's another such experiment with which it should be compared: separate but equal. By any measure, separate but equal was one of the most ambitious, large-scale, and fully implemented social experiments in the nation's history, and it was a complete flop. Given *that* experiment's past monstrous failures, and moral (more accurately, immoral) implications, the burden is on those who eschew desegregation to provide a convincing explanation of why they think separate but equal can be successful in the twenty-first century. Absent such an explanation, shouldn't school desegregation—with its moral obligations, educational benefits, and its opportunities to reap the benefits of diversity—be atop the educational reform agenda of both Charlotte and the nation as a whole?

APPENDIX A

Terminology

At the risk of getting too ensnarled in definitional, conceptual, and terminological thickets, we find it is useful to clarify some of the key concepts and terms that appear throughout the book.

Desegregation, Racial Balance, Integration, Diversity, Segregation, Racial Imbalance, and Racial Isolation

Of the thickets included in this note, this one might be the thorniest. Often used synonymously with *integration, desegregation* more precisely refers to the removal of the legal and social practices that divide students from different ethnic, racial, linguistic, and economic backgrounds into separate schools and classrooms. Integration, on the other hand, occurs only if there "then develops joint participation and mutual acceptance in all activities normally associated with school attendance."[1] There can thus be varying degrees of segregation, desegregation, and integration, as there can be of socioeconomic or racial balance and isolation. This variation can be analyzed by several quantitative measures. Chapters 1 and 2 use the dissimilarity index, chapter 7 uses the segregation index, and chapter 5 uses the imbalance index, which at the county and school system levels, is the same as the segregation index. Although the dissimilarity index produces values higher than the segregation index, "the two measures are highly correlated with each other."[2]

Integration, segregation/desegregation, and racial *balance/imbalance* have been staples of court decisions and the social science literature at least since *Brown v. Board of Education*. More recently, *diversity* has been added to the mix. Among this term's virtues, as James Ryan has pointed out, is that *diversity* more readily

connotes the benefits to all students of attending schools with those from different racial, ethnic, economic, and/or cultural backgrounds. In contrast, *desegregation* typically connotes eliminating the harms suffered by students of color
and/or poor students without connoting the benefits that others might receive.[3] These advantages of *diversity* notwithstanding, it obviously cannot be
used in all situations. To talk about the state-mandated antidiversity policies,
rather than the state-mandated segregation of Jim Crow, would euphemize
the monstrous harms of that era and make a mockery of historical understanding. Thus, in talking about harms, damages, and adverse consequences, this
book will generally use longstanding terms such as *segregation/desegregation, racial
balance/imbalance,* and so forth. But in talking about future policies, it will generally phrase its statements in terms of *diversity.* That said, in a multiauthored book
it's impossible to be fully consistent, and—mindful of Emerson's admonishment
about foolish consistencies—we won't try to be.

Educational Outcomes

The concept of *educational outcomes* encompasses academic and nonacademic
consequences of schooling that occur both in the short term while students
are still in school as well as over the long term after they leave formal schooling and enter adulthood. K–12 school academic outcomes (test scores, growth
scores, grades, courses taken) are the most commonly reported short-term academic outcomes. Educational aspirations and educational attainment (variously
operationalized as graduating from or dropping out of high school, college attendance and graduation, years of education) are the most common indicators
of long-term academic outcomes. Short-term nonacademic outcomes include
cross-race peers, cultural understanding, and reductions in fears and prejudice
among K–12 students. Labor force participation (occupational and income attainment), employment in integrated workplaces, adult cross-racial friendships,
residing in integrated neighborhoods, avoiding the criminal justice system, em-
bracing democratic values, and various forms of civic engagement are some
indicators of long-term outcomes that, across the life course, contribute to
cohesive, just, multiethnic democratic societies.

Race and Ethnicity

This book is primarily about the Charlotte-Mecklenburg Schools. In reporting the demographic characteristics of its students, CMS most recently uses the

categories American Indian, Asian/Pacific Islander, black, Hispanic, multiracial, and white, the last of which is a proxy for non-Hispanic white. Even though that proxy conflates race and ethnicity, this book will also use *white* as shorthand for non-Hispanic white. Although there can be important reasons for using Hispanic rather than Latino, those reasons generally do not apply to the issues discussed in this book, and we will use the two terms synonymously unless we specify otherwise. The same holds for black and African American, although here, too, in other contexts it may be important to use one term rather than the other. The pan-ethnic terms *Hispanic* and *Latino* embrace a wide range of peoples, cultures, races, and ethnicities, among which, in many contexts, it is crucial to distinguish. Similarly, *Asian* embraces a wide range of peoples, cultures, races, and ethnicities. But important as those contexts and distinctions are, they are generally beyond the scope of this book and unless otherwise specified, we will use the pan-ethnic categories of Hispanic or Latino and Asian, as does CMS in its administrative data reports.

Although there's a long history of *minority* being used by scholars and the lay public, we consider the term invidious. It's also illogical because demographic trends indicate that so-called minorities will soon outnumber whites. So we prefer *peoples of color*, but it's hard to use that term as an adjective, in which case *nonwhite* or *disadvantaged minorities* will generally be used. But, here, too, it's impossible to be fully consistent. Finally, although race is hardly a synonym for ethnicity, in the interest of brevity the book will often use race as a proxy for race and ethnicity.[4]

Socioeconomic Status, Social Class

In the social science and educational literatures, the term *socioeconomic status* (SES) often is used interchangeably with the term *social class* even though SES and social class are based on different sets of theoretical assumptions about the nature of stratification in society. The chapters in this book employ data that operationalizes SES in a variety of ways. Often, it uses the rather crude free-and/or reduced-lunch eligibility (FRL) measure. A better measure of SES is parental education, typically denoted by the mother's educational attainment. A superior indicator is a combination of parental educational and occupational attainment. As is true of studies of race, SES variables may refer to how the SES of individuals affects their outcomes as well as how the SES composition of their school is related to their outcomes.

Tracking and Ability Grouping

The widespread practices of elementary school *ability grouping* and secondary school *tracking* typically involve forms of curricular differentiation and, more often than not, segregation by race and SES as well. At the secondary level, tracking creates classroom learning environments that tend to be homogeneous with respect to student race, SES, and at times, language and immigrant status. Because of this within-school racial, ethnic, and linguistic and SES segregation, tracking creates what some researchers label *second-generation segregation*, as several chapters discuss.

APPENDIX B

List of Supplementary Materials

The book's Web site, yesterdaytodaytomorrowcms.com, contains supplemental materials for some of the chapters. Authors have directed readers to supplemental materials in the preface (Julius LeVonne Chambers interview) and in endnotes to relevant passages in their chapters.

Preface
Julius Chambers interview

Chapter 1
Appendix 1.a   Key Elements in the Nested State and National Policy Structures

Chapter 2
Figure 2.a   2013 CMS school closings by original identification for closure and outcomes of deliberative process and school poverty classification

Chapter 5
Appendix 5.a   Measuring Imbalance
Appendix 5.b   Calculating Between-School and Within-School Imbalance

Chapter 7
Appendix 7.a   Technical and Methodological Issues

Notes

Preface

1. See chapter 1, note 10, for additional discussion of unitary status.

Chapter 1

1. As quoted in Frye Gaillard, *The Dream Long Deferred* (Chapel Hill: University of North Carolina Press, 1988), xv.
2. *Charlotte Observer*, "You Were Wrong, Mr. President," October 9, 1984, 18A.
3. Jeremy Fiel, "Decomposing School 'Resegregation': Social Closure, Racial Imbalance, and Racial Isolation," *American Sociological Review* 78, no. 5 (2013): 828–848; John Logan, Elisabeta Minca, and Sinem Adar, "The Geography of Inequality: Why Separate Means Unequal in American Public Schools," *Sociology of Education* 85, no. 3 (2012): 287–301; Nancy McArdle, Theresa Osypuk, and Dolores Acevedo-Garcia, "Segregation and Exposure to High-Poverty Schools in Large Metropolitan Areas: 2008–9," *Poverty & Race* 19, no. 6 (2010): 6–8.
4. Green v. County School Board of New Kent County, 391 U.S. 430 (1968).
5. Swann v. Charlotte-Mecklenburg, 300 F. Supp. 1358, 1360 (W.D.N.C. 1969).
6. As a result of this arrangement, black children were typically bused at a younger age and for more years than white children (four as opposed to three), an asymmetry that many blacks and white liberals considered unfair but lacked the political clout to remedy.
7. However, there was a satellite in Eastover, a neighborhood that was home to some of Charlotte's most affluent and powerful white citizens. To show that even affluent and powerful white families would be included in the desegregation plan, CMS agreed to bus children from Eastover to West Charlotte, a historically black high school. However, CMS took several steps to make West Charlotte attractive to Eastover residents, including replacing its black principal with a white one and introducing an attractive curricular option, the Open Program (see chapter 3).
8. Stephen Samuel Smith, *Boom for Whom?: Education, Desegregation, and Development in Charlotte,* (Albany: State University of New York Press, 2004), 77–80. Notably, within-school segregation due to tracking began soon after the implementation of the *Swann* decision and, as chapter 5 indicates, continues to the present day. The history of tracking and ability grouping in CMS embodies the complicated relationships among equality of educational opportunity, desegregation, the practice of tracking, and achievement. In "Subverting *Swann*: First- and Second-Generation Segregation in the Charlotte-Mecklenburg Schools" (*American Educational Research Journal* 38, no. 2 [2001]: 215–252), Roslyn Arlin Mickelson reported the results of an investigation of the effects of school desegregation and tracking on the academic outcomes of 1997 high school seniors in all of CMS's high schools. Even though in 1997 CMS was a majority white school district, someone familiar with the historical relationship between tracking and race who observed any math, science, social studies, or English class in any of CMS's eleven regular high schools could accurately identify the academic level of the course simply by noting the classroom's racial composition. The top academic classes in CMS were disproportionately white, while the least rigorous classes were disproportionately black relative to the school's demographic mix. Moreover, Mickelson demonstrated that black and

white students with comparable academic abilities were found in different academic tracks. Blacks were far more likely to be in lower tracks than their similarly able white peers. Because lower-track classes characteristically offer less rigorous instruction, involve a more limited curriculum, and frequently are taught by less highly qualified teachers, the potential academic benefits of the desegregation mandated by the *Swann* decision were compromised—actually subverted—by the pervasive resegregation of secondary students into racially imbalanced tracked core academic classes. However, Mickelson also demonstrated that although the extensive second-generation segregation through tracking subverted *Swann*'s potential to augment educational outcomes, attending desegregated schools still had a positive relationship with both black and white students' achievement.

9. Jim Morrill, "Trial Brings School Case Full Circle," *Charlotte Observer,* April 18, 1999, 16A.

10. As Judge Potter, noted in his opinion, *unitary* has no fixed meaning (Capacchione v. Charlotte-Mecklenburg Schools 57 F. Supp. 2d, 228. 242 [W.D.N.C 1999]), but it is a crucial concept in desegregation law. Its importance comes from the 1968 *Green* decision (see endnote 4), in which the Supreme Court held that school boards previously operating state-compelled *dual* systems had an "affirmative duty to take whatever steps might be necessary to convert to a unitary system in which racial discrimination would be eliminated root and branch." By the time of Potter's ruling, desegregation law viewed a finding that a district was unitary as indicating that the vestiges of the state-mandated dual system had been eliminated to the extent practicable, and that the district was thus entitled to be released from court supervision and the legal obligation to pursue desegregation remedies.

11. To measure segregation, figure 1.1 employs a widely used measure, the dissimilarity index, which can be understood as the proportion of students who would have to change schools for every school's racial composition to be the same as that of the entire school system. The dissimilarity index ranges from 0 (complete racial balance) to 100 (complete segregation). There is a wide range of opinion about what constitutes "high" or "low" levels of racial balance, but a good working definition comes from the database on racial balance in districts nationwide that is currently maintained by Brown University's American Communities Project: "A value of 60 (or above) is considered very high... [v]alues of 40 or 50 are usually considered a moderate level of segregation, and values of 30 or below are considered to be fairly low" (http://www.s4.brown.edu/usschools2/DataSub.aspx?Schid=3702970). Figure 1.1 uses elementary school data because those schools' typically smaller attendance zones make them especially sensitive measures of segregation. It's important—as subsequent chapters indicate—to also consider socioeconomic segregation and segregation between other racial/ethnic groups. Figure 1.1 confines its analysis to black/white segregation for two reasons: they remain CMS's two largest racial groups and there's scant historical data on other kinds of segregation.

Desegregation can also be measured in other ways; e.g., the segregation index used in chapter 7 and the imbalance index used in chapter 5 (which at the school system or county level is the same as the segregation index). The dissimilarity index produces values higher than the segregation index, but the two "are highly correlated with each other" [Charles T. Clotfelter, *After Brown* (Princeton, NJ: Princeton University Press, 2004), 205].

Data in figure 1.1 for 2010 is from Charlotte-Mecklenburg Schools; for all other years, it is from the American Communities Project (http://www.s4.brown.edu/usschools2/DataSub.aspx?Schid=3702970).

12. "2011 Broad Prize Awarded to Charlotte-Mecklenburg Schools; North Carolina District Wins $550,000 in Scholarships, Three Finalist Districts Each Win $150,000" (press release of the Broad Foundation), http://www.broadeducation.org/asset/0-tbp%202011%20 winner%20release.pdf.

13. Ann Doss Helms, "CMS Tops Urban Districts in Reading, Math," *Charlotte Observer,* December 18, 2013, http://www.charlotteobserver.com/2013/12/18/4553390/cms-tops-urban-districts-on-national.html.

14. Ibid.

15. Eric Frazier and Susanna Booth, "CMS Test Scores Decline Steeply—Officials Cite Budget Cuts, Bigger Classes for Reversal After 4 Years of Increases," *Charlotte Observer,* July 22, 2011, 1B. The Prize was awarded in September 2011, and did not account for scores in the 2010–2011 academic year, which is the year the scores dropped so sharply.

16. See chapter 2 for a discussion of these closings.

17. According to a Broad Foundation spokeswoman there was no conflict of interest between CMS's seeking the Broad Prize and Gorman's serving on the Broad Center's board of directors because while the Broad Foundation funds both the Broad Prize and the Broad Center, the latter, she said, is a separate entity that's not involved at all in awarding the prize. Ann Doss Helms, "The Broad Barrage," *Charlotte Observer* "Your Schools" blog, May 8, 2011, obsyour schools.blogspot.com/2011_05_01_archive.html.

18. According to school board member Reverend Thomas Tate, many CMS board members and senior administrative staff also graduated from the Broad Academy's training programs, and CMS hosts Broad Institute interns (Thomas Tate, interview by editors, March 2013). In her chapter entitled "The Billionaires Boys' Club" historian Diane Ravitch describes the Gates, Walton, and Broad Foundations' vast influence over the reform agenda of American education through their strategic investments in school reforms. She points out that their reform strategies mirror the foundations' founders' own experiences with competition, choice, deregulation, incentives, and other market-oriented strategies, and she raises questions about the wisdom of relinquishing control of the direction of the *public* educational policy reform agenda to *private* foundations (Diane Ravitch, *Death and Life of the Great American School System* [New York: Basic Books, 2010], 200.)

19. Jaclyn Zubryzcki, "School Project Blurs Lines Between Public, Private," *Education Week,* January 9, 2013, http://www.edweek.org/ew/articles/2013/01/09/17projectlift.h32.html.

20. Stuart McAnulla, "Structure and Agency," in *Theory and Methods in Political Science,* 2nd ed., ed. David Marsh and Gerry Stoker (New York: Palgrave McMillan, 2002), 271. McAnulla provides an accessible account of the voluminous scholarly literature on the structure/agency relationship. Much of this literature draws on the work of Anthony Giddens (e.g., *The Constitution of Social Theory* [Cambridge, UK: Polity Press, 1984] and "Elements of the Theory of Structuration" in *Contemporary Social Theory,* ed. A. Elliot [Oxford, UK: Blackwell, 1999]). For critiques of Giddens, see Margaret Archer, *Realistic Social Theory: The Morphogenetic Approach* (Cambridge, UK: Cambridge University Press, 1995) and Bob Jessop, *State Theory: Putting the Capitalist State in Its Place* (Cambridge, UK: Polity Press, 1990).

21. McAnulla, "Structure and Agency," 271.

22. Potter's ruling drew heavily on the Supreme Court decisions in Board of Education of Oklahoma City v. Dowell (498 U.S. 237 [1991]) and Freeman v. Pitts (503 U.S. 467 [1992]). Eight years later, a sharply divided Supreme Court struck down as unconstitutional efforts by school districts in Seattle and Louisville, Kentucky, to increase diversity in their schools (Parents Involved in Community Schools v. Seattle School District No. 1 551 U.S. 701 [PICS; 2007]). The implications of this case for CMS—generally known as *PICS*—are discussed in chapters 10 and 11.

23. However, President Obama's proposed 2015 budget introduces a Race to the Top-Opportunity (RTT-Opportunity) initiative that includes attention to diversity and opportunity for underserved youth. U.S. Department of Education, "Obama Administration 2015 Budget Prioritizes

Education Investments to Provide Opportunities to All Americans" (press release), March 4, 2014, http://www.ed.gov/budget15.

24. Erica Frankenberg and Genevieve Siegel-Hawley, "A Segregating Choice?: An Overview of Charter School Policy, Enrollment Trends, and Segregation," in *Educational Delusions? Why Choice Can Deepen Inequality and How to Make Schools Fair,* ed. Gary Orfield and Erica Frankenberg (Oakland: University of California Press, 2013), 129–144. See chapters 2, 5, and 11 for a discussion of charter schools in CMS and North Carolina.

25. See, for example, David Berliner and Sharon Nichols, *Collateral Damage: How High Stakes Testing Corrupts America's Schools* (Cambridge, MA: Harvard Education Press, 2007).

26. Adam Gamoran, "Federal Policy, Educational Inequality, and the Role of Research in the Wake of No Child Left Behind" (keynote address, Sociology of Education Association, Pacific Grove, CA, February 22, 2014); Elementary and Secondary Education, ESEA Flexibility, http://www2.ed.gov/policy/elsec/guid/esea-flexibility/index.html. Also see *Education Week,* "NCLB Waivers: A State-by-State Breakdown," February 25, 2014, http://www.edweek.org/ew/section/infographics/nclbwaivers.html; Robert Garda and Derek Black, "The New Accountability? NCLB Waivers" (paper presented at the No Child Left Behind Symposium, Thurgood Marshall School of Law, Texas Southern University, Houston, TX, February 8, 2013); and the Department of Education's website describing waivers: http://www2.ed.gov/print/policy/elsec/guid/esea-flexibility/index.html

27. Leandro v. State (Leandro I), 346 N.C. 336, 342–43 (1997).

28. Three years after the Supreme Court's unanimous decision in *Swann,* it decided a case—Milliken v. Bradley, 418 U.S. 717 (Milliken I; 1974)—involving school desegregation in Detroit. Because the Detroit Public Schools were so heavily African American, a district court judge issued an order requiring desegregation between Detroit and its heavily white suburbs. However, by a 5–4 margin, the Supreme Court overturned the district court's decision on the basis that it involved desegregation between school districts rather than within a district (which is the issue with which *Swann* dealt). Given the differences between the racial compositions of central cities and suburbs in many metropolitan areas, *Milliken I* imposes high legal barriers to efforts to obtain meaningful desegregation in these areas.

29. Sean Reardon, "The Widening Academic Achievement Gap Between Rich and Poor: New Evidence and Possible Explanations," in *Whither Opportunity? Rising Inequality, Schools, and Children's Life Chances*, ed. Greg J. Duncan and Richard J. Murnane (New York: Russell Sage Foundation, 2011), 91–116.

30. Robert Frank, "The Vicious Circle of Income Inequality," *New York Times,* January 12, 2014, BU3, http://www.nytimes.com/2014/01/12/business/the-vicious-circle-of-income-inequality.html?_r=0. A recent study of upward mobility in the nation's fifty largest metropolitan areas found Mecklenburg County ranked last. Regions with the highest mobility were some of the whitest in the nation. In more heavily black areas like Mecklenburg County (32 percent black), low-income white youth also grow up to be low-income adults. See David Leonhardt, "The Complex Story of Race and Upward Mobility," *New York Times,* July 22, 2013, A1, http://economix.blogs.nytimes.com/2013/07/25/the-complex-story-of-race-and-upward-mobility/; David Leonhardt, "Geography Seen as Barrier to Climbing Class Ladder," *New York Times,* July 25, 2013, A1, http://www.nytimes.com/2013/07/22/business/in-climbing-income-ladder-location-matters.html?pagewanted=all.

31. Janice Petrovich and Amy Stuart Wells, *Bringing Equity Back: Research for a New Era in American Education Policy* (New York: Teachers College Press, 2005).

32. Common Core State Standards Initiative, *About the Standards,* 2012, http://www.core standards.org/about-the-standards; Lorraine M. McDonnell and M. Stephen Weatherford,

"Organized Interests and the Common Core," *Educational Researcher* 42, no. 9 (2013); 488–497. The technical appendix to chapter 1 that appears on the book's Web site provides a more detailed discussion of the status of No Child Left Behind, waivers, the Common Core State Standards, and the Race to the Top initiative.

33. Diane Ravitch, *Death and Life.*

34. Ibid.

35. The CMS Web page explaining its theory of action offers a link to the Broad Foundation and the National School Board Association: http://www.cms.k12.nc.us/boe/Pages/Theoryof ActionforChange.aspx.

36. Reverend Thomas Tate, interview by Amy Hawn Nelson and Roslyn Mickelson, March 28, 2013, Charlotte, NC.

37. *PICS*, 551 U.S. 701.

38. For a detailed explanation of why Justice Thomas is wrong and an analysis of the distortion of the social science record in two key *PICS* social science amicus briefs questioning the relationship between academic outcomes and the racial composition of schools and classrooms, see Roslyn Arlin Mickelson, "Twenty-First Century Social Science Research on School Diversity and Educational Outcomes," *Ohio State Law Journal* 69, no. 6 (2008): 1173–1228. Readers interested in reviewing for themselves the corpus of relevant scholarly literature can consult the searchable online database—the Spivack Archive (spivack.org)—that Mickelson has created. This archive contains over five hundred detailed synopses of social science articles relevant to the question of school and classroom compositional effects on short- and long-term academic and nonacademic outcomes. Each synopsis includes bibliographic information about the article as well as its research design, sample, data, analytic methods, and findings.

39. This summary of school and classroom compositional effects research relies on a growing body of high-quality scholarship that employed strong research designs, representative samples or populations of students, valid and reliable measures of outcomes, and appropriate statistical techniques to analyze the data. Rather than cite the voluminous studies, we refer readers to a series of recent literature synthesis of this broad corpus of scholarship conducted by many social scientists: Jomills Henry Braddock III and Tamela McNulty, "The Effects of School Desegregation," in *Handbook of Research on Multicultural Education*, ed. James Banks and Cherry A. McGee Banks (San Francisco: Jossey-Bass, 2003); Maureen Hallinan, "Diversity Effects on Student Outcomes: Social Science Evidence," *Ohio State Law Journal* 59, no. 3 (1998): 733–754; Robert Linn and Kevin Welner, *Race Conscious Policies for Assigning Students to Schools: Social Science Research and Supreme Court Cases* (National Academy of Education, 2007); Mickelson, "Twenty-First Century Social Science Research," 1173–1228; Roslyn Arlin Mickelson, Martha Cecilia Bottia, and Richard Lambert, "Effects of School Racial Composition on K–12 Mathematics Outcomes: A Metaregression Analysis," *Review of Educational Research* 83, no. 1 (2013): 121–158; Roslyn Arlin Mickelson and Mokubung Nkomo, "Integrated Schooling, Life Course Outcomes, and Social Cohesion in Multiethnic Democratic Societies," *Review of Research in Education* 36, no. 1 (2012): 197–238; Thomas Pettigrew and Linda Tropp, "A Meta-Analytic Test of Intergroup Contact Theory," *Journal of Personality and Social Psychology* 90, no. 5 (2006): 751–783; Janet Schofield, "International Evidence on Ability Grouping with Curriculum Differentiation and the Achievement Gap in Secondary Schools," *Teachers College Record* 112, no. 5 (2010): 1492–1528; Kevin G. Welner, "K–12 Race-Conscious Student Assignment Policies: Law, Social Science and Diversity," *Review of Research in Education* 76, no. 3 (2006); Reyn Van Ewijk and Peter Sleegers, "The Effects of Peer Socioeconomic Status on Student Achievement: A Meta-Analysis," *Educational Research Review* 5 no. 2 (2010): 134–150; Reyn Van Ewijk and Peter Sleegers, "Peer Ethnicity and Achievement: A Meta-Analysis into the Compositional Ef-

fect," *School Effectiveness and School Improvement* 21, no. 3 (2010): 237–265. However, Christine Rossell, David Armor, and Herbert Walberg's review of selective studies in their book *School Desegregation in the 21st Century* (New York: Oxford University Press, 2001) and the amicus briefs they authored for *PICS* reach different conclusions about desegregation and outcomes. Their long careers as expert witnesses against desegregation are important to consider in evaluating the scientific value of their writing. It is somewhat ironic that Christine Rossell once observed with regard to desegregation research, "when the available evidence is dispersed across multiple literatures and those reviewing the literature cite incomplete findings, conclusions drawn from social science can be distorted" (Christine Rossell, "Applied Social Science Research: What Does It Say About the Effectiveness of School Desegregation Plans?" *The Journal of Legal Studies* 12, no. 1 [1983]: 69–107).

40. Stephen Billings, David Deming, and Jonah Rockoff, "School Segregation, Educational Attainment, and Crime: Evidence from the End of Busing in Charlotte-Mecklenburg," *Quarterly Journal of Economics* 129, no. 1 (2014): 435–476; Jason Giersch et al., "Segregation, Tracking, and College Achievement Among 2004 Charlotte-Mecklenburg High School Graduates" (unpublished manuscript, Department of Sociology and Public Policy Program, University of North Carolina at Charlotte, 2014); Kenneth Godwin et al., "Sinking *Swann*: Public School Choice and the Resegregation of Charlotte's Public Schools," *Review of Policy Research*, 23, no. 5 (2005): 983–997; Chuang Wang, "Impacts of School Racial Composition on the Middle School Mathematics and Reading Achievement Gap in Post Unitary Charlotte-Mecklenburg Schools" (unpublished manuscript, College of Education, University of North Carolina at Charlotte, 2013).

41. C. Kirabo Jackson, "Student Demographics, Teacher Sorting, Teacher Quality: Evidence from the End of Desegregation," *Journal of Labor Economics* 27, no. 2 (2009): 213–256.

42. Prudence Carter, *Keepin' It Real* (New York: Oxford University Press, 2005); Brief for 65 Leading American Businesses as Amici Curiae Supporting Respondents, Gratz v. Bollinger, 539 U.S. 244 (2003) (No. 02-516), and Grutter v. Bollinger, 539 U.S. 306 (2003) (No. 02-241).

43. Amy Hawn Nelson, "Experiencing the Double-Edged Sword of Desegregation: Charlotte-Mecklenburg School Graduates from 1995–1998" (PhD dissertation, University of North Carolina at Charlotte, 2010).

44. Rucker C. Johnson, "Long-Run Impacts of School Desegregation and School Quality on Adult Attainments," (working paper 16664, National Board of Economic Research, 2011).

45. Consolidated brief of Joseph E. Brann, Daniel J. Coulombe, Edward F. David, Ronald Davis, Darrel Stephens as Amici Curiae in Support of the Respondents, *PICS*, 55 U.S. 701.

46. Billings, Deming, and Rockoff, "School Segregation," 2013.

47. Marco Basile, "The Cost-Effectiveness of Socioeconomic Integration," in *The Future of School Integration: Socioeconomic Diversity as an Education Reform Strategy*, ed. Richard Kahlenberg (New York: Century Foundation, 2012), 127–154; Johnson, "Long-Run Impacts"; Heather Schwartz, "Housing Policy Is School Policy: Economically Integrative Housing Promotes Academic Success in Montgomery County, Maryland," in *The Future of School Integration: Socioeconomic Diversity as an Education Reform Strategy*, ed. Richard Kahlenberg (New York: Century Foundation, 2012), 27–66.

Chapter 2

In discussing events prior to 2008, this chapter draws heavily on my book *Boom for Whom?: Education, Desegregation, and Development in Charlotte* (Albany: State University of New York Press, 2004) and "Development and the Politics of School Desegregation and Resegregation" in *Charlotte, NC: The Global Evolution of a New South City,* ed. William Graves and Heather Smith (Athens: University of Georgia Press, 2010), 198–219. References to events not explicitly cited here can be found in those two sources. An earlier version of this chapter was presented in a paper coauthored with Roslyn Arlin Mickelson that was presented at the April 2013 annual meeting of the Southern Sociological Society in Atlanta, Georgia.

1. Debbie Cenziper and Celeste Smith, "School Plan Is Greeted Cautiously," *Charlotte Observer,* February 14, 1999, 21A.
2. Hugh L. McColl, Jr., "What Is, and What We Hope For" (speech at the Governor's Emerging Issues Forum, Raleigh, North Carolina, February 24, 2000).
3. Stephen Smith, *Boom for Whom?: Education, Desegregation, and Development in Charlotte* (Albany: State University of New York Press, 2004), 61.
4. Ibid., 67.
5. Ibid., 67–68.
6. Tom Bradbury, "Direct Growth, for Schools' Sake," *Charlotte News,* October 25, 1979, 14A.
7. Thomas E. Norman, transcript of testimony in Capacchione v. Charlotte-Mecklenburg Schools, 57 F. Supp. 2d 228 (W.D.N.C. 1999), May 17, 1999.
8. Smith, *Boom for Whom?,* 98.
9. Ricki Morell, "Couple Symbolize City's Ambitions," *Charlotte Observer,* December 15, 1991.
10. These changes are illustrated by the neighborhood around East Mecklenburg High School. Located six and a half miles from downtown in the Independence Boulevard corridor, the high school is about one-quarter mile from three shopping centers on Independence. In the mid-1990s, those three shopping centers included a Target, Circuit City, Office Depot, Toys-R-Us, Barnes and Noble, Harris-Teeter, Service Merchandise, La-Z-Boy, T.J. Maxx, and an Eckerd drug store along with many small businesses. As the opening of the Outerbelt spurred growth on Mecklenburg's periphery, the first three of those big box stores closed their locations near East Mecklenburg High School in favor of ones several miles farther south along Independence. Within a few years, most of the other big stores closed as well.
11. Smith, *Boom for Whom?,* 224.
12. For example, in January 2014, Charlotte's city council approved a rezoning petition to build seventy low-income apartments on Mecklenburg's southern periphery, the first subsidized housing in that part of the county. But in 2010, efforts to build eighty-six units in Ballantyne area had failed in part because of neighborhood opposition, as had efforts to build ninety units at another location in the southwestern part of the county (Steve Harrison, "Rezoning OK'd for Low-Income Housing," *Charlotte Observer,* January 22, 2014).
13. Smith, *Boom for Whom?,* 104.
14. Smith, *Boom for Whom?,* 159. By the time the 1999 trial began, Capacchione had moved back to California. Although Capacchione and most of the white plaintiffs had, at the time of the trial, relatively shallow roots in Charlotte, the opposite was true of the two named African American plaintiffs who intervened in the litigation in support of CMS's pursuit of desegregation. One had been born in Mecklenburg, and the other had been raised in Charlotte, having arrived with his family while in elementary school.
15. Jennifer Wing Rothacker and Celeste Smith, "Busing As We Know It Today Will End," *Charlotte Observer,* August 24, 1999.
16. Jen Pilla, "1,500 People Attend Rally for Schools," *Charlotte Observer,* October 4, 1999.
17. Board members serve for four-year terms, and elections are staggered with the three at-large seats on the ballot one year, and the six district seats on the ballot two years later.
18. Smith, *Boom for Whom?,* 199–203.

19. This point is developed in Stephen Samuel Smith, Karen Kedrowski, and Joseph Ellis, "Electoral Structures, Venue Selection, and the (New?) Politics of School Desegregation," *Perspectives on Politics* 2, no. 4 (2004): 795–802.

20. Larry Gauvreau, "Diversity: America's Irrational Rationale," *Charlotte Observer*, March 7, 2001.

21. Figures 2.1 and 2.2 assess desegregation with the dissimilarity index, a widely used measure whose characteristics and relation to other measures are discussed in chapter 1, note 11.

22. In 2013–2014 the dissimilarity index between whites and all students of color was 59, that between whites and Hispanics was 64, and that between whites and blacks was 63. For additional discussion of trends in desegregation, see chapter 5. Although that chapter's method for computing desegregation differs from the one employed here, the two chapters' findings are consistent with each other.

23. Charlotte-Mecklenburg Schools, *Strategic Plan 2010: Educating Students to Compete Locally, Nationally, and Internationally* (2006), 7.

24. Ann Doss Helms, "Paperwork Trimmed on School Shuffle—CMS Assignment Process Easier, More Candid This Time Around," *Charlotte Observer*, November 22, 2005, 1B. For a fuller discussion of how the home school guarantee provided only a chimera of choice for most families seeking an alternative to their home school, see Roslyn Arlin Mickelson, Stephen Samuel Smith, and Stephanie Southworth, "The Chimera of Choice: Post-Unitary Charlotte's Rapid Resegregation" in *Court-Ended Desegregation: The Reconstitution of Schools and Communities*, ed. Claire Smrekar and Ellen Goldring (Cambridge, MA: Harvard Education Press, 2009), 129–156.

25. Leandro v. State (Leandro I), 346 N.C. 336, 342-43 (1997).

26. Tucker Mitchell, "Say a Prayer, Send More Mobiles," *Huntersville Herald*, August 12, 2004; Kaye McGarry et al., "Bonds Not Best Way to Build Schools—Defeat the Bonds to Ensure Schools Are Constructed Where Most Needed," *Charlotte Observer*, November 5, 2005.

27. Erica Beshears, "Talk Builds of School Split for N. Meck—400 People Meet in Church and Are Asked to Sign Petition," *Charlotte Observer*, February 18, 2005.

28. Celeste Smith and Ann Doss Helms, "With Rembert Loss, Chair Is Up for Grabs," *Charlotte Observer*, November 5, 2003.

29. Stephen Samuel Smith, "Resegregation, Development, and Regime Politics in Charlotte, North Carolina" (paper presented at the annual meeting of the American Political Science Association, Chicago, Illinois, 2007).

30. "Charlotte-Mecklenburg Board Of Education, Part II," *Charlotte Observer,* October 16, 2003, 15A.

31. Hugh McColl Jr., "Charlotte Needs Schools, Schools Need McGarry," *Charlotte Observer*, October 31, 2003; Richard Rubin and Ann Doss Helms, "Campaigns Have Raised 1.2 Million," *Charlotte Observer*, October 31, 2003.

32. Jim Morrill, "Ruling May Keep McColl Off Stand," *Charlotte Observer*, May 1, 1999.

33. *Mountain Xpress*, "A Q & A with Asheville Chamber CEO Kit Cramer (Full Transcript)," March 8, 2011, http://www.mountainx.com/article/1926/A-QA-with-Asheville-Chamber-CEO-Kit-Cramer-full-transcript.

34. David Mildenberg, "Shifting Demographics Take a Toll on Some Inner-City Schools," *Charlotte Business Journal*, May 13, 2004.

35. Ann Doss Helms, "Pughsley Points to 'Shifting Climate,' CMS Chief Says Those Who Remain Need the Will to Do the Right Thing," *Charlotte Observer*, April 22, 2005.

36. With the exception of Calvin Wallace, who was appointed as an interim superintendent a dozen years earlier, Pughsley was CMS's first and so far only black superintendent. Many blacks and liberal whites believed that the hostility of many white families toward CMS would

have been less sweeping and vitriolic had the superintendent been white, but as in many similar situations, it is difficult to assess with any precision the extent to which that was true.

37. Helms, "Pughsley Points to Shifting Climate."

38. American Institutes for Research, Cross & Joftus, LLC, *Findings and Recommendations of the Citizens' Task Force on Charlotte-Mecklenburg Schools* (Charlotte: Foundation for the Carolinas, 2005), i.

39. To be sure, the 2007 elections involved the three at-large seats, not the six district seats. The 2009 contests for the latter included black candidates, two of whom were elected from the district whose boundaries were drawn to facilitate black electoral success. That said, the absence of blacks on the 2007 ballot is still immensely significant. From 1970 until 1992, a period when all school board seats were at-large, at least one black candidate was on the ballot in every election, and a black candidate was elected in all but two of those elections. In the first three at-large elections (1995, 1999, and 2003) after the switch to the hybrid system, at least one black candidate was also on the ballot.

40. Fannie Flono, "With Gorman, Public Can Focus on Schools," *Charlotte Observer*, April 14, 2006.

41. See chapter 1 for additional discussion of CMS's receipt of the Broad Prize.

42. The results from the Strategic Staffing initiative were mixed. See Charlotte-Mecklenburg Schools, Office of Research and Evaluation, "Evaluation of the Strategic Staffing Initiative," January 2011, http://www.cms.k12.nc.us/cmsdepartments/accountability/REA/Documents/Stategic%20Staffing%20Evaluation%20Report%20January%202011.pdf.

43. Charlotte-Mecklenburg Schools, *Minutes of School Board Meeting of August 10, 2010.*

44. Figure 2.a on the book's Web site conveys the race and poverty composition of the schools that closed. Moreover, as indicated by figure 2.a, two schools with FRL-eligible enrollments of greater than 80 percent saw their student bodies dispersed, but the buildings remained open and became home to teachers, programs, and students (of whom less than 40 percent were FRL-eligible) of two schools whose previous buildings were permanently closed.

45. American Association of School Superintendents, "2012 AASA National Superintendent of the Year," http://www.aasa.org/content.aspx?id=23304.

46. http://www.pacificeducationalgroup.com/public/pages/home.

47. See Charlotte-Mecklenburg Schools, *2013–14 Guide to Magnet Programs* and *2014–2015 Schools Options Guide.*

48. Ann Doss Helms, "School Choice Boom Brings Options, Challenges," *Charlotte Observer*, January 11, 2014. Students are allowed to attend charter schools in counties different from the one in which they reside.

49. It is unclear just how towering these legal constraints are given Justice Kennedy's controlling opinion in *PICS* and the subsequent guidance on avoiding racial isolation that was issued by the Department of Justice and the Department of Education (see chapters 10 and 11).

Chapter 3

Parts of this chapter were originally written for "Listening for a Change: Transforming Landscapes and People," a 2001 conference presented by the North Carolina Humanities Council and the Southern Oral History Program at UNC Chapel Hill, and sponsored by the Z. Smith Reynolds Foundation, the National Endowment for the Humanities, and the First Union Foundation.

1. Gerson Stroud, interview by Pamela Grundy, May 26, 1999. All interviews cited in this essay are on deposit as part of the Southern Oral History Program archives at the Southern Historical Collection, Wilson Library, University of North Carolina, Chapel Hill.

2. West Charlotte High School, *The Lion* (Charlotte, NC: West Charlotte High School, 1986).

3. Lisa Hammersly, "School Desegregation's Historic Class of '82," *Charlotte Observer*, June 6, 1982, A1; Madge Hopkins, interview by Pamela Grundy, October 17, 2000; Samuel Haywood, interview by Pamela Grundy, November 15, 2000.

4. Pamela Grundy, *Lion Pride: West Charlotte High School, 1938–2013* (Charlotte, NC: West Charlotte High School National Alumni Association, 2013), 29; William Hamlin Jr., interview by Pamela Grundy, May 29, 1998.

5. West Charlotte High School, *The Lion* (Charlotte, NC: West Charlotte High School, 1974).

6. For descriptions of the political and community efforts that produced the new plan, see Frye Gaillard, *The Dream Long Deferred* (Chapel Hill: University of North Carolina Press, 1988) and Davison Douglas, *Reading, Writing and Race: The Desegregation of the Charlotte Schools* (Chapel Hill: University of North Carolina Press, 1995).

7. West Charlotte High School, *The Lion* (Charlotte, NC: West Charlotte High School, 1976); Gosnell White, interview by Pamela Grundy, March 29, 1999. Interviews indicate that many of the changes were made specifically to make the school more attractive to the well-off white families whose children had been assigned to the school. The Open School magnet program was operated as a small school-within-a-school, but most of West Charlotte's students, both black and white, were enrolled in the regular program.

8. Garfield Carr, interview by Laura Hajar, March 16, 1999.

9. Saundra Jones Davis, interview by Pamela Grundy, May 12, 1998.

10. Gaillard, *The Dream Long Deferred*, 33.

11. William B. A. Culp Jr., interview by Pamela Grundy, February 19, 1999.

12. Timothy Gibbs, interview by Pamela Grundy, May 27, 1998.

13. Latrelle McAllister, interview by Pamela Grundy, June 25, 1998; Brian Tarr, interview by Pamela Grundy, April 27, 1999.

14. Anna Spangler Nelson and Abigail Riggs Spangler, interview by Pamela Grundy, February 15, 1999. Anna Spangler Nelson is not related to Amy Hawn Nelson.

15. Betty Seizinger, interview by Jill Williams, June 22, 1999; Tarr, interview; William B. McMillan Jr., interview by Pamela Grundy, October 26, 2000; Haywood, interview.

16. John W. Love Jr., interview by Pamela Grundy, February 17, 1999.

17. Carrie Culp Abramson, interview by Pamela Grundy, February 21, 1999; Barbara Ledford, interview by Jill Williams, July 17, 1999.

18. Haywood, interview.

19. Patricia Sutherland, interview by Pamela Grundy, December 6, 2000. A description of the caring spirit found in many segregated African American schools can be found in Vanessa Siddle Walker, *Their Highest Potential: An African American School Community in the Segregated South* (Chapel Hill: University of North Carolina Press, 1996).

20. McAllister, interview.

21. Abramson, interview.

22. White, interview.

23. Nelson and Spangler, interview.

24. Abramson, interview.

25. Anthony Foxx, interview by Pamela Grundy, November 11, 2012.

26. Arthur S. Hayes, "Against the Odds: As Others Scale Back on School Integration, Charlotte Presses On," *Wall Street Journal*, May 6, 1991, A1; Hamlin Jr., interview.

27. For a lengthy account of the court case, as well as contemporary discussions over busing, see Debbie Cenziper and Ted Mellnik, "Deciding Desegregation," *Charlotte Observer*, January 10–14, 1999. For changes at West Charlotte, see Celeste Smith, "Bringing Back Respect," *Charlotte*

Observer, October 1, 2000, 8A. For an account of the political dynamics from the perspective of white suburban residents, see Matthew Lassiter, *The Silent Majority: Suburban Politics in the Sunbelt South* (Princeton, NJ: Princeton University Press, 2006), 301–329.

28. For one perspective on what desegregation did and did not accomplish at a variety of schools nationwide, including West Charlotte, see Amy Wells, *Both Sides Now: The Story of School Desegregation's Graduates* (Berkeley: University of California Press, 2009). For an analysis of the distribution of economic growth, see Stephen Samuel Smith, *Boom for Whom?: Education, Desegregation, and Development in Charlotte* (Albany: State University of New York Press, 2004), 210–234.

29. Gaillard, *The Dream Long Deferred*, 155–171.

30. Margaret "Maggie" Ray, interview by Pamela Grundy, November 9, 2000.

31. Culp Jr., interview.

32. Hamlin Jr., interview.

33. Love Jr., interview.

Chapter 4

1. Judge Howard E. Manning Jr., *Report from the Court: The High School Problem*, North Carolina General Court of Justice, Superior Court Division, 95 CVS 1158: Hoke County Board of Education et al., Plaintiffs and Asheville City Board of Education et al., Plaintiff-Intervenors v. State of North Carolina; State Board of Education, Defendants, May 24, 2005, 23.

2. Ibid.

3. The following year, 2012–2013, North Carolina's EOC tests assessed students on the state's new curriculum (aligned with the newly adopted Common Core State Standards), and almost all CMS students' scores plummeted. In 2012–2013, only 17.6 percent of West Charlotte students scored proficient on a composite of the new Math I, English II, and Biology exams, and the school ranked at the bottom of all CMS regular high schools. *Charlotte Observer*, "Chart: 2013 CMS High School Scores," November 10, 2013, http://www.charlotteobserver.com/2013/11/10/4455378/chart-2013-cms-high-school-scores.html#.UoAAno3QFPE.

4. Chapter 3 provides a rich portrait of the social, emotional, and cultural climate at WCHS during this era. Here, we augment that portrait with quantitative indicators similar to the ones used by Judge Manning. In 1986–1987, black students constituted 47 percent of West Charlotte's enrollment. Although higher than most other schools, it was well within CMS's desegregation guidelines. West Charlotte's rate of absenteeism and in-school suspensions were the lowest of all high schools. It was tied with two other schools for having the second lowest drop-out rate; and its SAT scores, percent of students taking the SAT, percent planning to go to college, percent of students eligible for FRL, and percent in basic-level courses were in the middle of the pack. The Open Program was thriving, and students from all across Mecklenburg County competed in the lottery to gain a seat in it. See Ricki Morell and Frye Gaillard, "Our Schools: Pass or Fail, Not Bad, but Not Equal," *Charlotte Observer*, April 23, 1988. According to Bill Anderson, EdD, a former teacher (1977–1988), and later an assistant principal and principal at Myers Park High School, during the early 1980s WCHS and MPHS were very comparable in terms of academic performance, scholarship dollars earned for their respective graduating classes, and competitive sports teams. Today Anderson is the executive director of MeckEd, a local nonprofit organization that informs the local community about key issues in public education. Personal correspondence with Roslyn Arlin Mickelson, May 15, 2014.

5. Charlotte-Mecklenburg Schools, *Summary of CMS Student Enrollment Data: Percent African-American Attendance by School, 1978–79 through 1998–99*. Defendant's Exhibit 47, Capacchione v. Charlotte-Mecklenburg Schools, 57 F. Supp. 2d 228 (W.D.N.C. 1999).

6. Roslyn Arlin Mickelson, "International Business Machinations: A Critical Examination of Corporate Involvement in School Reform," *Teachers College Record* 100, no. 3 (1999): 476–512.

7. In 2012 WCHS had a 54 percent cohort graduation rate (calculations generally based on entering ninth graders who complete twelfth grade). Denise Watts, interview by Stephen Samuel Smith, January 9, 2014, Charlotte, NC. CMS's graduation rate was 76 percent. Also see Justin Lane, "An Analysis of Dropout Trends in Charlotte Mecklenburg Schools: 1996–2012" (unpublished MA thesis, Department of Sociology, University of North Carolina at Charlotte, 2014).

8. Richard McElrath, interview by Stephen Samuel Smith and Roslyn Arlin Mickelson, December 28, 2013, Charlotte, NC. McElrath served on CMS's school board from 2009 to 2013.

9. Bill and Melinda Gates Foundation, "CMS Unveils Groundbreaking Initiative to Transform Teaching and Learning in Achievement Zone Schools," http://www.gatesfoundation. org/Media-Center/Press-Releases/2008/03/CMS-Unveils-Groundbreaking-Initiative-to-Transform-Teaching-and-Learning-in-Achievement-Zone-Schools. In 2013 CMS reorganized into seven learning communities organized by high school feeder patterns. Six of them have several high schools and their feeder middle and elementary schools. The seventh learning community is the Project LIFT zone. Charlotte-Mecklenburg Schools, *Learning Communities*, http://www.cms.k12.nc.us/LearningCommunities/Pages/default.aspx.

10. Charlotte-Mecklenburg Schools, *Per Pupil Expenditures 2010/2011*, 2011.

11. Charlotte-Mecklenburg Schools, *Strategic Staffing: "The Moral Thing to Do,"* Charlotte-Mecklenburg Schools, December 2009.

12. Frederick M. Hess, *Spinning Wheels: The Politics of Urban School Reform* (Washington, DC: Brookings Institution Press, 1998). Hess maintains that much of the problem with urban school systems is actually the result of continuous or fragmentary reforms driven by the political incentives that motivate superintendents to promote reforms. In contrast to policy churn, Charles M. Payne argues that urban school reforms have failed in the past thirty years largely because of their disconnect from the lived experiences of those who live in poor neighborhoods and the persistent dysfunctional organizational environments of urban school systems (*So Much Reform, So Little Change: The Persistence of Failure in Urban Schools* [Cambridge, MA: Harvard Education Press, 2008]). David Tyack and Larry Cuban take a much broader historical perspective on school reform than Hess. They examine a century of efforts to perfect public education, noting that Americans have long believed that education is an essential tool for transforming society and that such utopian dreams require restructuring public education from time to time. Because reform movements make only incremental improvements, restructuring requires continued efforts (*Tinkering Toward Utopia: A Century of Public School Reform* [Cambridge, MA: Harvard University Press, 1995]).

13. Ann Doss Helms, "R.I.P. FOCUS Schools," *Charlotte Observer* "Your Schools" blog, March 22, 2012, http://obsyourschools.blogspot.com/2012/03/rip-focus-schools.html.

14. Charlotte-Mecklenburg Schools, "West Charlotte Graduates Receive Anthony Foxx Scholarship," May 28, 2010, http://www.cms.k12.nc.us/news/pages/westcharlottegraduatesreceive anthonyfoxxscholarship05292010.aspx.

15. Charlotte-Mecklenburg Schools, "High School Challenge: A Strategic Business Plan to Improve Targeted High Schools in Charlotte-Mecklenburg Schools," September 2004.

16. Professor Kenneth Godwin, personal email communication, December 21, 2013. Professor Godwin was slated to evaluate the High School Challenge but was unable to do so because of the problems noted.

17. Minutes of the Regular Meeting of the Charlotte-Mecklenburg Board of Education, May 8, 2007; Ann Doss Helms, "Teacher Exodus Outpaces Recruiting," *Charlotte Observer*, May 9, 2007.

18. Foundation for the Carolinas, "Foundation Launches Effort to Explore Role for Pursuing Community's Public Education Goals" (press release), September 1, 2010, http://www.fftc.org/document.doc?id=1059.

19. Anna Spangler Nelson, interview by Stephen Samuel Smith and Stephanie Southworth, July 9, 2014, Charlotte, NC. Anna Spangler Nelson is not related to Amy Hawn Nelson.

20. Charlotte Mecklenburg School Investment Study Group, *Project LIFT Leadership and Investment for Transformation: Project Summary*, January 2011, http://www.fftc.org/Page.aspx?pid=2404.

21. Project L.I.F.T., *Strategic Plan 2012*, www.projectliftcharlotte.org; Jaclyn Zubrzycki, "School Project Blurs Line Between Public, Private," *Education Week*, January 9, 2013, http://www.edweek.org/ew/articles/2013/01/09/17projectlift.h32.html.

22. Watts interview.

23. Research for Action, *Project LIFT: Preliminary Implementation Findings*, August 15, 2013; Charlotte Mecklenburg School Investment Study Group, *Project LIFT Leadership*.

24. Elizabeth Kolb Cunningham and Alisa Chapman, *Induction Support Program for New Teachers in High-Need Schools* (report to the University of North Carolina General Administration), 2014. Confidential interviews with educational professionals working in the Project LIFT Zone and with administrative supervisors working with the Induction Support Program provided additional data for this section.

25. Minutes of the Regular Meeting of the Charlotte-Mecklenburg Board of Education, May 28, 2013, p. 8.

26. Ruby Payne writes and consults widely about education and poverty. Her works, like her book *Bridges Out of Poverty: Strategies for Professionals and Communities* (New York: Aha Processes, Inc., 2001), have been criticized as modern versions of discredited "culture of poverty" arguments. See Jennifer Ng and John L. Rury, "Poverty and Education: A Critical Analysis of the Ruby Payne Phenomenon," *Teachers College Record*, July 18, 2006, http://www.tcrecord.org/content.asp?contentid=12596; Paul Gorski, "The Classist Underpinnings of Ruby Payne's Framework" *Teachers College Record*, February 09, 2006, http://www.tcrecord.org/content.asp?contentid=12322; Randy Bomer et al., "Miseducating Teachers About the Poor: A Critical Analysis of Ruby Payne's Claims about Poverty," *Teachers College Record* 110, no. 11 (2008).

27. Nelson, interview.

28. *North Carolina State Board of Education Policy Manual*, "Policy Defining Course for Credit," Policy ID # GCS-M001, December 2, 2010.

29. Watts, interview.

30. Christian Friend, interview by Stephen Samuel Smith, December 23, 2013, Charlotte, NC.

31. Ibid.

32. Watts, interview.

33. McElrath, interview.

Chapter 5

1. We are grateful to Maria Marta Laurito for research assistance and to the North Carolina Education Research Data Center for access to administrative data for North Carolina public schools.

2. Capacchione v. Charlotte-Mecklenburg Schools, 57 F. Supp. 2nd 228 (1999).

3. In this chapter, the term *white* implies "non-Hispanic white." While the Census Bureau records Hispanic ethnicity distinctly from race, North Carolina's public schools treat Hispanic as a racial identity.

4. For details of the data used and analytic procedures employed to calculate between- and within-school segregation in North Carolina and CMS, see appendixes 5.a and 5.b on the book's Web site.

5. Sean F. Reardon, "The Widening Academic Achievement Gap Between the Rich and the Poor: New Evidence and Possible Explanations," in *Whither Opportunity? Rising Inequality and the Uncertain Life Chances of Low-Income Children*, ed. Richard Murnane and Greg Duncan (New York: Russell Sage, 2011).

6. The National School Lunch Program offers the free lunch benefit to students whose family income is 130 percent or less of the poverty level.

7. For further analysis of school segregation in the state of North Carolina, see Charles T. Clotfelter, Helen F. Ladd, and Jacob L. Vigdor, "Segregation and Resegregation in North Carolina's Public School Classrooms," *North Carolina Law Review* 81, no. 4 (May 2003): 1463–1511; Charles T. Clotfelter, Helen F. Ladd, and Jacob L. Vigdor, "School Segregation Under Color-Blind Jurisprudence: The Case of North Carolina," *Virginia Journal of Social Policy & the Law* 16, no. 1 (Fall 2008): 46–86; and Charles T. Clotfelter, Helen F. Ladd, and Jacob L. Vigdor, "Racial and Economic Diversity in North Carolina's Schools: An Update" (working paper, Sanford School, Duke University, Durham, NC, January 2013).

8. It is interesting to note that, despite the fact that there were only one hundred charter schools in the entire state in 2012 (the legislature has since lifted the cap), the statewide patterns depicted here raise by a noticeable amount the overall level of white/nonwhite imbalance in the state's schools. To determine the effect of charter schools on imbalance in the state's public schools, we recalculated the statewide white/nonwhite imbalance without charter schools. (This imbalance index without charter schools can be thought of as the imbalance index that would be obtained if all charter school students were redistributed to a county's regular public schools in proportion to each school's existing number of whites and nonwhites.) This recalculation produced an index of 0.15, which is lower than the 0.16 obtained when charter schools were included, implying that charter schools increase segregation as measured by racial imbalance within counties.

9. For a discussion of these cases, see John Charles Boger, "Willful Colorblindness: The New Racial Piety and the Resegregation of Public Schools," *North Carolina Law Review* 78, no. 6 (1999–2000): 1719–1796; Sean F. Reardon et al., "*Brown* Fades: The End of Court-Ordered School Desegregation and the Resegregation of American Public Schools," *Journal of Policy Analysis and Management* 31, no. 4 (Fall 2012): 876–904.

Chapter 6

1. Jack Michael McElreath, "The Cost of Opportunity: School Desegregation and Changing Race Relations in the Triangle Since World War II" (PhD thesis, University of Pennsylvania, 2002), 331.

2. Green v. County School Board, 391 U.S. 430 (1968); Alexander v. Holmes County Board of Education, 396 U.S. 1218 (1969).

3. Rob Christensen, "City, County Boards Trade School Bond Issue Views," *News & Observer*, July 23, 1973.

4. McElreath, "Cost of Opportunity," 402–416.

5. Matthew Lassiter, *The Silent Majority: Suburban Politics in the Sunbelt South* (Princeton, NJ: Princeton University Press, 2006), 296.

6. McElreath, " Cost of Opportunity," 338.

7. Ibid., 427–429.

8. Ibid., 439–441.

9. Linda Williams, "House OKs Merger Plan," *News & Observer*, June 7, 1975.

10. See Steve Berg, "Twiggs Vows to Bring School Boards Together," *News & Observer*, February 27, 1973, WA1; Williams, "House OKs Merger Plan."

11. Murphy served as the superintendent of CMS from 1990 to 1996. In 1997 he testified on behalf of the white plaintiff-intervenors in Capacchione v. Charlotte-Mecklenburg Schools (57 F. Supp. 2d, 228. 242 [W.D.N.C 1999]), who sought unitary status and the end of any race-conscious policies in the district.

12. Todd Silberman, *Wake County Schools: A Question of Balance* (unpublished monograph sponsored by the Spencer Foundation, Raleigh, NC).

13. John Murphy, "Magnet School Proposal, Exhibit A," minutes from Wake County Public School System Board Meeting, March 20, 1978, 255.

14. See Susan Leigh Flinspach and Karen E. Banks, "Moving Beyond Race: Socioeconomic Diversity as a Race-Neutral Approach to Desegregation in the Wake County Schools," in *School Resegregation: Must the South Turn Back?*, ed. John Charles Boger and Gary Orfield (Chapel Hill: University of North Carolina Press, 2005), 266–269, for more on this decision. See North Carolina Department of Public Instruction, SS100.Wake1.xls, as of September 26, 2007, for data on minority enrollment.

15. Todd Silberman, "Schools Facing Diversity Dilemma," *News & Observer*, December 26, 1999.

16. The Wake Education Partnership assessments are done every two years. The 2000 report is not available online and was obtained directly from the organization; Wake Education Partnership, *2000 Wake Public Education Community Assessment* (Raleigh: Wake Education Partnership, 2000).

17. Two cases were particularly important: Eisenberg v. Montgomery County Public Schools 197 F.3d 123 (4th Cir. 1999) and Tuttle v. Arlington County Schools 195 F.3d 698 (4th Cir. 1999). See also John Charles Boger and Elizabeth Jean Bower, "The Future of Educational Diversity: Old Decrees, New Challenges," Popular Government 66, no. 2 (2001): 2–16, http://sogpubs.unc.edu//electronicversions/pg/pgwin01/article1.pdf?.

18. Todd Silberman, "Schools Plan Adopted," *News & Observer*, January 11, 2000.

19. Eric A. Houck and Sheneka M. Williams, "'To Turn Back Would Be a Huge Mistake': Race, Class, and Student Assignment in Wake County Public Schools" (paper presented at the annual meeting of the American Education Research Association, Denver, CO, April 2010).

20. Wake County Public School System, *Measuring Up*, by the Evaluation and Research Department (Raleigh: Evaluation and Research Department of the Wake County Public School System, 2003).

21. T. Keung Hui, "Parents, Students Seek Changes in Plan," *News & Observer*, January 6, 2009.

22. Caroline M. Hoxby and Gretchen Weingarth, "Taking Race Out of the Equation: School Reassignments and the Structure of Peer Effects" (unpublished manuscript, Harvard University, 2006).

23. Keith Jordan, "Parents Challenge Reassignment Proposals," *News & Observer*, March 30, 1995.

24. Earl Black and Merle Black, *Rise of the Southern Republicans* (Cambridge, MA: Harvard University Press, 2003), 210–222; Thomas Byrne Edsall and Mary D. Edsall, *Chain Reaction* (New York: W. W. Norton & Co., 1991), 74–98; Matthew Lassiter, *The Silent Majority: Suburban Politics in the Sunbelt South* (Princeton, NJ: Princeton University Press, 2006), 225–241; Richard K. Scher, *Politics in the New South: Republicanism, Race and Leadership in the Twentieth Century, 2nd edition* (New York: M.E. Sharpe, 1997), 101–106.

25. Rob Christensen, *The Paradox of Tar Heel Politics: The Personalities, Elections, and Events That Shaped Modern North Carolina* (Chapel Hill: University of North Carolina Press, 2008), 227–234.

26. Byron Shafer and Richard Johnston, *The End of Southern Exceptionalism: Class, Race, and Partisan Change in the Postwar South* (Cambridge, MA: Harvard University Press, 2006).

27. T. Keung Hui, "Wake Voters Say Yes: Build More Schools," *News & Observer*, November 8, 2006.

28. Melissa M. Deckman, *School Board Battles: The Christian Right in Local Politics* (Washington, DC: Georgetown University Press, 2004), 10–30.

29. Arnold Shober, *The Democratic Dilemma of American Education: Out of Many, One?* (Boulder, CO: Westview Press, 2012).

30. Theda Skocpol and Vanessa Williamson, *The Tea Party and the Remaking of Republican Conservatism* (Oxford: Oxford University Press, 2012); Kate Zernicke, *Boiling Mad: Inside Tea Party America* (New York: Times Press, 2010).

31. See John Brehm and Wendy Rahn, "Individual Level Evidence for the Causes and Consequences of Social Capital," *American Journal of Political Science* 41, no. 3 (1997): 888–1023, http://www.jstor.org/stable/pdfplus/2111684.pdf?&acceptTC=true&jpdConfirm=true; Rodney Hero, *Racial Diversity and Social Capital* (New York: Cambridge University Press, 2007); Robert D. Putnam, *Bowling Alone: The Collapse and Revival of American Community* (New York: Simon and Schuster, 2000).

32. Population Studies Center, *Racial Residential Segregation Measurement Project: Year 1990 Index of Dissimilarity* (Ann Arbor: University of Michigan, 2014).

33. See chapter 2; Gerald Grant, *Hope and Despair in the American City: Why There Are No Bad Schools in Raleigh* (Cambridge, MA: Harvard University Press, 2009); Richard D. Kahlenberg, *All Together Now: Creating Middle-Class Schools Through Public School Choice* (Washington, DC: The Brookings Institution, 2001).

34. Roslyn Arlin Mickelson, "Subverting *Swann*: First-and Second-Generation Segregation in the Charlotte-Mecklenburg Schools," *American Educational Research Journal* 38, no. 2 (2001): 215–252, http://aer.sagepub.com/content/38/2/215.full.pdf+html.

35. Silberman, *Wake County Schools*.

36. John Portz, Lana Stein, and Robin R. Jones, *City Schools and City Politics: Institutions and Leadership in Pittsburgh, Boston, and St. Louis* (Lawrence: University of Kansas Press, 1999).

37. See chapter 2.

38. William S. Koski and Jeannie Oakes, "Equal Educational Opportunity, School Reform, and the Courts: A Study of the Desegregation Litigation in San Jose," in *From the Courtroom to the Classroom: The Shifting Landscape of School Desegregation,* ed. Claire E. Smrekar and Ellen B. Goldring (Cambridge, MA: Harvard Education Press, 2009), 71–102; Toby Parcel and Andrew Taylor, *The End of Consensus: Diversity, Community, and the Politics of Assigning Children to Wake County Public Schools* (Chapel Hill: University of North Carolina Press, forthcoming 2015); Claire Smrekar, "Beyond the Tipping Point: Issues of Racial Diversity in Magnet Schools Following Unitary Status," *Peabody Journal of Education: Issues of Leadership, Policy, and Organizations* 84, no. 2 (2013): 209–226, http://www.tandfonline.com/doi/pdf/10.1080/01619560902810153; Claire E. Smrekar and Ellen B. Goldring, ed., *From the Courtroom to the Classroom: The Shifting Landscape of School Desegregation* (Cambridge, MA: Harvard Education Press, 2009).

39. Stephen S. Smith, *Boom for Whom?: Education, Desegregation, and Development in Charlotte* (Albany: State University of New York Press, 2004).

40. The only federal court case affecting the desegregation of Wake schools was Holt v. City of Raleigh Schools 265 F.2d 95 (4th Cir. 1959) in which circuit and district courts upheld an administrative promulgation denying an African American high school student a transfer to an all-white school. The decision was narrowly drawn and effectively technical. A 2004 report by the U.S. Department of Education's Office for Civil Rights notes that Wake County

was under a "court-ordered desegregation plan until the district achieved unitary status in 1982" (http://www2.ed.gov/about/offices/list/ocr/edlite-raceneutralreport2.html). This is incorrect. There was no order and Wake County has therefore never been eligible to achieve unitary status; United States Department of Education Office for Civil Rights, *Achieving Diversity: Race-Neutral Alternatives in American Education* (Washington DC: U.S. Department of Education, Office for Civil Rights, 2004).

41. Silberman, *Wake County Schools.*

42. As Smith describes in chapter 2, the Charlotte black community has long mobilized to support desegregation, although as of this writing there is some debate in Charlotte's black community about the value of desegregation for educational improvement given CMS's recent track record among black students. The discussion of Project LIFT in chapter 4 further illustrates this tension in the black community.

43. Wendy M. Rahn and Thomas J. Rudolph, "A Tale of Political Trust in American Cities," *Public Opinion Quarterly* 69, no. 4 (2005): 530–560, http://poq.oxfordjournals.org/content/69/4/530.full.pdf+html.

Chapter 7

1. Parents Involved in Community Schools v. Seattle School District No. 1 et al., 551 U.S. 701 (PICS; 2007).

2. *Seattle, supra* at 735 quoting J. Kennedy, Freeman v. Pitts, 503 U.S. 495 (1992).

3. Freeman, supra at 495.

4. Charles H. Clotfelter, *After Brown: The Rise and Retreat of School Desegregation* (Princeton, NJ: Princeton University Press, 2004).

5. Clotfelter's descriptive findings are consistent with causal research examining housing prices along district boundaries (see Leah Platt Boustan, "School Desegregation and Urban Change: Evidence from City Boundaries," *American Economic Journal: Applied Economics* 4, no.1 [2012]: 85–108; Thomas J. Kane, Stephanie K. Riegg, and Douglas O. Staiger, "School Quality, Neighborhoods, and Housing Prices," *American Law and Economics Review* 8, no. 2 [2006]: 183–212; William T. Bogart and Brian A. Cromwell, "How Much Is a Neighborhood School Worth?" *Journal of Urban Economics* 47, no. 2 [2000]: 280–305); mechanisms of segregation and "white flight" (see Nathaniel Baum-Snow and Byron Lutz, "School Desegregation, School Choice and Changes in Residential Location Patterns by Race," *American Economic Review*, 101, no. 7 [2011]: 3019–3046); and district coverage of metropolitan areas (see Sarah Reber, "Court-Ordered Desegregation: Successes and Failures in Integrating American Schools since *Brown,*" *Journal of Human Resources* 40, no. 3 [2005]: 559–590).

6. See technical appendix 7.a on the book's Web site for details of how the index is calculated.

7. Ann Doss Helms, Ted Melnik, and Celeste Smith, "Historic Day Dawns in CMS Classrooms; with Monday's Opening Bell, Schools Face New Challenges," *Charlotte Observer*, August 18, 2002.

8. Roslyn Arlin Mickelson, Stephen Samuel Smith, and Stephanie Southworth, "Resegregation, Achievement, and the Chimera of Choice in Post-Unitary Charlotte-Mecklenburg Schools," in *From the Courtroom to the Classroom: The Shifting Landscape of School Desegregation*, ed. Claire E. Smrekar and Ellen B. Goldring (Cambridge, MA: Harvard Education Press, 2009), 129–156.

9. Ibid; Roslyn Arlin Mickelson, "The Academic Consequences of Desegregation and Segregation: Evidence from the Charlotte-Mecklenburg Schools," *North Carolina Law Review* 81, no. 4 (2003): 1513–1562; C. Kirabo Jackson, "Student Demographics, Teacher Sorting, and Teacher Quality: Evidence from the End of School Desegregation," *Journal of Labor Economics* 27, no. 2 (2009): 213–256.

10. Justine S. Hastings, Thomas J. Kane, and Douglas O. Staiger, "Preferences and Heterogeneous Treatment Effects in a Public School Choice Lottery" (working paper, National Bureau of Economic Research working paper No. 12145, 2009).

11. Jacob L. Vigdor, "School Desegregation and the Black-White Test Score Gap," in *Whither Opportunity? Rising Inequality, Schools, and Children's Life Chances*, ed. Greg J. Duncan and Richard J. Murnane (New York: Russell Sage Foundation, 2011), 443–464; Stephen B. Billings, David J. Deming, and Jonah Rockoff, "School Segregation, Educational Attainment and Crime: Evidence from the End of Busing in Charlotte-Mecklenburg," *Quarterly Journal of Economics* 129, no. 1 (2014): 435–476; Chuang Wang, "Impacts of School Racial Composition on the Mathematics and Reading Achievement Gap in Post-Unitary Charlotte-Mecklenburg Schools" (working paper, 2013).

12. Census 2000 Demographic Profile Highlights for Selected Population Groups in Mecklenburg County, NC. Retrieved from www.factfinder.census.gov.

13. Figure 7.a on the book's Web site presents the residential segregation index for CMS white and nonwhite families with elementary school students by year for 2000–2007.

14. See technical appendix 7.a at the book's Web site for details of our analyses.

15. Martin Carnoy and Susanna Loeb, "Does External Accountability Affect Student Outcomes? A Cross-State Analysis," *Education Evaluation and Policy Analysis* 24, no. 4 (2003): 305–331. Additionally, because of the provisions of North Carolina's "ABCs of Public Education" law, CMS had been publishing school-by-school performance disaggregated by student race for years prior to NCLB.

16. Douglas L. Lauen and S. Michael Gaddis, "Shining a Light or Fumbling in the Dark? The Effects of NCLB's Subgroup-Specific Accountability on Student Achievement Gains," *Educational Evaluation and Policy Analysis* 34, no. 2 (2012): 185–208.

17. Jeffrey Weinstein, "The Impact of School Composition on Neighborhood Racial Compositions: Evidence from School Redistricting" (working paper, Maxwell School of Citizenship and Public Affairs, Syracuse University, 2013).

18. Brown v. Board of Education, 347 U.S. 483 (1954).

Chapter 8

1. Charlotte-Mecklenburg Schools, "North Carolina Title III Application" (2013), available upon request from CMS ESL Services, Charlotte-Mecklenburg Schools.

2. Jerry Ingalls and Gary R. Rassel, "Political Fragmentation, Municipal Incorporation and Annexation in a High Growth Urban Area," *The North Carolina Geographer* 13, no. 1 (2005): 17–30.

3. John Rennie Short and Yeong-Hyun Kim, *Globalization and the City* (Upper Saddle River, NJ: Prentice Hall, 1999); Heather A. Smith and William Graves, "From Mill Town to Financial Capital: Charlotte's Global Evolution," in *Charlotte, NC: The Global Evolution of a New South City*, ed. William Graves and Heather A. Smith (Athens: University of Georgia Press, 2010), 1–9.

4. Department of Commerce, U.S. Bureau of the Census, 1990, 2000, and 2010 Decennial Census, and 2010 American Community Survey, retrieved from American FactFinder, http://factfinder2.census.gov.

5. To be consistent with other chapters in this volume we use the label *Latino* when referring to students of Latin American descent. Roberto Suro and Audrey Singer, *Latino Growth in Metropolitan America: Changing Patterns, New Locations* (Washington, DC: Brookings Institution Center on Urban and Metropolitan Policy, 2002); Audrey Singer, "Twenty-First Century Gateways: An Introduction," in *Twenty-First Century Gateways: Immigrant Incorporation in Subur-*

ban America, ed. Audrey Singer, Susan W. Hardwick, and Caroline B. Brettell (Washington, DC: Brookings Institution Press, 2004), 3–30.

6. Heather A. Smith and Owen J. Furuseth. "The 'Nuevo South': Latino Place Making and Community Building in the Middle Ring Suburbs of Charlotte," in Singer, Hardwick, and Brettell, *Twenty-First Century Gateways*, 281–307.

7. Heather A. Smith and Owen J. Furuseth, "Making Real the Mythical Latino Community in Charlotte, North Carolina," in *Latinos in the New South: Transformations of Place*, ed. Heather A. Smith and Owen J. Furuseth, (Burlington, VT: Ashgate Publishing, 2006), 191–216.

8. Ruben G. Rumbaut, "Assimilation and Its Discontents: Between Rhetoric and Reality," *International Migration Review* 31, no. 4 (1997): 923–960; Richard Alba and Victor Nee, "Rethinking Assimilation Theory for a New Era of Immigration," *International Migration Review* 31, no. 4 (1997): 826–874.

9. Suro and Singer, "Latino Growth"; Singer, "Twenty-First Century Gateways"; Smith and Furuseth, "The 'Nuevo South'"; Smith and Furuseth, "Making Real."

10. Tom Hanchett, "Salad-Bowl Suburbs: A History of Charlotte's East Side and South Boulevard Immigrant Corridors," in Graves and Smith, *Charlotte, NC*, 247–262.

11. U.S. Department of Education, National Center for Education Statistics, Common Core of Data (CCD), "Public Elementary/Secondary School Universe Survey," http://nces.ed.gov/ccd/elsi/.

12. Table 8.a on the book's Web site presents the twenty-five CMS schools with the highest percentages of Latino students for the 2008–2009 academic year.

13. Figure 8.a on the book's Web site is a map of Mecklenburg County displaying the ten schools most affected by increases in Charlotte's foreign-born population. It highlights in grey census tracts with Latino populations greater than 25 percent.

14. Table 8.b on the book's Web site presents the diversity among the LEP and ESL student population. Paul N. McDaniel, *Receptivity in a New Immigrant Gateway: Immigrant Settlement Geography, Public Education, and Immigrant Integration in Charlotte, North Carolina* (PhD dissertation, University of North Carolina at Charlotte, 2013).

15. Charlotte-Mecklenburg Schools, "North Carolina Title III Application."

16. See, for example, Swann v. Charlotte-Mecklenburg Board of Education (1971), which distinguished between blacks and nonblacks, lumping together whites and all other race/ethnic groups.

17. Title III—Language Instruction for Limited English Proficient and Immigrant Students," 2001, http://www2.ed.gov/policy/elsec/leg/esea02/pg39.html.

18. Angela Valenzuela, *Leaving Children Behind: How "Texas-Style" Accountability Fails Latino Youth* (Albany: State University of New York Press, 2005).

19. Laurie Olsen, *Made in America* (New York: The New Press, 1997).

20. Ibid.

21. Guadalupe Valdés, *Learning and Not Learning English: Latino Students in American Schools* (New York: Teachers College Press, 2001); Patricia Gándara and Russell Rumberger, "Immigration, Language, and Education: How Does Language Policy Structure Opportunity?" Teachers College Record 111, no. 3 (2009): 750–782.

22. James Crawford, "No Child Left Behind: Misguided Approach to School Accountability," in *Advocating for English Learners: Selected Essays*, ed. James Crawford (Clevedon, UK: Multilingual Matters, 2008), 128–138.

23. Ibid.

24. Jamal Abedi, "The No Child Left Behind Act and English Language Learners: Assessment and Accountability Issues," *Educational Researcher* 33, no. 1 (2004): 4–14.

25. Crawford, "No Child Left Behind."

26. James Cummins, "Cognitive/Academic Language Proficiency, Linguistic Interdependence, the Optimal Age Question and Some Other Matters," *Working Papers on Bilingualism* 19 (1979): 121–129.

27. North Carolina Department of Instruction, "NC Race to the Top," http://www.dpi.state.nc.us/rttt/lea-charter/plans?region=6.

28. Linda Darling-Hammond, *The Flat World and Education: How America's Commitment to Equity Will Determine Our Future* (New York: Teachers College Press, 2010).

29. The procedures for identifying and serving English language learners are found in part on the CMS Web site and in their entirety within the district's federal Title III application. Charlotte-Mecklenburg Schools, "North Carolina Title III Application"; Charlotte-Mecklenburg Schools, "Student Placement Enrollment Information," http://www.cms.k12.nc.us/cmsdepartments/StudentPlacement/Documents/2013-14%20Enrollment%20Packet%2 (English).pdf.

30. Ibid.

31. Abedi, "The No Child Left Behind Act."

32. WIDA, *Consortium Members,* 2014, http://wida.us/membership/states/.

33. Charlotte-Mecklenburg Schools, "North Carolina Title III Application."

34. North Carolina Department of Public Instruction, "Testing Policy and Procedure Information for First-Year LEP Students," http://www.ncpublicschools.org/docs/accountability/policyoperations/lep/lepfirstyrstudents11.pdf; North Carolina Department of Public Instruction, "North Carolina Procedures for the Identification of Limited English Proficient Students," http://wida.us/membership/states/NC/LEP_ID_Guidance_May2011.pdf.

35. Abedi, "The No Child Left Behind Act."

36. Jamal Abedi, "Classification System for English Learners: Issues and Recommendations," *Educational Measurement: Issues and Practices* 27, no. 3 (2008): 17–31.

37. Ibid.; Crawford, "No Child Left Behind."

38. Charlotte-Mecklenburg Schools ESL wiki, "LIEP Guidance on ESL Services," http://esl.cmswiki.wikispaces.net/file/view/LIEP%20Continuum%20of%20Services%20Rubric-%20Elem-Secondary.pdf/442768660/LIEP%20Continuum%20of%20Services%20Rubric-%20Elem-Secondary.pdf.

39. Charlotte-Mecklenburg Schools, "North Carolina Title III Application."

40. Charlotte-Mecklenburg Schools, "LIEP."

41. WIDA, WIDA ACCESS for ELLs, Developed by CAL, 2014, http://www.wida.us/assessment/ACCESS/#admin.

42. Abedi, "Classification System."

43. Ibid.

44. Charlotte-Mecklenburg Schools. "North Carolina Title III Application"; Jenelle Reeves, "'Like Everybody Else': Equalizing Educational Opportunity for English Language Learners," *TESOL Quarterly* 38, no. 1 (2004): 43–66.

45. Margarita Calderon, Robert Slavin, and Marta Sanchez, "Effective Instruction for English Learners," *The Future of Children* 21, no. 1 (2011): 103–127; Virginia P. Collier and Wayne P. Thomas, "Education Policies for English Learners Means Better Schools for All," *The State Education Standard* (Winter 2002): 31–36.

46. Ibid.

47. Tina L. Heafner and Michelle Plaisance, "Social Studies for Whom? A Qualitative Analysis of Curricular Access for ELLs" (paper presented at the American Educational Research Association Annual Meeting, San Francisco, CA, April 2013).

48. Charlotte-Mecklenburg Schools, "Middle School ESL Programs," http://esl.cmswiki. wikispaces.net/Middle+School+ESL+Programs; also see Jana Echievarria, Deborah Short, and Carla Peterson, *Using the SIOP®Model with Pre-K and Kindergarten English Learners* (New York: Pearson, 2012).

49. Charlotte-Mecklenburg Schools, "LIEP"; Heafner and Plaisance, "Social Studies."

50. Ibid.

51. Maria Dove and Andrea Honingsfeld, "ESL Coteaching and Collaboration: Opportunities to Develop Teacher Leadership and Enhance Student Learning," *TESOL Journal* 1, no. 1 (2010): 3–22.

52. Charlotte-Mecklenburg Board of Education, "Proposed Budget Recommendations," http:// www.cms.k12.nc.us/mediaroom/budget/201314%20Budget%20Information/201314%20 Proposed%20Budget%20Recommendation%20Budget%20Book.pdf.

53. Reeves, "Like Everybody Else."

54. North Carolina State Board of Education, "Policies on General Licensure Requirement," http://sbepolicy.dpi.state.nc.us/Policies/TCP-A-001.asp?pri=&cat=A&pol=001&acr=TCP.

55. Ibid.

56. Spencer Salas, Bernadette Musetti, and Michelle Plaisance, "Latino Transnationals (Not) in Advanced Academics: Asking Hard Questions Together," in *Talent Development for English Language Learners in Inclusive Settings*, ed. Michael Matthews and Jaime Castellano (Waco, TX: Prufrock PressShort, 2014), 87–100.

57. Ibid.; Charlotte-Mecklenburg Schools, "Middle School."

58. Charlotte-Mecklenburg Schools, "LIEP"; Ayana Allen, Abiola Farinde, and Chance Lewis, "The Landscape of Advanced Classes in CMS," http://plancharlotte.org/story/cms-high-school-ap-minority.

59. Center for Education Policy Research, *Teacher Employment Patterns and Student Results in Charlotte-Mecklenburg Schools*, Harvard University, 2010, http://www.gse.harvard.edu/~pfpie/ pdf/ Teacher_Employment_Patterns_and_Student_Results_in_CMS_Feb_23_2010.pdf.

60. Olsen, *Made in America*; Valdés, *Learning and Not Learning English.*

61. Charlotte-Mecklenburg Schools, "22 Task Force Recommendations for the Superintendent," http://www.cms.k12.nc.us/mediaroom/taskforce/Documents/22_Task_Force_Recommendations%20online%203.pdf.

62. Ibid.

63. Pedro R. Portes and Spencer Salas, "In the Shadow of Stone Mountain: Identity Development, Structured Inequality, and the Education of Spanish-Speaking Children," *Bilingual Research Journal: The Journal of the National Association for Bilingual Education* 33, no. 2 (2010): 241–248.

64. Virginia Collier and Wayne Thomas, "What Really Works for English Language Learners: Research-Based Practices for Principals," in *What Every Principal Needs to Know to Create Equitable and Excellent Schools*, ed. George Theoharis and Jeffrey Brooks (New York: Teachers College Press, 2012, 155–173.

65. Ibid., 244.

66. The Levine Museum of the New South's 2009 exhibit about Charlotte's changing demographics was entitled "Changing Places: From Black and White to Technicolor"; see http:// www.museumofthenewsouth.org/exhibits/detail/?ExhibitId=94.

Chapter 9

1. Curtis Sittenfield, "2 Principals to Be Suspended, State Teams on Way to Schools," *Charlotte Observer*, August 8, 1997.

2. See table 9.a on the book's Web site for a history of Shamrock Gardens' school improvement status from 2000 to 2012.

3. Ann Doss Helms, "20 CMS Magnet Schools Honored," *Charlotte Observer*, February 21, 2013.

4. See tables 9.b and 9.c on the book's Web site for details of Shamrock Gardens' academic performance from 2000 to 2012. Note that this longitudinal comparison is somewhat problematic because since 2011 the tests have become more rigorous than those used from 1998 through 2010.

5. "Shamrock Gardens Plaza Midwood Neighborhood Association," http://www.plazamidwood.org/shamrock.

6. Jason Koebler, "Charlotte-Mecklenbrug School District Wins Prestigious Broad Prize," *U.S. News and World Report*, September 20, 2011.

7. Jason C. Snipes, Fred Doolittle, and Corinne Herlihy, *Foundations for Success: Case Studies of How Urban School Systems Improve Student Achievement* (Washington, DC: Council of the Great City Schools, 2002); Pamela Derringer, "Charlotte-Mecklenburg's Roller-Coaster Ride to Prominence," *Scholastic Administrator* (Fall 2011).

8. Roslyn Mickelson, "The Academic Consequences of Desegregation and Segregation: Evidence from the Charlotte-Mecklenburg Schools," *North Carolina Law Review* 81, no. 4 (2003): 120–165.

9. Summary of CMS Student Enrollment Data, Capacchione v. Charlotte-Mecklenburg Schools, Defendant's Exhibit 47, 1998–1999. Figure 10.a on the book's Web site presents fluctuations in percent black in Shamrock Gardens and CMS from 1979 through1999.

10. Figure 9.b on the book's Web site compares Shamrock Gardens' proficiency levels and percent free or reduced lunch with nine other CMS Title I schools with similar demographic profiles in 2010–2011.

11. Peter Smolowitz, "If It Were Your Child, Would You Risk It?" *Charlotte Observer*, August 20, 2006.

12. City of Charlotte, "CMS Students Attending Neighborhood Schools," *Quality of Life Dashboard*, http://maps.co.mecklenburg.nc.us/qoldashboard/?npa=378&variable=k13.

13. This provision ended for all NC families, regardless of the school's performance, starting in 2013–2014. http://www.dpi.state.nc.us/newsroom/news/2011-12/20120530-01.

14. Because interviewees were assured that their interviews would be confidential, they have been assigned a pseudonym. Table 10.d on the book's Web site presents pseudonyms and descriptions of respondents by individual demographics, years of school involvement, and connection to Shamrock Gardens Elementary School.

15. See table 9.a on the book's Web site for details.

16. Peter Smolowitz, "Elementary's Troubles Trace Back to '80s," *Charlotte Observer*, August 21, 2006.

17. Ann Doss Helms, "CMS Grants 11 Principals New Freedom," *Charlotte Observer*, March 31, 2009.

18. Charlotte-Mecklenburg Schools, "Teacher Incentive Fund—Leadership for Educators' Advanced Performance," http://www.cms.k12.nc.us/cms departments/tif-leap/Pages/default.aspx

19. Charlotte-Mecklenburg Schools, "Per Pupil Expenditure Report 10–11," *School Progress Reports*, http://www.cms.k12.nc.us/cmsdepartments/accountability/spr/Pages/documents.aspx.

20. North Carolina Department of Public Instruction, "Average Class Size," *NC School Report Cards*, http://www.ncschoolreportcard.org/src/schDetails.jsp?pSchCode=527&pLEACode=600&pYear=2008-2009.

21. Table 9.e on the book's Web site presents teacher turnover rates at Shamrock Gardens and comparison elementary schools.

22. Helms, "Shamrock Gardens Blooms with Its Kids," *Charlotte Observer*, June 7, 2012.

23. North Carolina Department of Public Instruction, "Grade, Race, Sex," *Financial and Business Services*, http://www.dpi.state.nc.us/fbs/accounting/data/.

24. See http://seenfromtherock.blogspot.com/.

25. Coalition for Evidence-Based Policy, "Randomized Controlled Trials Commissioned by the Institute of Education Sciences Since 2002: How Many Found Positive Versus Weak or No Effects," http://coalition4evidence.org/wp-content/uploads/2013/06/IES-Commissioned-RCTs-positive-vs-weak-or-null-findings-7-2013.pdf.

26. National Center for Education Statistics, "The Condition of Education 2013," http://nces.ed.gov/pubs2013/2013037.pdf.

Chapter 10

1. Parents Involved in Community Schools v. Seattle School District No. *1* 551 U.S. 701 (2007); U.S. Dept. of Justice, U.S. Dept. of Education, "Guidance on the Voluntary Use of Race to Achieve Diversity and Avoid Racial Isolation in Elementary and Secondary Schools, http://www2.ed.gov/about/offices/list/ocr/docs/guidance-ese-201111.pdf.

2. For an example of this type of effort, see chapter 4's description and analysis of Project LIFT at West Charlotte High School.

3. Brown v. Board of Education 347 U.S. 483 (1954); Swann v. Charlotte-Mecklenburg Board of Education 402 U.S. 1 (1971).

4. *Swann* at 15.

5. *Swann* at 30. One seldom-appreciated aspect of the busing order is that CMS had been using busing to promote segregation, with white students taking long rides to avoid attending schools with black students.

6. Capacchione v. Charlotte-Mecklenburg Schools, 57 F.Supp. 2d 228 (W.D.N.C. 1999).

7. The judge later permitted two new black families to join the lawsuit as substitute plaintiffs, and the case was then renamed Belk v. Charlotte-Mecklenburg Bd. of Educ., 269 F.3d. 305 (4th Cir. 2001). Author Luke Largess was one of the attorneys representing the black plaintiffs in the reopened *Swann* litigation.

8. Board of Education of Oklahoma City v. Dowell 498 U.S. 237 (1991); Freeman v. Pitts 503 U.S. 467 (1992).

9. In chapter 7 Liebowitz and Page demonstrate that "white flight" can be indirectly linked to school board actions.

10. *Capacchione*, 57 F.Supp. 2d 228.

11. *Belk*, 269 F.3d. 305.

12. Laura Simmons and Claire Apaliski, "Mapping de facto Segregation in Charlotte-Mecklenburg," UNC Charlotte Urban Institute, September 23, 2010, http://ui.uncc.edu/story/mapping-de-facto-segregation-charlotte-mecklenburg-schools.

13. Leandro v. State (Leandro I), 346 N.C. 336, 342-43 (1997).

14. Leandro v. North Carolina, 122 N.C. App. 1, 11 (1996).

15. *Leandro I*, at 345 (emphasis added).

16. Ibid. at 347.

17. Ibid. at 349.

18. Justice Orr dissented from this part of the opinion, calling the endorsement of local funding a "cruel illusion," arguing that the constitutional language requiring "equal opportunities" must

account for funding disparities among districts. "To conclude otherwise would create arbitrary boundaries on educational opportunities based on geographical lines and local funding circumstances." *Leandro I*, at 362–363 (J. Orr, dissenting in part and concurring in part).

19. Memorandum of Decision, Hoke County v. State, Section I, pp. 189–191 (October 12, 2000).

20. Memorandum of Decision, Hoke County v. State, Section II, p. 42 (October 26, 2000).

21. Memorandum of Decision, Hoke County v. State, Section III, p. 79 (March 26, 2001).

22. Hoke County Bd. of Educ. v. State (Leandro II), 358 N.C. 605, 636 (2004) (quoting Memorandum of Decision, Hoke County v. State, Section IV, p. 111 (April 4, 2002).

23. Ibid. at 623–630.

24. Ibid. at 638.

25. Ibid. at 645. PreK was not the primary focus of the original litigation or *Leandro I* or *Leandro II*, but emerged as the centerpiece of the most recent *Leandro* ligation. In 2012, the court of appeals upheld a decision prohibiting the state from implementing portions of the budget that imposed substantial limitations on at-risk children seeking access to the state preK program developed after *Leandro II*. Hoke County Bd. of Educ. v. State, N.C. App., 731 S.E2d 691 (2012). The state appealed the decision to the state supreme court, which sidestepped the substantive issues of access or scope of the preK program. Although the program serves only a portion of eligible at-risk children, and was offered by the state as part of the remedy for its constitutional infirmities, because the legislation had been partially amended in the interim to remove some of the restrictions, the court dismissed the appeal as moot. Hoke County Bd. of Educ. v. State, 5PA-12, N.C., 2013 N.C. Lexis 1360 (2013).

26. Ibid. at 636–637.

27. Ibid. at 632, 640.

28. *Leandro II*, at 638. "The Court now remands to the lower court, and ultimately into the hands of the legislative and executive branches, one more installment in the 200-plus year effort to provide an education to the children of North Carolina." *Id.*, at 649.

29. See, for example, *Governor's Executive Order* (July 20, 2005); Greg Malhoit, "The Response to *Leandro* from the Legislative and Executive Branches: Full of Sound and Fury, Signifying Nothing or Real and Meaningful Change for Students?" in *The Leandro Case, What Does It Mean for N.C.'s Children?* (Cary: North Carolina Bar Association Foundation, 2006).

30. Order, Hoke County v. State, November 10, 2004 (reviewing composite data from DPI and funding needs of school districts); Order, Hoke County v. State, March 3, 2005 (reviewing the high school problem); Order, Hoke County v. State, July 11, 2005 (reviewing CMS composite data and calling a hearing on the district's *Leandro* compliance).

31. Judge Howard E. Manning, *Report from the Court: The High School Problem*, North Carolina General Court of Justice, Superior Court Division, 95 CVS 1158: Hoke County Board of Education et al., Plaintiffs and Asheville City Board of Education et al., Plaintiff-Intervenors v. State of North Carolina; State Board of Education, Defendants, May 24, 2005.

32. Ibid. at 6.

33. Ibid. Statewide, forty-eight high schools were below the 60 percent passage rate; with eight of its seventten below the passage rate, CMS schools composed 16 percent of the statewide group.

34. Ibid. at 21.

35. Ibid. at 23.

36. North Carolina Dept. of Public Instruction, "NC School Report Cards, Charlotte-Mecklenburg," http://www.ncreportcards.org/src/distDetails.jsp?Page=13&pLEACode=600&pYear=2003-2004&pDataType=1; Annie E. Casey Foundation, Kids Count Data Center, "Percent of Students Enrolled in Free and Reduced Lunch," http://datacenter.kidscount.org/data/tables/2239-

percent-of-students-enrolled-in-free-and-reduced-lunch?loc=35#detailed /10/5010-5124/ false/909,105,19,21/any/4682.

37. Manning, *Report from the Court*, 22–23.

38. Ibid. at 17 (emphasis appeared in the original report).

39. Ibid. at 23.

40. Plaintiff-Intervenors' Complaint, Hoke County v. State, February 9, 2005.

41. Ibid.

42. Order, Hoke County v. State, August 19, 2005.

43. Stay of Proceedings, Hoke County v. State, August 19, 2005.

44. See, for example, Howell v. Howell, 89 N.C. App. 115, 118, 365 S.E.2d 181, 183 (1988). "The refusal to grant permissive intervention is an interlocutory order . . . appellant may either bring a separate action . . . or appeal from a final order" (internal citation omitted).

45. Manning, *Report from the Court*, Exhibit A; North Carolina Department of Public Instruction (DPI), "Enrollments by LEAs, courses, race, and genders: 2003–04," http://beyond2020.dpi. state.nc.us/wds80_1/TableViewer/tableView.aspx?ReportId=25.

46. See, for example, Roslyn Mickelson, "The Incomplete Desegregation of Charlotte-Mecklenburg Schools and Its Consequences," in *School Resegregation: Must the South Turn Back?*, ed. John Charles Boger and Gary Orfield (Chapel Hill: University of North Carolina Press, 2005), 87–110; Gary Orfield, John Kucsera, and Genevieve Siegel-Hawley, *E Pluribus . . . Separation: Deepening Double Segregation for More Students* (Los Angeles: The Civil Rights Project, 2012), http://civilrightsproject.ucla.edu/research/k-12-education/integration-and-diversity/mlk-national/e-pluribus...separation-deepening-double-segregation-for-more-students. Also, see chapters 1, 8, and 9 in this volume for examples of how remedial measures are blunted by the structural limitations of a segregated school.

47. See chapter 4 for a discussion of Project LIFT's extraordinarily costly interventions designed to address the needs of students in the largely failing, high-minority-concentrated-poverty schools that feed into West Charlotte.

48. See chapter 2 for a discussion of the racial and social class politics and lobbying surrounding the school board's decision to close the ten schools.

49. Ann Doss Helms and Mark Price, "10 CMS Schools Will Be Closed," *Charlotte Observer*, November 10, 2010.

50. Ann Doss Helms, "Closings Saved Money, but Academic Value Unclear, Charlotte-Mecklenburg Schools Says," *Charlotte Observer*, September 26, 2012; and Frequently Asked Questions—Middle School Athletics, http://schools.cms.k12.nc.us/brunsavenueES/Documents/ Frequently AskedQuestions-Middle_School_Sports[1].pdf.

51. Parents Involved in Community Schools v. Seattle School District No. 1 551 U.S. 701 (*PICS*; 2007).

52. See, for example, Milliken v. Bradley, 418 US 717, 742 (1974) ("No single tradition in public education is more deeply rooted than local control over the operation of schools"); Dayton Board of Education v. Brinkman, 43 U.S. 406, 410 (1977) ("local autonomy of school districts is a vital national tradition").

53. *PICS*, at 716.

54. Ibid. at 733–735, 782. Kennedy's opinion is formally designated as "concurring in part and concurring in the judgment," meaning that he agreed with the Court's outcome in the case (striking down the Louisville and Seattle plans), but not with the *reasoning* of the majority opinion in reaching that outcome. This is distinct from a simple concurrence, where the concurring judge wants to include something additional to the majority opinion or further emphasize some particular aspect of the holding.

55. Ibid. at 746. Claiming that the use of race in this case was as pernicious as the legal segregation challenged in *Brown*, the Chief Justice wrote, "When it comes to using race to assign children to schools, history will be heard."

56. Ibid. at 788–89 (J. Kennedy, concurring in part and concurring in the judgment).

57. Ibid. at 789 (J. Kennedy, concurring in part and concurring in the judgment).

58. U.S. Department of Justice, U.S. Department of Education, "Guidance on the Voluntary Use of Race to Achieve Diversity and Avoid Racial Isolation in Elementary and Secondary Schools," http://www2.ed.gov/about/offices/list/ocr/docs/guidance-ese-201111.pdf

59. Ibid. at 5.

60. Ibid. at 1.

61. Ibid at 6–7.

62. Ibid. at 6.

63. The guidelines are available in appendix 10.a on the book's Web site. They are also available at http://www.cms.k12.nc.us/boe/Documents/Guiding %20Principles %20 for%20Student %20Assignment.pdf.

64. Ibid.

65. See, for example, Frye v. Brunswick County Bd. of Educ., 612 F.Supp.2d 694, 708 (E.D.N.C. 2009) (declining to extend *Leandro* to a lawsuit arising out of teacher's sexual relationship with student. "A federal court should not create or expand a State's public policy or elbow its way into a controversy to render . . . an interpretation of state law."); Fothergill v. Jones County Bd. of Educ., 841 F.Supp.2d 915 (E.D.N.C. 2012).

66. King v. Beaufort County Bd. Educ. 364 N.C. 368, 377 (2010).

67. Ibid.

68. On racial disparities and student discipline generally, see Dan Losen and Tia Elena Martinez, "Out of School and Off Track: The Overuse of Suspensions in American Middle and High Schools," Civil Rights Project, UCLA, http://civilrightsproject.ucla.edu/resources/ projects/ center-for-civil-rights-remedies/school-to-prison-folder/federal-reports/out-of-school-and-off-track-the-overuse-of-suspensions-in-american-middle-and-high-schools/Outof-School-OffTrack_UCLA_4-8.pdf.

69. Richmond County Bd. of Educ. v. Cowell, N.C. App., 739 S.E.2d 566 (2013); Craig v. New Hanover County. Bd. of Educ., 363 N.C. 334 (2009).

70. William Shakespeare, *Hamlet*, act 3, scene 1. The phrase "the law's delay" comes from Hamlet's "To be or not to be" soliloquy, wherein he laments the many burdens of this "so long life."
To be, or not to be—that is the question:
Whether 'tis nobler in the mind to suffer
The slings and arrows of outrageous fortune
Or to take arms against a sea of troubles
And by opposing end them. To die, to sleep—
No more—and by a sleep to say we end
The heartache, and the thousand natural shocks
That flesh is heir to. 'Tis a consummation
Devoutly to be wished. To die, to sleep—
To sleep—perchance to dream: ay, there's the rub,
For in that sleep of death what dreams may come
When we have shuffled off this mortal coil,
Must give us pause. There's the respect
That makes calamity of so long life.
For who would bear the whips and scorns of time,

Th' oppressor's wrong, the proud man's contumely
The pangs of despised love, the law's delay,
The insolence of office, and the spurns
That patient merit of th' unworthy takes,
When he himself might his quietus make
With a bare bodkin?

Chapter 11

1. Charlotte-Mecklenburg School Board, "Minutes of Meeting of September 10, 1991."
2. http://www.cms.k12.nc.us/boe/Documents/Vision,%20Mission%20and%20Core%20 Beliefs.pdf.
3. The civil rights movement gave rise to the 1964 Civil Rights Act, which authorized the federal government to withhold aid to segregated school districts. The following year, Congress passed the Elementary and Secondary Education Act, which provided the federal government with unprecedentedly large amounts of federal aid for local school districts. The stick of the 1964 Civil Rights Act combined with the carrot of the 1965 Elementary and Secondary Education Act resulted in many districts desegregating. Moreover, executive branch guidelines about acceptable measures and level of desegregation influenced the federal courts in deciding what constituted constitutionally acceptable desegregation (Davison M. Douglas, *Reading, Writing, and Race: The Desegregation of the Charlotte Schools* [Chapel Hill: University of North Carolina Press, 1995], 125).
4. Among the many accounts of the turmoil that engulfed Boston's schools in the wake of a federal court's desegregation order is Ronald P. Formisano, *Boston Against Busing* (Chapel Hill: University of North Carolina Press, 1991). At the height of Boston's violent reaction to court-ordered desegregation, a group of West Charlotte students traveled to that city, and some Boston students came to Charlotte to witness the successful desegregation experience at West Charlotte High School.
5. This conflict was especially evident in the set of decisions that resulted in the location of an interstate highway, the Outerbelt, I-485. Developers and key members of the corporate class successfully pushed for the road to be built in the far south of the county, which fueled sprawling development of outlying and predominantly white neighborhoods. CMS was aware of the difficulties such development posed for desegregation and took various steps to address these developments such as in the 1992 adoption of what was called the "10-Percent Rule," which stated flatly that "the Board shall not proceed with construction of new schools in any census tracts that have less than a 10 percent black population." (Charlotte-Mecklenburg School Board, "Minutes of Meeting of September 10, 1991," 8). But the surging development in outlying areas and political pressure from residents of these areas helped create conditions that precluded CMS from observing its own policy. Between the passage of the 10-Percent Rule and Judge Potter's 1999 decision, CMS built five schools violating the rule.

   The history of one of these five schools, Hawk Ridge Elementary, illustrates another aspect of the interplay between agency and structure—in this case, fiscal constraints, especially those arising from the governmental structure that deprives CMS of taxing authority. Because CMS must rely on the county commission to issue bonds and provide approximately 30 percent of its operating revenue, the county commission frequently uses its control of the purse strings to influence CMS policy and has made crystal clear its aversion to CMS's looking gift horses like "free land" too closely in the mouth. The land for Hawk Ridge was such a gift horse; it was donated by a developer whose development—Ballantyne—would benefit from easy access to a new and nearby school. Moreover, Ballantyne's initial development had been fueled by the far-south location of the Outerbelt, and the developer's political influence had played a key role in securing that location. The motion to accept the donation passed by a 5–4 vote of the board. Three of the affirmative votes come from board members who several years earlier had voted for the 10-Percent Rule, but for whom financial considerations now trumped that rule. Unsurprisingly, when the school opened, black students constituted just 2 percent of its enrollment, though they constituted 42 percent of CMS's total enrollment (Stephen Samuel Smith, *Boom for Whom?: Education, Desegregation, and Development in Charlotte* [Albany: State University of New York Press, 2004], 148–149).

6. The reverse process was blatantly manifest in the 1970s. As CMS desegregated, racially correlated tracking became so pronounced that the Department of Health, Education, and Welfare withheld federal money from the district. Tom Bradbury, "HEW's Mandate: Racial Balance over Education," *Charlotte News*, July 29, 1977; Charlotte-Mecklenburg Schools, "Class Counts for High School English Classes," (unpublished report, November, 11, 1981); Capacchione v. Charlotte-Mecklenburg Schools, Defendant's Exhibit No. 61 (1999).

7. Samuel R. Lucas, "Effectively Maintained Inequality: Education Transitions, Track Mobility, and Social Background Effects," *American Journal of Sociology* 106, no. 6 (2001): 1642–1690.

8. See appendix 1.a on the book's Web site for a detailed discussion of NCLB and its status as of early 2014.

9. David Berliner and Sharon Nichols, *Collateral Damage: How High-Stakes Testing Corrupts America's Schools* (Cambridge, MA: Harvard Education Press, 2007); Adam Gamoran, "Federal Policy, Educational Inequality, and the Role of Research in the Wake of No Child Left Behind" (keynote address, Sociology of Education Association, Pacific Grove, CA, February 22, 2014); Roslyn Arlin Mickelson (presentation to Secretary of Education Arne Duncan about school integration and K–12 educational outcomes, Washington, DC, March 18, 2011).

10. Gary Orfield, "Conclusion," in *Integrating Schools in a Changing Society*, ed. Erica Frankenberg and Elizabeth DeBray (Chapel Hill: University of North Carolina Press, 2011), 318.

11. Parents Involved in Community Schools v. Seattle School District No. 1 551 U.S. 701 (*PICS*; 2007).

12. Sean F. Reardon, "The Widening Achievement Gap Between Rich and Poor: New Evidence and Possible Explanations," in *Whither Opportunity*, ed. Greg Duncan and Richard Murnane (New York: Russell Sage Foundation, 2011), 91–116.

13. In 2013–2014, the black/Latino dissimilarity index was 35. By contrast, the white/black dissimilarity index was 63, and the white/Latino index was 64. Indices involving Asians were generally in the 40s.

14. Thomas Tate, interview by Roslyn Arlin Mickelson and Amy Hawn Nelson, March 15, 2013, Charlotte, North Carolina.

15. Ericka Ellis-Stewart, interview by Stephen Samuel Smith, February 14, 2014, Charlotte, North Carolina.

16. Heath Morrison, interview by Roslyn Arlin Mickelson, March 7, 2014, Charlotte, North Carolina

17. Ellis-Stewart interview.

18. Julius Chambers, interview by Roslyn Arlin Mickelson, March 11, 2013, Charlotte, North Carolina

19. Ellis-Stewart, interview.

20. Arthur Griffin, interview by Roslyn Arlin Mickelson and Stephen Samuel Smith, January 31, 2014, Charlotte, North Carolina.

21. Marco Basile, "The Cost-Effectiveness of Socioeconomic Integration," in *The Future of School Integration: Socioeconomic Diversity as an Education Reform Strategy*, ed. Richard Kahlenberg

(New York: Century Foundation, 2012), 127–154; Rucker C. Johnson, "Long-Run Impacts of School Desegregation and School Quality on Adult Attainments" (working paper 16664, National Board of Economic Research, 2011); Heather Schwartz, "Housing Policy Is School Policy: Economically Integrative Housing Promotes Academic Success in Montgomery County, Maryland," in *The Future of School Integration: Socioeconomic Diversity as an Education Reform Strategy*, ed. Richard Kahlenberg (New York: Century Foundation, 2012), 27–66.

22. See chapter 2.

23. For a comprehensive discussion of federal and state policies that would significantly increase educational diversity, see Amy Stuart Wells, *Seeing Past the "Colorblind" Myth of Education Policy*, National Education Policy Center, March 20, 2014, http://nepc.colorado.edu/publication/seeing-past-the-colorblind-myth.

24. There are important methodological differences between the CMEF and UI polls that make comparisons only suggestive. In particular, the CMEF surveys were of registered voters and the UI survey was of county residents.

25. All questions used a 10-point Likert scale. Responses 8 through 10 were collapsed into the category Strong Support.

26. Data for 1995–2001 comes from Charlotte-Mecklenburg Education Foundation, *2001 Community Assessment*, Graph 9, page 24. Data for 2013 comes from the University of North Carolina Urban Institute 2013 Annual Survey.

27. In a 2007 Pew poll, a nationally representative sample was asked, "Which is more important— to have students go to racially mixed schools even if many of the students don't live nearby or to have students go to local community schools even if it means most students are of the same race?" Fifty-nine percent chose the latter, as cited in Erica Frankenberg and Rebecca Jacobsen, "School Integration Polls," *Public Opinion Quarterly* 75, no. 4 (2011), table 6.4. If the responses to the question in the UNCC poll are dichotomized, the corresponding percentage for blacks (26) and for whites (46) is lower.

28. Because of the manner in which data is presented in the 2001 report from CMEF (as well as in its earlier reports), we cannot make any additional comparisons between 2013 and any years earlier than 2001.

29. All members serve four-year terms, but elections are staggered so that the three at-large seats are on the ballot one year, and the six district seats are on the ballot two years later.

30. Moreover, in the 1999 election one of the losing candidates was the most outspoken of the white plaintiffs who had just prevailed in the reopened *Swann* case.

31. Smith, *Boom for Whom?*, 179–184.

32. Edward Glaeser and Jacob Vigdor, "The End of the Segregated Century: Racial Separation in America's Neighborhoods, 1890–2010 (New York: Manhattan Institute for Policy Research, 2012), https://www.manhattan-institute.org/html/cr_66.htm.

33. The schools are Berewick, Grand Oak, River Gate, River Oaks, and Stoney Creek. Data on their racial composition comes from CMS's *2013–14 Grade/Race/Sex Report*.

34. Richard Kahlenberg, ed., The Future of School Integration: Socioeconomic Diversity as an Education Reform Strategy (New York: Century Foundation, 2012).

35. *PICS*, 788–789.

36. U.S. Department of Justice and U.S. Department of Education, *Guidance on the Voluntary Use of Race to Achieve Diversity and Avoid Isolation in Elementary and Secondary School*, http://www2.ed.gov/about/offices/list/ocr/docs/guidance-ese-201111.html. For additional discussion of these strategies, see chapter 10.

37. Carol Corbett Burris and Delia T. Garrity, *Detracking for Excellence and Equity* (Alexandria, VA: Association for Supervision and Curriculum Development , 2008); Kevin Welner and Carol

Corbett Burris, "Alternative Approaches to the Politics of Detracking," *Theory into Practice* 45, no. 1 (2006): 90–99; Jeannie Oakes, *Keeping Track* (New Haven, CT: Yale University Press, 2005); Elizabeth G. Cohen and Rachel Lotan, *Designing Groupwork: Strategies for the Heterogeneous Classroom* (New York: Teachers College Press, 2014).

38. Lucas, "Effectively Maintained Inequality."

39. See endnote 5.

40. Motoko Rich, "Magnet Schools Find a Renewed Embrace in Cities," *New York Times*, February 17, 2014, A9, http://www.nytimes.com/2014/02/17/us/magnet-schools-find-a-renewed-embrace-in-cities.html?_r=0.

41. Stephanie Moller et al., "Collective Pedagogical Teacher Culture and Mathematics Achievement: Differences by Race, Ethnicity, and Socioeconomic Status," *Sociology of Education* 86, no. 2 (2013): 174–194.

42. Charlotte-Mecklenburg Schools, *Board of Education—2010 Guiding Principles* (see appendix 10.a on the book's Web site); Charlotte-Mecklenburg School Board, "Minutes of Meeting of October 22, 2013." The rubric for awarding points appears in *Report to Board of Education, Boundaries, Student Assignment, New Options and School Programs,* October 22, 2013, http://www.cms.k12.nc.us/sites/agenda/Lists/Agenda%20Items/Attachments/1999/1%20-%20Student%20Assignment%20Presentation.pdf.

43. Marta Tienda, "Diversity ≠ Inclusion: Promoting Integration in Higher Education," *Educational Researcher* 42, no. 9 (2013): 467–475. Chapter 9 describes how these dynamics unfolded at Shamrock Gardens Elementary School.

44. Jennifer Hochschild and Bridget Scott, "Trends: Governance and Reform of Public Education in the United States," *Public Opinion Quarterly* 62, no. 1 (1998): 79–120; Gary Orfield, "Public Opinion and School Desegregation," *Teachers College Record* 96, no. 4 (1995), 654–670. For in-depth interviews with CMS graduates, see chapter 3 in this volume. Also see Amy Hawn Nelson, "Experiencing the Double-Edged Sword of Desegregation: Charlotte-Mecklenburg School Graduates from 1995–1998" (PhD dissertation, University of North Carolina at Charlotte, 2010) and Amy Stuart Wells et al., *Both Sides Now: The Story of Desegregation's Graduates* (Berkeley: University of California Press, 2009), which features a chapter about graduates from West Charlotte High School's class of 1980.

45. Stephen Samuel Smith was a member of this task force. For additional information about it, see Smith, *Boom for Whom?*, 153–159.

46. For examples of some of these plans, designed by the team now at the Haas Institute and that have been successfully implemented, see http://kirwaninstitute.osu.edu/opportunity-communities/education/.

47. Clarence N. Stone, *Introduction: Urban Education in Political Context,* in *Changing Urban Education,* Clarence N. Stone, ed. (Lawrence: University Press of Kansas, 1998), 12.

48. Stephen Samuel Smith, "Still Swimming Against the Resegregation Tide? A Suburban Southern South District in the Aftermath of *Parents Involved,*" *North Carolina Law Review* 88, no. 3 (2010): 1145–1208.

49. Lynn Moody, interview by Stephen Samuel Smith, Rock Hill, SC, January 23, 2006.

50. Ken Spears, interview by Stephen Samuel Smith, Rock Hill, SC, January 18, 2006.

51. Ibid.

52. H. Stephen Shoemaker, "School Bonds Will Reveal If Charlotte Has a Soul," *Charlotte Observer*, October 16, 2000, p. 11A.

53. Chambers, interview.

54. See http://www.upcch.org/downloads/PastoralLetter.pdf and http://www.naacpnc.org/sign_passover_open_letter.

55. A key aspect of the group's efforts involve Oakhurst Elementary, an older school located in a diverse neighborhood and adjacent to other diverse neighborhoods. As of the spring of 2014, when this book went to press, Oakhurst was being rebuilt with money from a bond referendum that designated the reopened Oakhurst as a full magnet. Fearing that a full magnet at Oakhurst would siphon educationally active parents from the Oakhurst and other diverse neighborhoods and thus decrease the diversity of these neighborhoods and their schools, group members have met with board members and CMS senior leadership. It is now likely that Oakhurst will reopen as a partial magnet.

56. Barry Sherman, CMS veteran school social worker at one of the West Charlotte High School feeder schools. Personal communication with Roslyn Arlin Mickelson, April 28, 2014.

57. Wells et al., *Both Sides Now*, 232.

Appendix A

1. Robin M. Williams Jr., *Mutual Accommodation: Ethnic Conflict and Cooperation* (Minneapolis: University of Minnesota Press, 1977), 95.

2. Charles T. Clotfelter, *After Brown: The Rise and Retreat of School Desegregation* (Princeton, NJ: Princeton University Press, 2004), 205.

3. James Ryan, *Talking About Diversity*, http://furmancenter.org/research/iri/ryan. Ryan's remarks are part of an exchange with Charles Clotfelter, Richard Kahlenberg, and Richard Rothstein, all of whose comments are illuminating on this topic.

4. We readily acknowledge the social construction of the concept of *race* but employ it nonetheless because of its common use in popular and scholarly discourse.

Acknowledgments

We begin our thanks with our contributors, who not only provided us with their superb original scholarship but also cheerfully responded to our many requests for edits and rewrites. Next, we thank staff members at the University of North Carolina at Charlotte's Urban Institute for their technical assistance with the preparation of this manuscript. They transcribed interviews, edited manuscripts, and generally kept the many pieces of this project from getting out of control. In particular, we acknowledge the tireless research and editorial contributions of Diane Gavarkavich and Selena Skorman. Their commitment to this project shines through every page in this book, especially the tables, figures, and graphs.

A great many CMS educators and citizens of Mecklenburg County permitted us to interview them, sometimes even if the interview could potentially put them at some professional risk. They shared their time and insights with us, for which we are grateful. Our colleagues tolerated our focus on completing this book even though it meant we could not participate as fully in other aspects of our jobs as we would have liked. Mickelson's work on the book was facilitated by a sabbatical she received from UNC Charlotte, as was Smith's work by a sabbatical he received from Winthrop University. Caroline Chauncey, our patient editor at Harvard Education Press, supported us, encouraged us, and brought out the best in us as scholars. Her incisive guidance and ruthless recommendations for eliminating some chapters made the book more focused, for which we are very grateful.

And last but certainly not least, we are grateful to our friends and families for cheering us on throughout the process. Fincher Louisa Nelson was born a month before this manuscript was delivered to Harvard Education Press. We hope that the CMS school she attends in five years will be as good as the ones that David Michael Smith and Virginia Gail Smith attended in the 1980s and 1990s.

The book's dedication recognizes those who have fought for racial and social justice and the distinctive role Julius LeVonne Chambers played in that struggle in Charlotte and nationally. Chambers was a founding partner, with

James Ferguson II, of the law firm Ferguson Stein Chambers Gresham & Sumter, P.A. During his career, he successfully litigated several cases that changed the contours of civil rights law, including *Swann v. Charlotte-Mecklenburg Board of Education* (1971), and two employment discrimination cases, *Griggs v. Duke Power* (1971) and *Albemarle Paper Co. v. Moody* (1975). He served as the head of the NAACP's Legal Defense and Education Fund, Chancellor of North Carolina Central University, and professor of law at UNC Chapel Hill. He was the founder and first director of the UNC Center for Civil Rights. He practiced law in Charlotte until his death in August 2013. The life and work of this eminent civil rights champion touched our lives in many ways and changed this nation for the better.

Roslyn Arlin Mickelson
Stephen Samuel Smith
Amy Hawn Nelson

About the Editors

Roslyn Arlin Mickelson is a Professor of Sociology, Public Policy, and Women's and Gender Studies at the University of North Carolina at Charlotte. She completed a postdoctoral fellowship in child development and social policy at the University of Michigan, Ann Arbor. Prior to receiving her PhD from the University of California, Los Angeles, she taught high school social studies in Inglewood, California, for nine years. Her research interests include minority educational issues, desegregation, gender and education, educational policy, and pathways to science, technology, engineering, and mathematics (STEM). Mickelson has investigated school reform in Charlotte-Mecklenburg Schools since 1989, chronicling its transformation from a desegregated to a resegregated school system.

Stephen Samuel Smith is a Professor of Political Science at Winthrop University and author of *Boom for Whom?: Education, Desegregation, and Development in Charlotte* (State University of New York Press, 2004). He received his PhD from Stanford in 1990, having returned to academia after fifteen years doing blue-collar work, most of them in Detroit-area factories. He served as an expert witness in the 1999 reopened *Swann* litigation and has written about education policy in numerous professional journals and edited volumes. He has published widely about urban civic capacity, urban regimes, and the politics of desegregation. In addition to his continuing interest in the politics of education, he writes about antiwar movements, resistance by U.S. soldiers to military authority during the war in Iraq, and the ideological and analytic shortcomings of the term *social capital.*

Amy Hawn Nelson is a community researcher and career educator who has served as a teacher, mentor, and school leader in traditional, private, and charter schools. She is a Charlotte native and graduate of Charlotte-Mecklenburg Schools. She is currently the Director of Research for the UNC Charlotte Urban Institute and the Director of the Institute for Social Capital, Inc., whose mission is to advance university research and increase the community's capacity for data-based planning and evaluation. She received her PhD in urban education and a master's in school administration from UNC Charlotte, and a master's in teaching from Johns Hopkins University. Her research interests include long-term schooling outcomes, data-informed decision making, and integrated data systems.

About the Contributors

Charles T. Clotfelter is the Z. Smith Reynolds Professor of Public Policy Studies and Professor of Economics and Law at Duke University's Sanford School of Public Policy. During the 2013–2014 school year he was a Straus Fellow at the Straus Institute for the Advanced Study of Law and Justice at New York University. Clotfelter is also a research associate for the National Bureau of Economic Research and the director of the Center for the Study of Philanthropy and Voluntarism at Duke.

Mark Dorosin is the managing attorney at the University of North Carolina Center for Civil Rights. He also teaches a course in political and civil rights at the University of North Carolina School of Law in Chapel Hill. Much of his work at the Center has focused on issues of school segregation and resegregation in North Carolina.

Pamela Grundy is an independent historian living in Charlotte, North Carolina. She received her PhD in history from the University of North Carolina at Chapel Hill, and her work on education history has been supported by the Spencer Foundation, the National Endowment for the Humanities, and the Southern Oral History Program.

Joshua A. Hendrix is a doctoral student and instructor in sociology at North Carolina State University. His research interests are in family processes and child and adolescent well-being, with special emphases on the ways that parental work schedules, parental availability, and other household characteristics shape family and child outcomes. His 2013 publication in the *Journal of Family Issues* examines how the timing of parental work schedules influences parent/child bonds and adolescent children's delinquent behaviors.

Helen F. Ladd is the Edgar Thompson Professor of Public Policy Studies and Professor of Economics at Duke University. Most of her current research focuses on topics in education policy including school accountability, parental choice and market-based reforms, charter schools, school finance, and teacher labor markets. With colleagues at Duke, she has explored the relationship between teacher credentials and student test scores, the effects of accelerating algebra, school segregation, and the effects of early childhood initiatives. She is a past president of the Association for Public Policy Analysis and Management and a member of the National Academy of Education.

Luke Largess, along with James Ferguson and others at Ferguson Stein Chambers Gresham & Sumter, P.A., represented the class of black families in the 1999 trial that resulted in the vacating of the original *Swann* orders. He is now a partner at Tin Fulton Walker & Owen in Charlotte.

David Liebowitz is the principal of Joseph A. Browne Middle School in Chelsea, Massachusetts. He was formerly a middle school teacher and a policy analyst at the Massachusetts Executive Office of Education and the New York State Education Department, and is currently a doctoral candidate at the Harvard Graduate School of Education.

Paul McDaniel is a research fellow with the Immigration Policy Center at the American Immigration Council in Washington, DC. His research interests include urban social geography and immigrant settlement, new immigrant destinations and metropolitan regions, and immigrant integration and community receptivity. McDaniel holds a PhD in geography and urban regional analysis from the University of North Carolina at Charlotte.

Elizabeth Morrell is a doctoral candidate in the University of North Carolina at Charlotte's Department of Geography and Earth Sciences. Her research focuses on the political, economic, and social aspects of neighborhood change. She has extensive experience in both education and community organizing.

Lindsay C. Page is a Research Assistant Professor of Education at the University of Pittsburgh. Her work focuses on quantitative methods and their application to questions regarding the effectiveness of educational policies and programs across the preschool to postsecondary spectrum.

Toby L. Parcel is a Professor of Sociology in the Department of Sociology and Anthropology at North Carolina State University. She has published studies of the effects of social capital at home and at school on child and adolescent academic and social well-being in journals such as the *American Journal of Sociology*, *Social Forces*, and *Journal of Marriage and Family*. With Andrew Taylor, she is co-author of *The End of Consensus: Diversity, Neighborhoods, and the Politics of Public School Assignments* (University of North Carolina Press, 2015).

Michelle Plaisance is a former teacher of English language learners for Charlotte-Mecklenburg Schools. She is Assistant Professor of English and Teaching English to Speakers of Other Languages (TESOL) at Greensboro College, where she also is the Director of the TESOL program. She received her PhD in urban education from the University of North Carolina at Charlotte in spring 2014.

Stephanie Southworth received her PhD in public policy from the University of North Carolina at Charlotte in 2008. Her research interests include the social context of education, social stratification, race and ethnicity, urban sociology, and social problems. She teaches sociology at Clemson University.

Andrew J. Taylor is a Professor of Political Science in the School of Public and International Affairs at North Carolina State University. For the most part, his work focuses on national governmental institutions. He is coauthor, with Toby L. Parcel, of *The End of Consensus: Diversity, Neighborhoods, and the Politics of Public School Assignments* (University of North Carolina Press, 2015).

S. Lorén Trull holds a JD from the University of North Carolina School of Law and has been admitted to the State Bar of New Jersey. She is currently a doctoral student in the Public Policy program at the University of North Carolina at Charlotte. Her research interests include education policy and school reform, with a focus on race, social class, and gender equity.

Jacob L. Vigdor is a Professor of Public Policy and Economics at Duke University, a research associate at the National Bureau of Economic Research, an adjunct fellow at the Manhattan Institute for Policy Research, and an external fellow at the Centre for Research and Analysis of Migration.

Index